College
Mathematics
Through Baseball

FRED WORTH

McFarland & Company, Inc., Publishers
Jefferson, North Carolina

LIBRARY OF CONGRESS CATALOGUING-IN-PUBLICATION DATA

Worth, Fred, 1958–
    College mathematics through baseball / Fred Worth.
       p.   cm.
    Includes index.

    ISBN 978-0-7864-9776-8 (softcover : acid free paper) ⓧ
    ISBN 978-1-4766-2011-4 (ebook)

    1. Mathematics—Study and teaching (Higher)   2. Mathematical
statistics—Study and teaching (Higher)   3. Games in mathematics
education.   4. Baseball—Mathematics.   I. Title.

QA135.6.W667 2015
510—dc23   2015031691

BRITISH LIBRARY CATALOGUING DATA ARE AVAILABLE

Front cover: Red Sox designated hitter David Ortiz (Second
Print Productions)

Printed in the United States of America

McFarland & Company, Inc., Publishers
  Box 611, Jefferson, North Carolina 28640
  www.mcfarlandpub.com

To my mom, Gay Worth, who taught me long division
in first grade so that I could do batting averages.

To my father, Ed Worth, and my brother,
Richard Worth, who shared my love for baseball.

To my undergraduate professor, Glen Bernet, for helping
me see the beauty of theoretical mathematics.

To my dissertation advisor, W. T. Ingram,
for helping me become a mathematician.

To my almost-completely-perfect wife, Beth Worth, for her
loving and faithful encouragement over the past 30 years.

To my lord and Savior, Jesus Christ, for helping me
through life's troubles, both mathematical and otherwise.

Acknowledgments

Thanks to the Department of Mathematics and Computer Science at Henderson State University for their openness to trying the course that gave rise to this text. Thanks also to M. Frank, Norm Ginsberg, Dave Goss, Lee Ann Grace, John Greene, Howard Henry, Jan Larson, Lloyd Moyo, David Mummy, Cliff Otto, Dwight Oxley and Alan Reifman for proofreading portions of the text.

College
Mathematics
Through Baseball

Table of Contents

Preface

When I was in high school, or maybe it was junior high, I was told that the algebra I was learning was very important. In fact, I was told, as many students have been since, "You will use it every day for the rest of your life." I suspect there are some days that I do not use algebra, so I do not believe it was literally true but it was probably close to 95 percent true. However, I am a mathematician. There were other kids in those classes. And not all of them were going to be mathematicians. Most of them were not going to go into technical fields. Some, if they went to college at all, may have been English majors or history majors. They were lied to. I seriously doubt they use that algebra from high school more than once or twice a year.

Don't misunderstand me. I think algebra is important. Even if someone is not going to go to college in a technical field, algebra, specifically, and mathematics, generally, are very important. Even if it is for no other reason than that mathematics teaches problem solving skills that work in every area of life. However, there is a subset of mathematics that really will be used by many people pretty much every day for the rest of their lives.

Sociology majors and political science majors will read about statistical studies or polls. Art majors will use geometry. Everyone will need to be able to think logically and realize when they are being manipulated by faulty logic. This book is an attempt to provide that subset of mathematics from the perspective of sports, primarily baseball. There are many people who do not like mathematics, who would probably prefer a root canal with no Novocain to a mathematics class, but do like sports. Combining the two may make the mathematics more enjoyable, even if mathematics already is enjoyed by the student.

"*Correct thinkers think that 'baseball trivia' is an oxymoron: Nothing about baseball is trivial.*"

George Will

"*There have been only two authentic geniuses in the world. Willie Mays and Willie Shakespeare.*"

Tallulah Bankhead

1—Logical Fallacies

"There is always hope when people are forced to listen to both sides."—John Stuart Mill

"Bad reasoning as well as good reasoning is possible; and this fact is the foundation of the practical side of logic."—Charles Sanders Peirce

In many areas of life, people attempt to convince other people of things. They may be trying to convince people to accept their point of view on some topic. They may be trying to convince people to buy a particular product.

Baseball is a topic where arguments come up frequently. In fact, the phrase "Hot Stove League" illustrates this well. The Hot Stove League refers to the baseball-related arguments that fans might have during the winter while sitting around a hot stove for warmth. Since the baseball season would not be going on, the only competition is in the arguments of the fans. Which player is the best? Which team has done the most to improve its chances to win the pennant next season? Does Ron Santo belong in the Hall of Fame?

One of the most famous arguments of this nature would take place in New York City in the 1950s. That was the end of the era when New York was home to three teams, the New York Giants, the Brooklyn Dodgers and the New York Yankees. During the 1950s, each of those teams had a Hall of Fame center fielder. Willie Mays played for the Giants, Duke Snider for the Dodgers and Mickey Mantle for the Yankees. With three such outstanding players playing the same position, it was inevitable that the teams' respective fans would argue over who was the best. That argument even gave rise to one of many wonderful baseball songs, "Talkin' Baseball" by Terry Cashman (listen at www.youtube.com/watch?v=fWKA9Zi5-_Y), mentioning "Willie, Mickey and the Duke."

Logic is the general study of the structure of arguments. In this chapter we will look at examples of faulty logic. There are many ways of using faulty logic. We will look at only a small number of those ways. Before we look at those, however, it should be noted that faulty logic does not necessarily result in an incorrect conclusion.

Suppose we wanted to reduce the fraction $\frac{16}{64}$ to lowest terms. Suppose that we did this by "canceling" the 6s.

Though the approach is horribly incorrect, the answer is correct. In the same way, an argument can be logically flawed yet still have a correct conclusion.

$$\frac{16}{64} = \frac{1\cancel{6}}{\cancel{6}4} = \frac{1}{4}$$

Another important thing to note is that a particular statement may fall victim to more than one logical fallacy. It is entirely possible that two or more fallacies may be involved in the same statement. Lastly, it is important to keep in mind that we are not going to consider ALL of the different kinds of logical fallacies. If you look on the web, you can find sites listing dozens of logical fallacies.

Always keep in mind that any argument has reasons and a conclusion. It is very helpful to identify these parts of the argument.

Logical Fallacy #1—Appeal to Authority

In an **appeal to authority**, one may cite a well-known authority to support one's argument or comment on a topic. That person has an opinion. Therefore, that person's opinion must be right. In *The Skeptical Essays*, philosopher/mathematician Bertrand Russell wrote, "Even when the experts all agree, they may well be mistaken."

This does not mean it is unwise to seek out opinions of knowledgeable people. It just means that we should not stop thinking just because an "expert" speaks.

Example—During an ESPN broadcast, John Kruk says "a sacrifice bunt is the best play here."

Conclusion—"a sacrifice bunt is the best play"
Reason—"John Kruk said so"

Yes, John Kruk is a former professional baseball player. Yes, he has been involved in baseball broadcasting for a number of years. Yes, he knows a lot about baseball. Yes, he may even be right! But we still need to think for ourselves.

Another occurrence of this appeal to authority fallacy occurs when a person is an expert in one area but speaks about another area.

Example—"We should pay attention to what Sally Field says about organized labor because she played a union organizer in the movie *Norma Rae.*"

Conclusion—"pay attention to what Sally Field says about organized labor"
Reason—"she played a union organizer in a movie"

Just because an actor or actress plays a part in a movie does not make that person an expert on the topic involved in the role.

Even if someone IS an expert in a field, that person can still be wrong. Here is a list of exceptionally bad predictions from experts. It is excerpted from crazy-frankenstein.com/top-80-bad-predictions-about-the-future.html.

"Man will not fly for 50 years."—Wilbur Wright, American aviation pioneer, to brother Orville, after a disappointing flying experiment, 1901 (their first successful flight was in 1903).

"Democracy will be dead by 1950."—John Langdon-Davies, *A Short History of the Future*, 1936.

"The Americans are good about making fancy cars and refrigerators, but that doesn't mean they are any good at making aircraft. They are bluffing. They are excellent at bluffing."—Hermann Göring, commander-in-chief of the Luftwaffe, 1942.

"It will be gone by June."—*Variety*, passing judgment on rock 'n' roll, 1955.

"And for the tourist who really wants to get away from it all, safaris in Vietnam."—*Newsweek*, predicting popular holidays for the late 1960s.

"Such startling announcements as these should be deprecated as being unworthy of science and mischievous to its true progress."—Sir William Siemens, on Edison's light bulb, 1880.

"That the automobile has practically reached the limit of its development is suggested by the fact that during the past year no improvements of a radical nature have been introduced."—*Scientific American*, January 2, 1909 edition.

"Heavier-than-air flying machines are impossible."—Lord Kelvin, British mathematician and physicist, president of the British Royal Society, 1895.

"Where a calculator on the ENIAC is equipped with 18,000 vacuum tubes and weighs 30 tons, computers in the future may have only 1,000 vacuum tubes and weigh only 1.5 tons."—*Popular Mechanics*, March 1949.

"There is no reason anyone would want a computer in their home."—Ken Olson, president, chairman and founder of Digital Equipment Corp. (DEC), maker of big business mainframe computers, arguing against the PC, 1977.

"Space travel is utter bilge."—Richard Van Der Riet Woolley, upon assuming the post of astronomer royal in 1956.

"The cinema is little more than a fad. It's canned drama. What audiences really want to see is flesh and blood on the stage."—Charlie Chaplin, actor, producer, director, and studio founder, 1916.

"This 'telephone' has too many shortcomings to be seriously considered as a means of communication. The device is inherently of no value to us."—Memo at Western Union, 1878 (or 1876).

"Transmission of documents via telephone wires is possible in principle, but the apparatus required is so expensive that it will never become a practical proposition."—Dennis Gabor, British physicist and author of *Inventing the Future*, 1962.

Please understand that the purpose of discussing appeal to authority is not to cause total distrust of anyone saying anything about any topic. The opinions of experts should be given considerable respect and attention. But we ought not blindly follow such people all of the time.

Logical Fallacy #2—Appeal to Emotion

A common ploy in argumentation is to try to associate a very positive emotion or a very negative emotion with a particular argument, product or view. By an **appeal to emotion** the speaker hopes to convince the hearer to conform to the speaker's opinion.

Example—"If we do not work to preserve our forests, then our children will never know the joy of taking a walk in the woods."

Conclusion—"our children will never know the joy of taking a walk in the woods"
Reason—"we must preserve our forests"

In this statement, the speaker argues for taking care of forests by associating with it the very negative feeling of seeing "our children" deprived of "a walk in the woods."

Example—"Anyone who thinks Alex Rodriguez is the best ballplayer of all time is a fool."

Conclusion—"Alex Rodriguez is not the best ballplayer"
Reason—"thinking he is would be foolish"

Surely no one desires to be considered foolish. Therefore, the speaker seeks to associate "foolishness" with the position that "Alex Rodriguez is the best ballplayer of all time." The emotion is the only support the speaker has for this assertion.

Appeal to emotion is a very common fallacy in commercials and advertisements. We have all seen ads showing a man using a particular brand of shampoo, beer, car, etc. The ad closes with a beautiful woman with the man, implying that the only reason he got the girl was his use of that product.

Political campaigns also use appeal to emotion regularly. Candidates tell us of the wonderful things that will happen if they are elected. Or the awful things that will happen if their opponent is elected. Barack Obama's 2008 campaign slogan, "Yes we can," gave many people a feeling of power and optimism, thus appealing to emotion.

Logical Fallacy #3—Appeal to Popularity

We have all seen commercials or other advertisements that said something like "Go out and buy the most popular car in America." That is an appeal to popularity. The idea is "Everybody else is doing this, or buying this, or thinking this way, or…." Since "everyone else is" then you should, too. We have all used this fallacy. Think back to when you were a child and told your mother, "But everyone else is going." And give Mom credit since she probably did not fall for your appeal to popularity.

Example—"Buy the new Dodge truck, the most popular truck in America."

Conclusion—"the Dodge truck is something you should buy"
Reason—"a lot of other people have bought it"

The purpose of such an ad is to get you to think that EVERYONE else is doing something. And because EVERYONE else is doing it, there must be a good reason for doing it.

Example—"The Yankees are the best team in major league baseball because more fans attend their games than those of any other team."

Conclusion—"the Yankees are the best team in major league baseball"
Reason—"more fans attend their games than those of any other team"

Number of fans attending games does not necessarily translate into the quality of the team. In the early 1960s, the Mets became a very popular team among fans even though they were losing over 100 games every year.

Appealing to the fact that others are, or aren't doing something, is the fallacy of appeal to popularity.

Logical Fallacy #4—Circular Reasoning

Every argument has two parts to it. There is a conclusion. There is a reason. Sometimes the reason and conclusion are simply rewordings of the same thing.

Example—"Clayton Kershaw is the best pitcher in baseball because there is no pitcher better than Clayton Kershaw."

Conclusion—"Clayton Kershaw is the best pitcher"
Reason—"Clayton Kershaw pitches better than anyone"

In this statement, the conclusion the speaker wants us to draw is that "Clayton Kershaw is the best pitcher in baseball." The "support" for this conclusion is "there is no pitcher better than Clayton Kershaw." Both of these are simply variations on "Clayton Kershaw is the best."

Whenever we work with an argument, it is instructive to identify the reason and the conclusion. It is particularly important here. Whenever we do this, if we notice that the reason and conclusion are rewordings of each other, then we have an example of **circular reasoning**. Keep in mind that we do not have circular reasoning solely because words are repeated.

Example—"Babe Ruth is the best player of all time. He was an outstanding pitcher. His home run hitting changed the way the game was played. His on-base percentage and slugging percentage are among the best all time. He is certainly the best player of all time."

Conclusion—"Babe Ruth is the best player of all time"
Reason—"good pitcher, good hitter"

Note that "best player of all time" is repeated. In this case, however, the speaker simply repeated the conclusion at the end to re-emphasize what was being asserted. There are several reasons stated so the speaker's conclusion is supported by reasons, not the repetition of "best player of all time."

Logical Fallacy #5—Diversion

As mentioned above, every argument has two parts, a conclusion and a reason. To present a strong argument, the reason and conclusion should be related. That is not always the case.

This fallacy, sometimes called "Red Herring," is known as **diversion**.

Example—"Miguel Cabrera is overrated as a hitter. After all, last week he committed three errors in just six games."

Conclusion—"Miguel Cabrera is overrated as a hitter"
Reason—"he committed three errors"

The two topics mentioned here, Cabrera's hitting ability and the three errors, have nothing to do with each other. His fielding has nothing to do with his hitting.

In diversion, the speaker diverts the attention from the actual topic to something else. Often this will happen because the speaker is not thinking clearly about what he or she is saying. Other times it is because the speaker does not have a good argument about the topic under consideration so starts grasping at anything that can be said about the person or entity involved.

Logical Fallacy #6—False Cause

A common mistake many people make is assuming that event A preceding event B means that event A caused event B. Superstitions are a great example.

Many baseball players will not step on the foul line when leaving or going onto the field. Oliver Perez would give a dramatic leap to avoid stepping on the line. Why do they do this? Because someone, somewhere, at some time decided stepping on the line was bad luck. Why? Most likely there was a day, perhaps in 1876, that some player stepped on the line and immediately made two errors and struck out his next two times up. "Oh, that must have happened because I stepped on the line."

Example—"The Tampa Bay Rays changed their name from the Devil Rays to Rays and suddenly ended up in the World Series. Taking 'Devil' out of the name made the difference."

Reason—"the name change preceded the change to a winning team"
Conclusion—"the name change caused the change to a winning team"
Just because one event precedes another it does not follow that the one caused the other. To assert otherwise is **false cause**.

Example (quoted from *Baseball Gold* by Dan Schlossberg)—"Yankees coach Jim Hegan once told Mel Stottlemyre that avoiding the fouls lines was a silly superstition. The pitcher agreed and stepped on one deliberately. He had immediate regrets: 'The first batter was Ted Uhlaender. He hit a line drive off my left shin. It went for a hit. Rod Carew, Tony Oliva, and Harmon Killebrew followed with extra-base hits. The fifth man hit a single and scored and I was charged with five runs. I haven't stepped on a foul line since.'"

Reason—"stepping on the line preceded getting bombed by the Twins"
Conclusion—"stepping on the line caused getting bombed by the Twins"
It actually didn't happen the way Stottlemyre remembered. The only time he allowed five runs in one inning against the Twins, during the time that Uhlaender and Carew both played for the Twins, happened on August 23, 1969. According to www.retrosheet.org, the first inning went as follows: "Uhlaender singled to pitcher; Tovar out on a sacrifice bunt (pitcher to first) [Uhlaender to second]; Oliva doubled to left [Uhlaender scored]; Killebrew

homered [Oliva scored]; Reese doubled to right; Nettles doubled [Reese scored]; Roseboro flied out to left; Cardenas singled to left [Nettles scored]; KEKICH REPLACED STOTTLEMYRE (PITCHING); Perry struck out."

Example (quoted from *Baseball Gold* by Dan Schlossberg)—"Washington Senators first baseman Mickey Vernon picked up pennies he found on the field; he regarded them as omens of base hits to come. 'I can't recall a time that I found a penny and did not get a hit,' he said. 'Why doesn't the manager throw pennies onto the field near first base? That's the catch. The penny had to be found by accident. You can't fool around with this superstition stuff and get away with it.'"

Logical Fallacy #7—Hasty Generalization

All of us have heard, experienced and, probably, engaged in perpetuating stereotypes. Jeff Foxworthy has made a career by giving amusing stereotypes about rednecks. We have all heard racial or ethnic stereotypes. Stereotypes typically come from a person encountering someone from another group and noticing a behavior, then assuming that the behavior is common to all people from that group.

Example—"In 2006, Miguel Olivo struck out 103 times and walked nine times. Guys from the Dominican Republic don't know how to work the count and get walks."

Conclusion—"players from the Dominican Republic don't draw walks"
Reason—"one Dominican player is cited as not drawing walks"

In this example of **hasty generalization**, the speaker sees one person (or two or three people) from a group exhibiting a trait and assumes all people from that group exhibit that trait. It ignores people who do not fit the pattern. In this example, it ignores people like Albert Pujols who, in 2007, struck out only 58 times while walking 99 times.

Logical Fallacy #8—Limited Choice

Sometimes people are asked to make a choice but the question is worded in a way that excludes some legitimate responses.

Example—"Obviously Jimmy Rollins was the best shortstop in the National League in 2007. After all, he was better than Khalil Greene and Hanley Ramirez."

Conclusion—"Jimmy Rollins was the best"
Reason—"he was better than two particular players"

All of these choices are legitimate choices but the wording excludes other possibilities like Jose Reyes or Troy Tulowitzki. To assert Rollins was the best, we would have to consider all shortstops.

To be certain you really have identified an example of **limited choice**, be sure to identify another reasonable option that was excluded by the statement. In the above example, you should say something like "This is an example of limited choice because the speaker didn't consider other great shortstops like Jose Reyes."

Just having limited choices does not mean we have an example of **limited choice**.

Example—"Are you over six feet tall or not?"

This is NOT an example of limited choice. True, the choices "yes" and "no" are limited. But those are the only possible responses. You are either over six feet tall or you are not. There are no other options.

Logical Fallacy #9—Personal Attack

Personal attacks, or *ad hominem* arguments, are arguments or statements that, instead of dealing with the actual topic or argument, attack the person involved. Usually such a fallacy occurs when one does not have a decent response to an argument so attacking the person gives the appearance of a legitimate response.

Example—"Alex Rodriguez is an over-rated fielder. After all, he allegedly cheated on his wife."

Conclusion—"Alex Rodriguez is over-rated"
Reason—"he allegedly cheated on his wife"

Rather than dealing with the fielding issue, the speaker attacks Rodriguez personally. Whether Rodriguez cheated on his wife or not, the statement attacks his morals and does not speak to whether or not his fielding skills are over-rated. So this is a personal attack.

This example could also be classified as a diversion. It is not uncommon for a statement to actually exhibit multiple fallacies. Therefore it will be important for you to give a good explanation of why you think a particular fallacy is exhibited.

Logical Fallacy #10—Straw Man

This next fallacy is similar to diversion but there is a significant difference.

Example—"Senator Watson opposes abortion. He just wants to keep women barefoot, pregnant and chained to the stove."

Reason—"Senator Watson opposes abortion"
Conclusion—"Senator Watson wants to keep women barefoot, pregnant and chained to the stove"

In a **straw man** argument, the speaker takes a person's beliefs and extends or exaggerates them. Opposing abortion is a long way from thinking women should be kept barefoot, pregnant and chained to the stove.

The point of a straw man argument is that by exaggerating a person's position, it becomes easier to argue against the position. Straw man typically happens when one does not really understand another's position or simply doesn't have a good response to an argument and therefore is forced to exaggerate the position in order to be able to respond.

Logical Fallacy #11—Guilt by Association

This fallacy is similar to **hasty generalization** but typically focuses on negative characteristics.

Example—"Johnny has been hanging out with Bob and Dave lately. Bob and Dave use drugs so Johnny must have started using drugs."

Reason—"Johnny hangs out with drug users"
Conclusion—"Johnny must use drugs."

In a **guilt by association** argument, the speaker assumes that if one person group shares any characteristic with another person or group, then any negative traits of the person or group must also be shared.

Logical Fallacy #12—Gambler's Fallacy

Quoting www.Nizkor.org's fallacy pages, "The **gambler's fallacy** is committed when a person assumes that a departure from what occurs on average or in the long term will be corrected in the short term."

Example—"Ichiro hasn't gotten a hit in his last six at-bats. That means he's got to get a hit now."

Reason—"Ichiro gets a lot of hits but hasn't gotten one lately"
Conclusion—"he must be about to get a hit"

We will talk more about this later but a batting average is, in a sense, a probability of a batter getting a hit in a particular at-bat. Theoretically, whether or not a batter gets a hit in a particular at-bat has nothing to do with whether or not he got a hit in his previous at-bat.

"He's due for a hit." "Lebron James has been hitting all of his shots lately so he'll make this one." These are kinds of expressions that are frequently heard in sports. They are occurrences of the gambler's fallacy.

This is called the gambler's fallacy because it occurs in gambling. If a particular casino game has been resulting in a particular way lately, a gambler assumes it will act differently now. Assuming the game is run fairly (possibly not a good assumption), the next occurrence will have nothing to do with what happened in previous occurrences.

Chapter 1—Exercises

In the following exercises, an argument, statement or advertisement is given. For each exercise identify one of our fallacies that is exhibited in that argument, statement or advertisement. Give a detailed explanation to justify your choice.

1. A former Miss Alabama said, "I would not live forever, because we should not live forever, because if we were supposed to live forever, then we would live forever, but we cannot live forever, which is why I would not live forever."

2. Earl Weaver's managing philosophy was said to be "pitching, defense, and the three-run homer." So obviously Weaver didn't care what kind of batting averages his players had.

3. Every time I've watched the Red Sox play at Fenway Park, the Red Sox have always lost. The Red Sox play at Fenway tomorrow but I won't watch the game because I really want them to win.

4. Former major league pitcher Ross Grimsley, nicknamed Scuzz, would not wash or change any part of his uniform as long as the team was winning, believing that washing or changing anything would jinx the team.

5. Gosh, officer, I know I made an illegal left turn, but please don't give me a ticket. I've had a hard day, and I was just trying to get over to my aged mother's hospital room, and spend a few minutes with her before I report

to my second full-time minimum-wage job, which I have to have as the sole support of my 37 children and the 19 members of my extended family who depend on me for food and shelter.

6. I don't like the Tigers and they are from Michigan. Therefore, Michigan must be a terrible place to go for a vacation.

7. I know that guy hit a lot of home runs during the 1990s but that is when everyone was using steroids so steroids must be why he hit so many.

8. I wore a hat during the last test and made the highest grade I've made all semester. I'll wear a hat on the final so I'll get a good grade on the final.

9. Ichiro Suzuki was elected to the All-Star team in 2003, so obviously he was the best right-fielder in the game.

10. If you didn't pick Andrew McCutchen as the best center fielder in baseball then you must have picked Mike Trout.

11. In 1977, a prosecuting attorney said, "I submit to you that if you can't take this evidence and find these defendants guilty on this evidence then we might as well open all the banks and say, 'Come on and get the money, boys, because we'll never be able to convict them.'"

12. In 1980, Billy Martin managed the Athletics and his pitchers had 94 complete games. Martin won a lot of games as manager so obviously having pitchers come out of games so early is a bad strategy.

13. In 2004, Jacque Chirac, then president of France, said, "History does not repeat itself and it is very difficult to compare historical situations that differ because history is not repetitive."

14. LeBron James once said, "I think, team first. It allows me to succeed, it allows my team to succeed." He obviously didn't mean that when you consider the miserable attitude he showed when leaving the Cavaliers.

15. Mariano Rivera said Dustin Pedroia is a better second baseman than Robinson Cano. Rivera played with Cano so he must know what he is talking about.

16. Most of the pitchers the Mets had in the 1960s were not very successful so Tom Seaver, Nolan Ryan and Jerry Koosman must not have been very good.

17. Obviously the only solution to the designated hitter problem is to eliminate the DH completely or adopt it in both leagues.

18. Only a fool would oppose the new drug testing rules that Major League Baseball is instituting.

19. Shoeless Joe Jackson was at one of the meetings with the gamblers before the 1919 World Series so he must have tried to throw the series the way Lefty Williams did.

20. That is the third time this week some guy in a pickup truck has cut me off on the interstate. Obviously rednecks don't know how to drive.

21. The Astros have won five straight games. There is no way they can win another because they are due to lose one.

22. The best baseball team must be the Yankees since so many people are going to see them.

23. The Boston Strangler and Jack the Ripper were both left-handed so obviously all left-handed people are at least borderline psychotic killers.

24. The Cubs haven't won the World Series since 1908 so they must win it sometime soon.

25. The senator's views on gun control are flawed. After all, he's one of the people who supported the latest revision of the tax code.

26. You had better agree that the new company policy is the best if you expect to keep your job.

2—Unit Conversions

"A man went to his doctor to find out why he had been having such severe headaches. The doctor ran some tests and after a few hours called the man into his office. 'I have terrible news,' he told the patient. 'Your condition is terminal.' 'Oh, no!' the man wailed.

'How long do I have?'

'Ten … ' began the doctor.

'Ten what?' the patient interrupted. 'Days? Months? Years?'

'Nine,' said the doctor, 'eight, seven, six…'"—*Contributed by Bob Fajardo,* Reader's Digest, *November 1997*

"Baseball is a game of inches."—*Branch Rickey*

Any time we count something, we are using units. If we are counting apples, we have some number of apples. When we measure things, we are using units. If we are measuring length, we could be working in inches, feet, yards or miles. We could be using meters, millimeters or kilometers.

Various considerations help us determine which units we should use. Again looking at length, our location can affect the units we use. If we are in the United States, we would likely use feet, inches, miles or some other English unit. If we are in Europe, we would use metric units, like meters, centimeters or kilometers.

Another consideration is how big something is. If I am measuring my height, it would be silly to use miles. If I did, I would have to say, "I am 0.001144 miles tall." No one would have any idea how tall I am from that comment. If I am talking about driving from Arkadelphia, Arkansas, to Little Rock, Arkansas, I am not going to say, "The distance is 4,245,120 inches." No one is going to have any idea how long that trip would take based on that comment.

We also seek to be consistent in units. If you are measuring your living room in order to buy carpet, you would not say the living room is 14 feet by 5 yards. Those measurements may very well be correct but we do not want to use different units for two different sides of a rectangle. We would instead say 14 feet by 15 feet. After all, we would be interested in the area of the room. When we say 14 feet by 15 feet we would multiply to get (14)(15) feet × feet or 210 feet squared. When we say 14 feet by 5 yards and multiply we would get (14)(5) feet × yards or 70 feet-yards, whatever that is.

Lastly, units can also help us know the format for an answer. If we do a problem that involves division, perhaps our answer on our calculator is 25.62753432. How many decimal places should we use? The answer to that question can be given by units. If the unit involved is dollars, we would give an answer of $25.63 because dollars only make sense to the hundredths place (unless we're talking about gasoline prices). If the problem involved the population of a city, the unit might be people, so our answer would be 26 people. We do not allow fractions when our unit is "people." If the unit is grams, then eight decimal places from the original calculation would be fine.

A Brief History of Units

When was it decided that an inch would be the length that it is? When was it decided that a foot would be the length that it is? And why 12 inches in a foot? Originally, an "inch" was the width of one's thumb. A "foot" was the length of one's foot.

There are obvious problems with that approach. Whose thumb? Whose foot? At various times the person whose dimensions determined these things changed. People finally realized such ambiguity was not helpful and the lengths were standardized. The inch became what it is now. The foot became what it is now. Twelve inches happened to be the same as one foot. Similar conventions were established for other units.

Most of the world uses the metric system. The meter is the basic unit of length. Originally the meter was defined as 1/10,000,000 of the distance from the equator to the north pole on the longitudinal line through Paris, France. In 1983, it was redefined as the distance light travels in a vacuum in 1/299,792,458 of a second.

The liter is the basic unit of volume. It is equal to 0.001 cubic meters.

The kilogram is the metric system's basic unit of mass. It is defined as roughly equal to the mass of one liter of water.

Conversions

There are various reasons to do conversions from one set of units to another. If I am trying to communicate with my friend in New Zealand, it is helpful for him if I refer to temperatures in Celsius rather than Fahrenheit. If I am communicating with a colleague in France, I should use meters and liters rather than feet and gallons. If I am buying something from someone in Mexico, it is helpful if I am familiar with pesos and how they relate to dollars.

In sports, there are times that units of interest are determined by the topic at hand. We say that Randy Johnson used to throw a 100 mile per hour fastball. That is a nice way to explain how fast the ball is going. But if I am the batter and want to know how much time I have to react in order to hit that ball, miles and hours make no sense. Feet and seconds are more appropriate for that discussion.

We are going to look at a couple of simple conversions in order to set up a method for doing conversions in general. But before we do that, let us first talk about the arithmetic of units. Units can be multiplied and added. They can be subtracted and divided.

Suppose I have (3 feet) × (4 feet). Obviously I have 12 somethings. Just like we multiply the numbers together, we also multiply the units together. If we had y times y, we might call that y^2, or "y squared." So if we have feet × feet, we have feet^2 or "square feet." So (3 feet) × (4 feet) = 12 feet^2.

In algebra, if we have $\frac{6x}{5x}$ we divide the numerator and denominator by x to get $\frac{6}{5}$. Units work the same way. If I have $\frac{4\ feet}{3\ feet}$, the "feet" divide out leaving $\frac{4}{3}$.

Example—Suppose I want to convert four yards to feet. We all know the answer is 12 feet. But we will look at the problem one step at a time in order to help set up a process we can use for other conversions. The way we approach the problem is by looking at the units I have and the units I want. Right now I have 4 *feet* = $\frac{4\ feet}{1}$ (we will find it helpful to always view these as fractions).

The unit I have is feet. The unit I want is yards. Looking at the table, I see the expression 1 yard = 3 feet. If two quantities are equal, then putting one over the other in a fraction produces a fraction equal to 1. All of the following equal 1.

$$\frac{2}{2} \qquad \frac{2+2}{4} \qquad \frac{12\ inches}{1\ foot} \qquad \frac{3\ feet}{1\ yard} \qquad \frac{1\ yard}{3\ feet}\ (*)$$

We call a fraction equal to 1 a "unit fraction." Also note that multiplying a quantity by 1 does not change the quantity. It may change the appearance of the quantity, but the quantity is unchanged.

Look again at the fraction we have.

$$\frac{4\ yards}{1}$$

I want to multiply it by a unit fraction. But I want that unit fraction to help eliminate the unit I do not want and introduce the unit I do want. Of the unit fractions in (*), two deal with the units we want. One of the last two is what we want. Notice that the unit, yards, that we do not want is in the numerator of our fraction. If we want it to divide out, we need to introduce it in the denominator of our fraction. So we will multiply our fraction by

$$\frac{3\ feet}{1\ yard}.$$

This gives us $\dfrac{4\ yards}{1} \dfrac{3\ feet}{1\ yard}$.

Yards divide out giving us $\dfrac{4\ \cancel{yards}}{1} \dfrac{3\ feet}{1\ \cancel{yard}} = 12\ feet$.

One very important thing in any academic endeavor is knowing what the words mean. There is a word that we use often in mathematics but may not think about what it means. We say drove some number of "miles PER hour." Or someone is paid some amount of "dollars PER hour." What does "per" mean?

If I drive 100 miles in two hours, what was my average speed? We know it would be 50 miles per hour. How did we get that? We divided.

If a woman is paid $48 for working four hours, how much was she paid? She was paid $12 per hour. How did we get that? We divided.

If you buy four loaves of bread for $6, how much did you pay? You paid $1.50 per loaf. How did we get that? We divided.

The word "per" means division.

Example—If Randy Johnson threw a fastball 100 miles per hour, what would the speed be in feet per second?

Since "per" means division, the quantity we have right now is $\dfrac{100\ miles}{hour}$.

This expression has two units, one for distance and one for time, neither of which we want. Consider one unit at a time. We will consider distance first. We have "miles" and we want "feet." From the chart, we know 1 mile = 5280 feet. That means that $\dfrac{5280\ feet}{1\ mile} = \dfrac{1\ mile}{5280\ feet} = 1$. Which unit fraction do we want? In our fraction above, mile is the unit we have and do not want. It is in the numerator. To have it divide out, we need to multiply by a unit fraction that has that unit in the denominator. Thus, we have $\dfrac{100\ miles}{hour} \dfrac{5280\ feet}{1\ mile}$.

With that, miles divide out, leaving feet, which is what we want.

Now we need to fix the time unit. We have hours and we want seconds. We do not normally talk about how many seconds are the same as some number of hours. In this case there is a unit, minutes, in between. So we will take the conversion in two steps, first eliminating hours by inserting minutes, then eliminating minutes by inserting seconds. Notice hour is in the denominator so we have to multiply by a fraction that has hour in the numerator. After we do that, we will have minutes in the denominator so we will have to multiply by a fraction that has minutes in the numerator.

The unit fractions we will use are $\dfrac{1\ hour}{60\ minutes}$ and $\dfrac{1\ minute}{60\ seconds}$.

$$\frac{100\ miles}{hour}\ \frac{5280\ feet}{1\ mile}\ \frac{1\ hour}{60\ min}\ \frac{1\ min}{60\ sec}=\frac{100\times5280\ feet}{60\times60\ sec}=\frac{146.6667\ feet}{sec}$$

Calculator Note—Proper use of parentheses is important when using your calculator to do the arithmetic in a problem. In the problem above, we do not see any parentheses but there are some implied by how we are supposed to handle order of operations. If you are not certain how to handle the arithmetic, a simple rule to go by is this:

Any time you have a fraction with more than one number in the numerator or denominator, put parentheses around the entire numerator and put parentheses around the entire denominator.

In other words, for the above calculation, you should type this:

$$(100 \times 5280) / (60 \times 60).$$

In order to do conversions between metric units, it is essential that we understand what the metric prefixes mean and how to use them.

Consider the metric unit kilometers. It is the distance unit "meters" together with the prefix "kilo-." Note from the chart that "kilo-" means "thousand." Thus "kilometer" means "one-thousand meters." Mathematically this would mean 1 km = 1000 m.

Now we can turn this expression into a unit fraction by putting either side of the above equivalence over the other side.

$$\frac{1000\ m}{1\ km},\ \frac{1\ km}{1000\ m}$$

Consider the metric unit centigrams. It is the weight unit "grams" together with the prefix "centi-." Note from the chart that "centi-" means "hundredth." Thus "centigram" means "one-hundredth of a gram." Mathematically this would mean $1\ cg = \dfrac{1}{100}g$.

In doing conversions, we are already working with unit fractions. We do not want to have to create unit fractions involving fractions since that would mean we would have complex fractions. Therefore, let us take the equivalence above and simplify it by multiplying both sides by 100. This gives us 100 *cg* = 1*g*.

Now we can turn this expression into a unit fraction by putting either side of the above equivalence over the other side.

$$\frac{100\ cg}{1\ g},\ \frac{1\ g}{100\ cg}$$

Example—If Randy Johnson threw a fastball 100 miles per hour, what would the speed be in meters per second?

$$\frac{100\ miles}{hour}\ \frac{1\ hour}{60\ minutes}\ \frac{1\ minute}{60\ seconds}\ \frac{1.6093\ km}{1\ mile}\ \frac{1000\ meters}{1\ km} = 44.70278\ meters\ per\ second$$

Example—In 2007, Jose Reyes of the New York Mets hit an inside the park home run. He was timed at 13 seconds for his run around the bases. What was his approximate average running speed in miles per hour?

We know that it is 90 feet between bases on a baseball diamond. That would give 360 feet from home to home. We also know that, when running full speed, a runner does not run directly from base to base but rounds the bases a bit. So let us estimate that Reyes ran 400 feet.

$$\frac{400\ feet}{13\ seconds}\ \frac{60\ seconds}{1\ minutes}\ \frac{60\ minute}{1\ hour}\ \frac{1\ mile}{5280\ feet} = 20.97902\ miles\ per\ hour$$

As we have noted, units are multiplied and divided just like numbers or just like algebraic variables. We will discuss the idea of area in greater detail in a later chapter but we know that when we give measures of area we give them in squared units, such as square feet or square miles.

Example—Convert the area inside the base paths into centimeters.

We know the baseball diamond is a square that is 90 feet along each side. Thus, its area is 90 feet × 90 feet or 8100 ft².

Note that the unit "feet" is squared. Therefore, we need to have feet divide out two times. That means we will have to multiply by a new unit fraction twice each time we try to change the units.

$$8100\ ft^2\ \frac{12\ inches}{1\ foot}\ \frac{12\ inches}{1\ foot}\ \frac{2.540\ cm}{1\ inch}\ \frac{2.540\ cm}{1\ inch} = 7,525,146.24\ cm$$

Example—Jorge Cantu of the Florida Marlins made $500,000 in 2008. Cantu is from Mexico. What was his 2008 salary in Mexican pesos?

$$\$500,000\ US\ \frac{1\ peso}{\$.0723\ US} = 6,915,629\ pesos$$

Example—Suppose Cantu is traded to the Toronto Blue Jays. All players are paid in U.S. dollars. Suppose, however, Cantu's salary is $1,000,000 Can. What would his salary be in Mexican pesos?

We do not have a conversion for pesos to $ Can. So we will convert to $ U.S. and then to pesos.

$$\$1,000,000\ Can\ \frac{\$.817\ US}{\$1\ Can}\ \frac{1\ peso}{\$.0723\ US} = 11,300,138\ pesos$$

Example—How many centimeters are in one light year?

First, it is necessary to figure out what one light year is. A light year is the distance that light can travel in one year. From science we know that light can travel 186,000 miles per second in a vacuum. We can convert from miles to kilometers to centimeters using our charts below. We can convert from seconds to minutes to days easily.

How to convert from days to years is actually sort of a trick question. A year has 365 days, most of the time. A leap year has 366. A year, scientifically, is the amount of time it takes the earth to make one revolution around the sun. This is where leap years come in. The actual amount of time it takes the earth to revolve around the sun is approximately 365.25 days. That extra .25 days adds up to an extra day every four years. That is why we have leap year.

How do we tell if a given year is a leap year? The year 2008 was a leap year because 2008 is evenly divisible by four. So a year is a leap year if it is evenly divisible by four? Not quite. A year is not exactly 365.25 days. It is a little less. So every so often we do not have a leap year. The year 1900 should have been a leap year. But a year is a leap year if it is divisible by four unless it is divisible by 100. So 1900 was not a leap year. The year 2000 was a leap year. The leap year rule is "a year is a leap year if it is divisible by four, but not if it is divisible by 100, unless it is divisible by 400." And that is not even perfect. To adjust for the inexact nature of things, every so often a "leap second" is added to a year to finish making the adjustment. The year 2008 had a leap second added to it.

Anyway, back to the problem.

$$\frac{186,000\ miles}{second}\ \frac{60\ seconds}{1\ minute}\ \frac{60\ minutes}{1\ hour}\ \frac{24\ hours}{1\ day}\ \frac{365.25\ days}{1\ year}\ \frac{1.6093\ km}{1\ mile}\ \frac{1000\ m}{1\ km}\ \frac{100\ cm}{1\ m} =$$

$9.446 \times 10^{17}\ cm$

Temperature Conversions

We will consider the last conversion, those involving temperature, because they are the only ones we will consider that do not involve unit fractions.

Most of the world uses the Celsius temperature scale. In the United States, we use the Fahrenheit temperature scale. In order to make the conversions, we use the following formulas.

Temperature Conversions

$$C = \frac{5}{9}(F - 32) \qquad \bigg| \qquad F = \frac{9}{5}C + 32$$

Which formula is used when? We use whichever formula has the unknown temperature's scale on the left.

Example—The Houston Astros are playing a home game. It is a very hot day and, unfortunately, the retractable roof on the stadium is stuck open. The only thermometer available gives the temperature 46° C. What is the temperature in Fahrenheit?

We know the Celsius temperature so we use the second of the two formulas.

$$F = \frac{9}{5}C + 32 = \frac{9}{5}46 + 32 = 114.8°F$$

Note that in evaluating, it is wise to let the calculator do all the work by simply typing in the entire expression at once. Be sure to use any parentheses in your formula and not use parentheses if there are not any in your formula.

Example—The average "normal" body temperature for a person is 98.6° F. What would that be in Celsius?

Since we know the Fahrenheit temperature, we will use the first formula.

$$C = \frac{5}{9}(F - 32) = \frac{5}{9}(98.6 - 32) = 37°C$$

Currency Exchange Rates (as of December 31, 2008)

Country/Continent	Exchange Rate
Australia	0.6989 U.S. Dollars = 1 Australian Dollar
Canada	0.817 U.S. Dollars = 1 Canadian Dollar
China	0.1466 U.S. Dollars = 1 Chinese Yuan Renminbi
Great Britain	1.442 U.S. Dollars = 1 British Pound

Country/Continent	Exchange Rate
Europe	1.4088 U.S. Dollars = 1 European Euro
Japan	0.0111 U.S. Dollars = 1 Japanese Yen
Mexico	0.0723 U.S. Dollars = 1 Mexican Peso

Lengths

1 foot (ft.) = 12 inches (in.)
1 yard (yd.) = 3 feet
1 fathom = 6 feet
1 rod = 5.5 yards
1 furlong = 40 rods = 1/8 mile
1 marine league = 3 nautical miles
1 land league = 3 miles
1 nautical mile = 1.15 miles = 6076.1 feet
1 mile (mi.) = 1760 yards = 5280 feet

Volumes

1 cup = 8 fluid ounces
1 quart = 2 pints = 57.75 in^3
1 tablespoon =3 teaspoons
1 fluid ounce = 2 tablespoons = 1.805 in^3
1 gallon = 4 quarts
1 pint = 16 fluid ounces = 28.88 in^3
1 barrel of petroleum = 42 gallons
1 barrel of liquid = 31 gallons

Area   1 acre = 43,560 square feet

Metric Prefixes

Prefix	Abbreviation	Value	Value	Prefix	Abbreviation	Value	Value
Deci	d	10^{-1}	tenth	Deca	da	10^1	ten
Centi	c	10^{-2}	hundredth	Hecto	h	10^2	hundred
Milli	m	10^{-3}	thousandth	Kilo	k	10^3	thousand
Micro	μ	10^{-6}	millionth	Mega	M	10^6	million
Nano	n	10^{-9}	billionth	Giga	G	10^9	billion
Pico	p	10^{-12}	trillionth	Tera	T	10^{12}	trillion

U.S.—Metric Conversions

1 inch = 2.540 cm
1 foot = 0.3048 m
1 yard = 0.9144 m
1 mile = 1.6093 km

1 pound = 0.4536 kg
1 fl. oz. = 29.574 milliliters
1 qt. = 0.9464 liters
1 gal = 3.785 liters

Temperature Conversions

$$C = \frac{5}{9}(F - 32) \quad \bigg| \quad F = \frac{9}{5}C + 32 \quad \bigg| \quad K = C + 273.15$$

Chapter 2—Exercises

Do the following unit conversion problems. Be sure to show the use of units.

1. Suppose a pitcher weighs 110 kg. In order to attain an incentive clause in his contract, he must weigh no more than 215 pounds. Does he qualify for the incentive clause? If not, how much weight must he lose in order to qualify?

2. Betty is 5.2 feet tall. How many meters is that? Suppose Betty is 5 feet, 2 inches tall. How many meters is that?

3. At their concession stands, the Padres have started selling Billy Bob's combination motor oil/salad dressing for $5.49 (U.S.) per gallon. Due to their proximity to the Mexican border, they also want to start selling the product in Mexico. What will the price be in pesos per liter?

4. Dave is driving 40 miles per hour. Convert his speed to meters per second.

5. The part of a baseball diamond inside the bases is a square that is 90 feet on each side. Find the area inside the basepaths and convert it to meters.

6. Aroldis Chapman has thrown a baseball unofficially clocked at 106 miles per hour. If he did that in Toronto they might want to know what that would be in meters per second. What would it be?

7. On September 10, 1960, Mickey Mantle hit a home run against Paul Foytack that cleared the right-field roof at Tiger Stadium. Based on where it was found, it was later estimated to have traveled 643 feet. How many millimeters did the ball travel?

8. Tom threw a baseball 42.7 meters per second. Dave threw a ball 94 miles per hour. Who threw the ball faster, Tom or Dave? Be sure to show all necessary work.

9. Suppose you drive a distance of 480 miles at a speed of 50 miles per hour. How many hours does this take?

10. CC Sabathia is reported to weigh 311 pounds. A few years ago he signed a contract with the New York Yankees for $161 million. Convert his weight to centigrams and the contract amount to Mexican pesos.

11. Convert 27 degrees Fahrenheit to degrees Celsius.

12. Convert 15 degrees Celsius to degrees Fahrenheit.

13. Suppose you need to put carpet in a rectangular room that measures 18 feet by 12 feet. At a price of $16.50 per square yard and assuming that you can buy precisely the amount of carpet you need, how much will the carpet for the room cost?

14. Guttenberg, New Jersey, has a population of 10,807 people in 0.24 square miles. This gives a population density of 45,029 people per square mile. What is the population density in people per square kilometer?

15. According to Genesis 5:27, Methusaleh was 969 years old when he died. How many seconds old was Methusaleh when he died?

16. A Canadian Football League field is 110 yards by 65 yards. A National Football League field is 100 yards by 160 feet. Using meters as your unit, how much bigger is the Canadian Football League field?

17. Eddie Gaedel, who played for the St. Louis Browns on August 19, 1951, was listed as being 3'7" tall. Randy Johnson was listed as 6'10" tall. How much taller was Johnson

    a. in inches?

    b. in feet?

    c. in meters?

    d. in millimeters?

18. A National Football League field is 100 yards by 160 feet. How many acres is that?

19. If the price of gasoline is \$3.44–9/10 per gallon, what would the price be in euros per liter?

20. Mickey Mantle was once timed running to first base in 3.1 seconds. It is 90 feet from home to first. What would Mantle's speed be

    a. in feet per second?

    b. miles per hour?

    c. meters per minute?

21. In 1851, a yacht race was held in England that was a precursor to the America's Cup Yacht Race. The distance of the race was 53 nautical-miles. What is that distance in

    a. marine leagues?

    b. miles?

    c. land leagues?

    d. furlongs?

22. In 2010, Alex Rodriguez was paid \$33,000,000. He had 595 plate appearances that year.

    a. How much money was he paid per plate appearance?

    b. He saw an average of 3.94 pitches per plate appearance that year. How much money was he paid per pitch thrown to him?

23. When a ballplayer is tested for performance enhancing drugs, he must submit a urine sample. Most labs require at least 1.5 fluid ounces of urine to do the test. What is that amount in

    a. teaspoons?

    b. milliliters?

    c. cups?

3—Statistics:
Introduction, Statistical
Studies, Reliability, History

"It is the mark of a truly intelligent person to be moved by statistics."—
George Bernard Shaw

"Be able to analyze statistics, which can be used to support or undercut
almost any argument."—Marilyn vos Savant

"You can prove anything with statistics." This is a common complaint
when statistics are used. The reason the statement is made is the fact that
many people use statistics in inappropriate ways. There can be unintentional
misuse of statistics. There can be intentional misuse of statistics. In either
case, the statement is false. You cannot PROVE something with statistics if
it is not true. But you can confuse people into believing all kinds of things if
you use statistics incorrectly and they do not understand how to analyze the
argument effectively.

One goal in this chapter will be to discuss what statistics are and talk
about how they are collected, calculated and presented so that you will learn
to identify statistics that are used well and statistics that are used poorly.

Section 3.1—Introduction

Before we get into baseball statistics, we will begin by talking about statistics in general. Statistics has two definitions. There is the field of statistics
which is defined as the science of collecting, analyzing and reporting data.
The collected data are also called statistics. So breaking all the rules we were
taught in school about using a word in its own definition, we can define statistics as collecting and analyzing statistics.

These data generally fall into two categories. There are **quantitative sta-**

tistics and **qualitative statistics**. Quantitative statistics are statistics that measure things that can be numerically described. How big? How heavy? How many? How old? Things that can have such questions asked about them are described using quantitative statistics. Qualitative statistics are used to describe things that do not have an obvious numerical description. For instance, if I ask someone, "What color are your eyes?" an answer of "Five" makes no sense. Eye color is not a quantity, but a quality. We can count how many people have a particular eye color. We can, while doing a study of eye color, decide to record "five" whenever anyone says "blue." But the color of someone's eyes does not have an inherent numerical description. There is nothing in a color that has any obvious numerical meaning. Responses to opinion polls are qualitative statistics as well. Anything that does not have an obvious numerical association can be viewed as a qualitative statistic.

We will spend most of our time looking at quantitative statistics since baseball has so many things that can be counted or numerically described such as batting average, number of home runs, earned run average, WHIP, win shares, and VORP. Baseball, more than any other sport, is intimately associated with the numbers that describe it. If you have paid any attention to baseball, there are numbers that are important. Things like .300 batting average, 20 wins, 300 career wins, 56-game hitting streak and 2.00 earned run average. All of these numbers immediately convey something very meaningful.

Section 3.2—Statistical Studies

The casual fan may not think of statistical studies when thinking of sports. Even the rabid fan may not. But there are many people who do a lot of statistical study and analysis of sports, particularly baseball. The Society for American Baseball Research (SABR) studies all aspects of baseball but much of its research focuses on statistics.

Statistics and statistical studies have a great deal of importance outside of sports as well. If you spend any time reading or watching the news, you regularly hear reports of statistical studies. Studies deal with effectiveness of medical treatments, crime rates in various locales, people's opinions on social issues, the person for whom people are going to vote in an election and just about anything else you can imagine.

Typically a statistical study has the goal of determining something about a group. We call that group the **population** of interest. Generally the population is too large or spread out for us to be able to actually obtain the statistic of interest from every member of the population. Or it may be too costly or time consuming to survey the entire population. Because of that, researchers will work with a **sample**. A sample is a smaller subset of the population. The desired information is then obtained from the sample, and, if the study is done well, conclusions are then drawn about the population from the results from the sample.

Samples can be done in a variety of ways.

1. Random sampling—A person studying a population can randomly choose members of the population. This can be done by randomly choosing names from the phone book or by questioning people as the researcher walks down the street.

2. Systematic sampling—This is not much different from random sampling except that some system is set up to help determine which members of the population to include in the sample. Instead of randomly choosing names from a phone book, I may choose every 75th name.

3. Convenience sampling—If I am interested in finding out college students' attitudes about some issue, it would be easy for me to simply poll my classes. Convenience sampling simply chooses an easily accessible subset of the population for a sample.

4. Stratified sampling—Sometimes the measurement of interest can vary widely between different subgroups in the population. To be sure the sample is representative, we want to be sure that each of those subgroups are represented in the sample in proportion to their size in the general population. So the person doing the study will do a random sample with each subgroup. If one subgroup makes up 30% of the general population, we will want it to represent 30% of our sample. In some sense, we're making the sample "look like" the general population.

Other considerations are also important when considering how to do a study or determining whether or not to put confidence in a study. There are various ways that a statistical study can be biased or skewed in favor of a particular response.

1. Wording—The way a survey is worded can easily bias the results. Perhaps I am interested in finding out if people think Barry Bonds should get into the Hall of Fame. I could word the question "Do you think Barry Bonds, the all-time home run champion and the only player to have over 500 homers and stolen bases, belongs in the Hall of Fame?" Or I could word the question "Do you think Barry Bonds belongs in the Hall of Fame in spite of the allegations of steroid use, anti-social behavior and fights with teammates?" It is entirely possible that the two questions would produce different results.

2. Participation bias—Sometimes, due to the way a survey is done, a certain group of participants may be more or less likely to participate. Many groups do polls on websites or by having people watching a television show call in to register their opinion. There are immediate problems with such polls. Only people accessing that website or watching that show will have the chance to participate. And only those who feel strongly about the particular issue will be likely to respond. I once saw a web-based poll asking "Do you hunt or fish?" The poll is immediately questionable because it was on the website of the Arkansas Game and Fish Commission. People visiting that website are much more likely to hunt or fish than the general population. A poll on the Colorado Rockies' website seeking opinions on the National League Most Valuable Player is far more likely to find people choosing Troy Tulowitzki than a survey on the New York Mets' website.

3. Who is doing the study?—A research study on the effects of second-hand tobacco smoke is suspect if it is done by the American Tobacco Institute. If the person or group doing a study has an agenda or strong interest in the results of the study, there is a possibility of that agenda affecting the results of the study.

4. Definitions of terms—Consider a survey asking, "Who is the best hitter in the American League?" Is it Mike Trout? Is it David Ortiz? Miguel Cabrera? Dustin Pedroia? The problem here is that we have no clear definition of what is meant by "best hitter." Is it batting average? Is it power? Is it on-base percentage? If a term in a survey is not clearly defined it can make the survey's results far less valuable.

5. Knowledge—It is important that people answering a survey have sufficient knowledge to be able to intelligently answer the questions. In 2000, CNN's website ran a series of articles talking about CNN's choice for the "century's best" in a variety of categories like athletes, musicians, etc. They would then run polls to see if people agreed. One such poll asked, "Do you agree with our choice for America's best paleoanthropologist?" It is highly unlikely that many of the people answering the poll know enough about paleoanthropology to intelligently answer that question. If you are trying to find out who people think is the best baseball player of all time, it would be nice if respondents knew something about baseball and had heard of people like Ty Cobb, Babe Ruth and Willie Mays in addition to current ballplayers.

Often people are skeptical of statistical studies because a sample of 1000 may be used to draw conclusions about a population of millions. However, such a sample can, if done properly, actually give a good approximation to the quantity or quality of interest in the general population. More specific information about assurances of this reliability is beyond the scope of this book.

Section 3.3—History of Statistics

IN GENERAL

Since one aspect of statistical study is the simple matter of counting things, it is obvious that rudimentary statistics have been around for millennia. But the generally recognized beginnings of formal statistical study were related to demographic and economic data. In 1662, John Graunt published "Observations on the Bills of Mortality" to track and warn about the bubonic plague. The major mathematical underpinnings of statistical study began in the 17th century as well, thanks to the development of probability theory in the work of Blaise Pascal and Pierre de Fermat. The 18th century saw more efforts to accumulate and analyze data as a means of determining what has happened and seeking to predict what would happen.

IN BASEBALL

Before someone gets very far into baseball statistics, certain things will become obvious. One of those is that numbers are not at all consistent over the years in baseball.

Let's look at a couple of statistical examples to make this clear.

This first chart shows the National League leaders in at-bats from 1877 and 1977.

1877 National League				1977 National League		
		AB				*AB*
1	George Wright	290		1	Pete Rose	655
2	Jumbo Latham	278		2	Dave Cash	650
3	Jack Burdock	277		3	Steve Garvey	646
4	Tom Carey	274		4	Dave Parker	637
5	Andy Leonard	272		5	Bill Russell	634
6	Joe Start	271		6	Enos Cabell	625
7	George Hall	269		T7	Larry Bowa	624
8	Jim Devlin	268		T7	Ivan DeJesus	624
T9	Mike Dorgan	266		9	Garry Templeton	621
T9	Cal McVey	266		10	Warren Cromartie	620
T9	Deacon White	266				

It is not hard to notice something different between the two data sets. George Wright led the 1877 National League with a total that was less than half of that of the 1977 leader. In fact, Wright's total would have placed him

101st in the league in 1977. What was the difference? Teams in the 1877 National League played between 57 and 60 games. In the 1977 National League, all teams played 162 games.

Our next chart shows the top ten single season strikeout totals by pitchers.

		Year	SO	IP
1	Matt Kilroy	1886	513	583
2	Toad Ramsey	1886	499	588.2
3	One Arm Daily	1884	483	500.2
4	Dupee Shaw	1884	451	543.1
5	Old Hoss Radbourn	1884	441	678.2
6	Charlie Buffinton	1884	417	587
7	Guy Hecker	1884	385	670.2
8	Nolan Ryan	1973	383	326
9	Sandy Koufax	1965	382	336
10	Bill Sweeney	1884	374	538

Again, it does not take much to notice something different. All but two of these totals occurred in 1884 or 1886. What happened? In 1884, for the first time, pitchers were allowed to throw with any motion, including overhand. Up to that point, pitchers were not allowed to throw overhand. Considering the mound was also only 50 feet away, instead of the modern 60 feet, 6 inches, it is not hard to see why there was a huge number of strikeouts. It is also not hard to notice the pitchers from the 1880s all pitched significantly more innings than the two more modern pitchers.

In 1887, Tip O'Neill led the major leagues with a .492 batting average. But if you look at the lists of top averages of all time you will see Hugh Duffy's .440 from 1894 listed at the top, with O'Neill's 1887 average listed as .435. What happened? For that one season, walks were counted as hits. The statistics for that season were adjusted to eliminate those tainted statistics. Of course, .435 is still a pretty good batting average.

In 1879, John Peters had 379 at-bats and only one walk. How could that be? Was he that much of a free-swinger? In fact, from 1876 to 1884, there were 17 other players with at least 300 at-bats and no more than two walks. What was different? During those years, it took seven, eight or nine balls to earn a walk.

The game has obviously changed. And with those changes, there are a number of changes in values of certain statistics and which statistics are valued by people involved in the game.

Chapter 3—Exercises

For each of the exercises marked with an asterisk (*), you will be using www.baseball-reference.com.

1. (*) Look at the annual stolen base leaders over the years. What do you notice? Pay particular attention to the 1930s through the 1950s. What do you think explains the differences?

2. (*) Look at the American League batting average leaders in 1968. Compare that to other years. Why were the averages so low?

3. (*) Look at the league leading saves totals over the years. What do you notice? Using some other resource, find out when the save became an official statistic.

4. (*) For the years 1970, 1975, 1980, 1985, 1990, 1995, 2000, 2005 and 2008, find the number of innings pitched for the major league leader in saves. What do you notice? What do you think explains the differences? (Note: We might suspect that the change in the way relief pitchers are used [middle relief, set-up men, closers] would mean that teams are doing a better job of protecting leads than would previously have been the case. Interestingly, this is not the case. David Smith, founder of retrosheet.org, once wrote an email to SABR members saying the following: "Gabriel Schechter has done some wonderfully detailed work on relievers in the last few months, some of which he has shared with this list. He and I have consulted somewhat and one of the conclusions we have both reached is that the advent of the 'closer age' and 'structured bullpen' has not had the result that one would expect. That is, teams are no more likely to hold on to a 9th inning lead now than they were 30, 60 or 90 years ago.")

5. For each of the following, classify the statistic as either qualitative or quantitative.
   a. team on which a player is playing
   b. number of teams on which a player has played
   c. brand of baseball glove
   d. number of batting gloves a player wears while batting
   e. home runs hit during August
   f. votes received during All-Star Game voting
   g. position played
   h. in golf, percentage of drives a player hits that land within the fairway
   i. in football, kinds of penalties an offensive lineman incurs
   j. in basketball, number of pairs of shoes a player uses during the year
   k. country of origin for players

6. Review the difference between quantitative and qualitative statistics.
   a. Give examples of five different quantitative statistics from baseball (other than ones mentioned in #5 above).
   b. Give examples of five different quantitative statistics from basketball (other than ones mentioned in #5 above).

    c. Give examples of five different quantitative statistics from football (other than ones mentioned in #5 above).

    d. Give examples of two different qualitative statistics that are often reported for athletes (other than ones mentioned in #5 above).

7. Explain why the survey question "Who is the best defensive second baseman in baseball?" is flawed.

8. Explain why the survey question "Who is the best manager?" is flawed. (Exercises 7 and 8 are not intended to imply that discussions of "Who is the best defensive second baseman in baseball?" or "Who is the best manager?" are not valid questions to ask in a discussion format. The problem is that for a scientifically valid study, they are flawed. For discussion or argument, they are fine questions.)

9. (*) Honus Wagner played shortstop for the Louisville Colonels (1897–1899) and Pittsburg Pirates (1900–1917). John Peters played shortstop for the Chicago White Stockings (1874–1877, 1879), Milwaukee Grays (1878), Providence Grays (1880), Buffalo Bisons (1881) and Pittsburg Alleghenys (1882–1884). Ozzie Smith played shortstop for the San Diego Padres (1978–1981) and St. Louis Cardinals (1982–1996). Look at some of the defensive statistics for these players and then explain some of the problems in comparing the defensive abilities of these three players.

10. Suppose you were interested in finding out the percentage of high school baseball players from California who end up playing major league baseball.

    a. What is the population you are studying?

    b. What are some difficulties one would encounter in attempting to do such a study?

    c. Do you think there would be a different final if you were doing the study on high school ball players from Alaska instead of California?

    d. Do you think there would be differences in percentages between northern and southern California? between urban and rural ballplayers?

11. A few years ago I saw a poll that asked the question, "Do you feel safe when confronted by a police officer?" Explain why this wording is flawed.

12. Suppose major-league baseball decided to cut expenses involved with All-Star game voting by only shipping paper ballots to teams to the east of the Mississippi River. Explain how this would bias the results of the voting.

13. Go online and find out how the All-Star game voting was problematic in 1957. How was the voting process changed after 1957?

14. The text discussed the difficulties in answer the question "Who is the best hitter in the American League?" Compile a list of statistics or criteria

that you think are important in answering that question and devise a system that uses those statistics to produce a single "best hitter in the league" number.

15. Cricket is another game that has some aspects common with baseball. The two games may very well share a common ancestor in devising the rules and process of play. Explain why doing a survey for "best cricket batsman of all time" at major league baseball ballparks would be a poor idea.

16. (*) Do some online research into rules regarding walks, strikeouts and how pitching was done. Also consider how many innings pitchers tended to pitch. Then break up the years from 1871 to 2014 into blocks of years that would allow for reasonable comparisons of pitchers' walks and strikeout totals.

17. (*) Look at fielding percentages for third baseman from 1871 to 1930. Then look online for rules or practices involved in use of fielding gloves by baseball players. See if you notice any patterns in the fielding percentages compared to glove usage. (Related trivia—Who was Jerry Denny?)

4—Different Kinds of Statistics

"Statistics is the grammar of science."—Karl Pearson

"Statistics are to baseball what a flaky crust is to Mom's apple pie."—Harry Reasoner

Every sport has statistics associated with it. But statistics are more a part of baseball than any other sport. There are all kinds of numbers in baseball that have significant meanings. Football has the 1000-yard running back. Basketball has the 50-point game. But baseball has so many. They can be signs of excellence, like 20 wins, 3000 hits, 500 home runs or a .300 batting average. They can be signs of futility, like 20 losses, a .200 batting average or a .400 winning percentage. There are numbers of mythic proportions due to the performance associated with them, like Babe Ruth's 714 home runs (even though it is no longer the record), Joe DiMaggio's 56-game hitting streak, Ty Cobb's .366 batting average and Cal Ripkens 2,632 consecutive games played.

There are statistics for everything that happens on a baseball diamond. Before we get into the different kinds of statistics, there are a couple of preliminary mathematical topics we must consider.

Section 4.1—Percentages

Percentages are one of the most common kinds of mathematics encountered by people in their daily lives. Loans involve percentages. Sales involve percentages. Taxes involve percentages. The mathematics involved in percentages is actually fairly simple. It is a basic example of what we call proportional reasoning. Simply stated, that means that we have two fractions set equal to each other. Since fractions are a part over a whole, this means a proportional problem can be written this way.

$$\frac{part}{whole} = \frac{PART}{WHOLE}$$

Since a percentage is a fraction over 100, then every percentage problem can be written this way.

$$\frac{part}{100} = \frac{PART}{WHOLE}$$

What we need to do in order to solve a particular problem is to figure out what numbers go where in the other three spots.

Example—What is 32% of 150?

We are told that we are working with 32%. So obviously the 32 is the part on the percentage side.

$$\frac{32}{100} = \frac{PART}{WHOLE}$$

The wording of the problem shows that 150 is the "WHOLE" and the "PART" is unknown. So we have $\frac{32}{100} = \frac{x}{150}$ and $\frac{32\,(150)}{100} = x$ or $x = 48$.

Example—32 is what percent of 98?

The percentage is unknown. Percentages are fractions over 100 so x is a part and 100 is a whole.

$$\frac{x}{100} = \frac{PART}{WHOLE}$$

The wording of the problem shows that 32 is the "PART" and the "WHOLE" is 98. So we have $\frac{x}{100} = \frac{32}{98}$ and $x = \frac{32\,(100)}{98}$ or x is roughly 32.65. So 32 is approximately 32.65% of 98.

Example—32 is 47% of what number?

Percentages are fractions over 100 so 47 is a part and 100 is a whole.

$$\frac{47}{100} = \frac{PART}{WHOLE}$$

The wording of the problem shows that 32 is the "PART" and the "WHOLE" is unknown. So we have $\frac{47}{100} = \frac{32}{x}$ and $x = \frac{32\,(100)}{47}$ or x is approximately 68.09. Hence, 32 is 47% of (roughly) 68.09.

One other thing to remember is that, since percentages can be greater than 100, the "PART" may be greater than the "WHOLE." Just read the problem carefully and the wording will tell what is the "PART" and what is the "WHOLE."

Example—132 is what percent of 98?

The percentage is unknown. Percentages are fractions over 100 so x is a part and 100 is a whole.

$$\frac{x}{100} = \frac{PART}{WHOLE}$$

Be careful not to assume that 98 is the "PART" and 132 the "WHOLE" just because 132 is bigger than 98. The wording of the problem shows that 132 is the "PART" and the "WHOLE" is 98. So we have $\frac{x}{100} = \frac{132}{98}$ and $x = \frac{132\,(100)}{98}$ or x is roughly 134.69. So 132 is approximately 134.69% of 98.

One problem with percentages is that they generally cannot be added like regular numbers. This is due to the likelihood that their reference values are not the same.

Example—A jacket is priced at $100. It goes on sale for 15% off. A week later it is reduced another 10%. What is the price now?

It would be easy to say that "10% + 15% = 25%" and conclude that the jacket's price is now $75, having subtracted $25, which is 25% of $100. But that is wrong. We will take the problem one step at a time.

First, the price is reduced 15%.

$$\frac{part}{whole} = \frac{PART}{WHOLE}$$

$$\frac{15}{100} = \frac{x}{100}$$

Solving this gives $x = 15$ so the reduced price is $100 − 15 = $85. Notice that now, the 10% reduction is based on a price of $85, not the original $100. This is the problem with adding the percentages in this problem.

$$\frac{part}{whole} = \frac{PART}{WHOLE}$$

$$\frac{10}{100} = \frac{x}{85}$$

Solving this gives 8.5 so the current price is $85 − $8.50 = $76.50.

Another thing that can help solve percentage problems is drawing pictures of the fractions. Consider the problem below.

Example—A jacket is on sale at 25% off. The price of the jacket is now $45. What was the original price?

I've chosen the numbers so the problem isn't particularly hard. If we just go to $\dfrac{part}{whole} = \dfrac{PART}{WHOLE}$, we can have a problem here. Let's see why. Since the discount is 25%, the "part" on the percentage side could be 25 while the "whole" is 100.

$$\frac{25}{100} = \frac{PART}{WHOLE}$$

The only other number we are given is 45. Where does it go? Let's draw a picture.

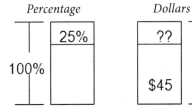

Notice that the 25% and the $45 do not refer to the same thing. The 25% is the amount of discount. The $45 is the amount left AFTER the discount. But neither does the $45 refer to the 100%. So we actually have to add another number to the problem.

So we now call the "WHOLE" on the money side × since it relates to 100% on the percentage side. This gives us $\dfrac{75}{100} = \dfrac{45}{x}$. Solving this equation will give us the original price of $60. The picture helps us to see what the "PART" and "WHOLE" need to be.

One more item should be mentioned when it comes to percentages. When percentages are reported, there can be errors. There can also be the appearance of errors. Consider the following data.

Category	%
A	39
B	33
C	16
D	13

You may notice that these percentages add up to 101. That appears to be wrong. This can simply be a result of rounding off. Here are the same data, given to one decimal place.

Category	%
A	38.6
B	32.7
C	15.8
D	12.9

They add up to 100, as they should.

Consider this set of data.

Category	%
A	48
B	45
C	33
D	32

These percentages add up to 158. There is no way that rounding off can account for that much difference from 100. But sometimes, there can be overlap in categories. For instance, suppose these data categories are courses being taken by college students.

Category	%
mathematics	48
English	45
history	33
geography	32

It is certainly possible that some students are taking two or more of these classes so some students may be reported in more than one category. Therefore a sum of more than 100% may not be an error.

I did, however, once see a poll reported in the *Arkadelphia* (Arkansas) *Siftings Herald*. It asked "How would you rate the cleanliness of Arkadelphia. The first day the results were reported we were told:

Results: 5 votes

Excellent—0%
Good—0%
Fair—5%
Poor—0%

It appears that it reported the number of votes for each category rather than the percentages. However, the next day, the following results were reported:

Results: 31 votes

Excellent—66%
Good—19%
Fair—52%
Poor—23%

That is not the number of votes in each category. Also, it is more than a round off error. Though I am not sure, my guess is that the 66% for "excellent" should be 6%. If that is the case, the percentages add to 100% and those percentages are possible with 31 total votes, with 2 votes for "excellent," 6 votes for "good," 16 votes for "fair" and 7 votes for "poor."

Section 4.2—*Mean, Median and Mode and "Five Number Summary"*

We have all heard the word "average" in reference to numerical quantities. Test averages, income averages, etc. What many people do not know is that there are different "averages." When most people think of "average" they are thinking of adding up the numbers and dividing by the number of numbers. For example, if a student takes four tests and scores 78, 90, 85 and 84, the student's test average is (78 + 90 + 85 + 84)/4 = 84.25. When most people hear the word "average" that is the kind of mathematics they think of. But in many statistical reports, "average" means something else.

Suppose you receive an offer to work for a company. You are told that the average salary at the company is $100,000 per year. That sounds appealing. But suppose the company has five employees and the incomes are $440,000, $18,000, $15,000, $14,000 and $13,000. Adding those numbers up and dividing by five would give $100,000. But that number does not give a good idea of what the majority of the data are. Because of that, a different "average" is often used.

The "average" with which most people are most familiar, the one where we add the numbers and divide by the number of numbers, is called the **mean**. Therefore, the mean of the salary data at are fictional company is $100,000. In many cases, though, the mean does not really give a good idea of what "most of the data are like." In that case we use the **median**. A simple definition of median is "the middle number." So for our company, with salaries of $440,000, $18,000, $15,000, $14,000 and $13,000, the "middle number" is $15,000.

A small problem arises when we try to calculate the median by thinking of the "middle number." That problem occurs if we have an even number of data points. Consider the numbers 4, 5, 6, 7, 8, 9. There is no "middle number." It isn't 6, because there are two numbers less than six but three greater. It isn't 7, because there are two greater and three less. When we have an even number of data points, we take the middle TWO numbers, add them together and divide by 2. So, in this case, the median is (6 + 7)/2 = 13/2 = 6.5.

There is another "average" that is particularly useful for qualitative data, data that does not have any obvious numerical meaning. For instance, eye color is not a quantitative concept. So if we wanted to decide what the "average" eye color is, the mean and median are of no help. Suppose a group of people was evaluated for eye color, producing the following results.

Color	Quantity
blue	23
brown	18
green	12
plaid	2

The most common eye color is blue. We would call blue the **mode**. The mode of a data set is the most common value. Data need not be qualitative for the mode to be of value.

Example—The following data are the top nine players for triples from 1974.

Larry Bowa	10
Dave Cash	11
Willie Davis	9
Ralph Garr	17
Roger Metzger	10
Al Oliver	12
Amos Otis	9
Mickey Rivers	11
Reggie Smith	9

To calculate the mean, we add the numbers and divide by 9 (the number of data values).

$$\frac{10+11+9+17+10+12+9+11+9}{9} = \frac{98}{9} = 10.88$$

To calculate the median, we must first put the values in numerical order.

$$9 \quad 9 \quad 9 \quad 10 \quad 10 \quad 11 \quad 11 \quad 12 \quad 17$$

Choosing the "middle number" yields a median of 10, since the fifth number from both the left and the right is 10.

The mode is the number that appears the most, which, in this case, is 9.

\-

Example—The following are the National League home run leaders from 1964 to 1973

1964	Willie Mays	47
1965	Willie Mays	52
1966	Hank Aaron	44
1967	Hank Aaron	39
1968	Willie McCovey	36
1969	Willie McCovey	45
1970	Johnny Bench	45
1971	Willie Stargell	48
1972	Johnny Bench	40
1973	Willie Stargell	44

First, the mean is $\dfrac{47 + 52 + 44 + 39 + 36 + 45 + 45 + 48 + 40 + 44}{10} = \dfrac{440}{10} = 44.$

The median cannot be found until we first put the numbers in order.

36　　39　　40　　44　　44　　45　　45　　47　　48　　52

Since we have an even number of numbers, we find the middle two, 44 and 45, add them together and divide by 2, giving (44 + 45) / 2 = 89/2 = 44.5.

The mode in this case is a little different. Two numbers, 44 and 45, both occur twice. So the mode in this case is both 44 and 45. In such cases we say the data set is **bimodal**.

The following are looking at calculator usage (TI-82, 83 or 84) for finding the mean and median.

Data into a List

Press <STAT> and choose "Edit."

Enter the data into Ll or Ll and L2 depending on the kind of problem. Enter a number and press down arrow or <ENTER>.

You will find a table with headings Ll and L2.

If you are just putting in one set of numbers, they should all be in Ll. If you are entering a second data set, use right arrow in order to enter data in another list using the same method as we did for Ll.

Getting the Statistical Analysis of List Data

Put the data into a list as above. Usually you want to use Ll but that is not required

Choose "1-Var Stats"

The following tells what each item means

Press <STAT> and choose "CALC"

If your data was in Ll, then all you need to do is press <ENTER>

$\bar{x}$	mean	Σx	sum of data
Σx^2	sum of squares of data	Sx	standard deviation
σx	another standard deviation	n	number of data entries

Using down arrow shows more statistical information

The following tells what each item means   minX smallest data   Q1 lower quartile
                                                  Med   median   Q3 upper quartile
                                                  maxX largest data value

If the data is not in L1, then one thing would be different. After you have "1-Var Stats," add L2 (or whatever list holds the data) by pressing <2nd> L2. Then proceed as above.

The calculator is not programmed to find the mode. Therefore you will still have to do that yourself.

One other way of describing a set of data is what is called the **Five Number Summary**. One of the calculator screens shown above gives all of the data for the Five Number Summary.

As mentioned above, "minX" is the smallest data value, "Q1" is the lower quartile, "Med" is the median, "Q3" is the upper quartile and "maxX" is the largest data value. "Lower Quartile" is known as the 25th percentile. That means that approximately 25% of the data values will be below that value. As mentioned above, the median is the middle value. It is also known as the 50th percentile, meaning approximately 50% of the data are below that value. "Upper Quartile" is known as the 75th percentile. That means approximately 75% of the data are below that value. These five values give the Five Number Summary of the data.

Section 4.3—Counting Statistics

Some of the simplest baseball statistics are "counting statistics." Those are statistics like games played, home runs, strikeouts, etc., where all that is reported is how many times something happened.

Some examples:

1. Through 2008, Mark Teixeira had 203 career home runs.
2. For his career, Robin Yount had 251 home runs.
3. For his career, Gavvy Cravath had 119 home runs.
4. In 1999, Billy Wagner struck out 124 batters.
5. In 1925, Dazzy Vance struck out 221 batters.

It is certainly true that counting statistics tell exactly what they mean. As with all statistics, however, context can be important. From the information above, it could be concluded that Robin Yount was a better home run hitter than Mark Teixeira and that Teixeira is a better home run hitter than Gavvy Cravath. It could be concluded that Dazzy Vance was a much better strike out pitcher in 1925 than Billy Wagner was in 1999.

Let us now look at some context for those statistics.

1. Through 2008, Mark Teixeira had 203 career home runs in 3414 at-bats.
2. For his career, Robin Yount had 251 home runs in 11008 at-bats.
3. For his career, Gavvy Cravath had 119 home runs in 3951 at-bats.
4. In 1999, Billy Wagner struck out 124 batters in 74⅔ innings pitched.
5. In 1925, Dazzy Vance struck out 221 batters in 265⅓ innings pitched.

We might now conclude that Teixeira is the best home run hitter of the three hitters and that Wagner was a better strikeout pitcher than Vance. But there is still more context that might be of interest.

- From 1908 through 1918, Gavvy Cravath had three of the four highest single season home run totals in the major leagues.
- When he retired, Cravath was the fourth leading home run hitter of all time.
- Cravath played in the Dead Ball Era, when the ball was not as lively and a single ball might have stayed in play for nearly the entire game.
- In 1915, Cravath led the National League with 24 home runs. The entire rest of the league only hit 201 home runs. In 2001, the National League had 25 players with at least 30 home runs.
- In 1925, Vance led the National League in strikeouts. Second place in the league was 140. Third was 93.

As we saw in Chapter 3, the game has changed over the years so when we look at statistics, context will be important.

Some counting statistics are a little more complicated. Consider Total Bases. In 1922, Rogers Hornsby had 250 hits. Among these were 46 doubles, 14 triples and 42 home runs. It is not hard to see that he must have had 148 singles. Total bases gives the total number of bases accumulated by a hitter on his hits. So every single would count as one, every double would count as two, every triple would count as three and every homer would count as four. So Hornsby had 1 * 148 + 46 * 2 + 3 * 14 + 4 * 42 = 450 Total Bases. This happens to be the second highest single season total of all time, trailing only Babe Ruth's 457 from 1921.

One oddity in statistical reporting is that IP, unlike other counting statistics, can include fractions. That can be displayed in a variety of ways. If a pitcher throws 25 and one-third innings, you may see it written 25⅓, 25.333, or 25.1. For many years in baseball, the official statistics would round off innings so 25⅓ was reported as 25. This was changed when a pitcher won an ERA title that he shouldn't have won because rounding benefited him while hurting another pitcher.

Section 4.4—Percentage Statistics

Quite a few common baseball statistics percentage statistics, although very few are actually written the way we normally write percentages.

In 1919, Slim Sallee had a win-loss record of 21–7. If we wanted to figure out the percentage of his decisions that ended in a win, we would set up the following equation.

$$\frac{x}{100} = \frac{21}{28}$$

Doing the arithmetic would tell us that Sallee won 75% of his games. In most cases, however, that is not how baseball reports winning percentage.

Usually, the formula will be $winning\ percentage = \dfrac{wins}{decisions} = \dfrac{wins}{(wins + losses)}$.

Notice that this is the usual percentage formula except for dividing by 100 on the percentage side.

Batting average is handled similarly. In 1924, Goose Goslin had 199 hits in 579 at-bats. The percentage of his at-bats resulting in a hit would be given by $\dfrac{x}{100} = \dfrac{199}{579}$ for an answer of 34.4%. The formula for batting average is $batting\ average = \dfrac{hits}{at\ bats}$. Again, same formula as for the percentage except for dividing by 100. So, Goslin's batting average was $x = \dfrac{199}{579} = .344$. Since a player cannot have more hits than at-bats, the highest possible batting average is 1.000.

Most of the time, batting average will be displayed using three places to the right of the decimal point. There are a few cases where this was not sufficient. In 1949, George Kell (from Swifton, Arkansas) and Ted Williams both finished with batting averages of .343. In order to determine the league champion, more decimal places were used.

	AB	H	AVG
George Kell	522	179	.3429
Ted Williams	566	194	.3427

Each player's average is still reported as .343 but Kell was the batting champion.

Slugging Percentage is another of this sort of statistic. The formula here is $slugging\ percentage = \dfrac{total\ bases}{at\ bats}$. We saw above that Rogers Hornsby had 450 total bases in 1922. Since he had 623 at-bats, his slugging percentage was $x = \dfrac{450}{623} = .722$.

It should be noted that slugging percentage, unlike batting average, can be higher than 1.000. This would happen if a player has more total bases than at-bats. For example, if a player bats twice and has a single and a double, that would be three total bases in two at-bats for a slugging percentage of 1.500. It is not unlimited. The best slugging percentage possible would be 4.000, obtained when a player homers in every at-bat.

Another useful offensive statistic is On Base Percentage. The way to win baseball games is to score runs. The way to score runs is to get runners on base. It does not matter whether the batter gets on by a hit or a walk, as long as he gets on base. That is what on base percentage measures. It is calculated by

$$OBP = \frac{(hits + walks + hit\ by\ pitch)}{(at\ bats + walks + hit\ by\ pitch + sacrifice\ flies)}.$$

In 1979, Gary Templeton of the Cardinals batted .314, ranking 6th in the National League. However, his OBP was only .331, ranking 40th in the league. Mike Schmidt, the Hall of Fame third baseman, had a batting average of only .253. However, Schmidt's OBP was .386, more than 16% higher than Templeton's. If "value" is determined by batting average, then Templeton was a much better player than Schmidt. If it is getting on base, then Schmidt was a much better player. As mentioned above, slugging percentage also factors into value. When a player gets a hit, it is better if it is for more bases. Templeton's slugging percentage was .458, good for 18th in the league. But Schmidt's was .564, second best in the league.

As with counting statistics, percentage statistics require context to be truly informative. In 2000, Esteban Yan had a slugging percentage of 4.000. Todd Helton's slugging percentage was .698. That would seem to say that Yan was a better hitter than Helton. Context, however, is enlightening. Yan, a pitcher, batted once and hit a home run, thus giving him the highest possible slugging percentage. Helton batted .372 with 59 doubles and 42 home runs. Helton led the major leagues in slugging in 2000 for players with 500 or more plate appearances. No major league manager would take Yan over Helton for hitting.

Section 4.5—Other Baseball Statistics

As mentioned above, simply looking at counting statistics does not give enough context to allow us to compare performance as much as we would like. Consider the example of Ralph Branca and Joe Coleman in 1947. Branca allowed 83 earned runs. Coleman allowed 77 earned runs. Without any context, we might conclude that Branca was not as effective as Coleman that year. But things change when we note that Branca pitched 280 innings while Coleman pitched 160. We would like a better idea of how much better Branca was than Coleman. One way to do that would be to consider how many games each pitcher pitched. But using games is still problematic. If a pitcher typically pitches 7 or 8 innings in a game, we would expect him to allow more runs per game than a pitcher who pitches only 1 inning per game. Thus, we use Earned Run Average (ERA) which became an official statistic in 1912. ERA is a "rate" statistic. It tells how many earned runs a pitcher allows for every nine innings he pitches.

	ER	IP
Ralph Branca	83	280
Joe Coleman	77	160

It is not hard to see that Branca allowed $\dfrac{83}{280} = 0.296429$ runs per inning while Coleman allowed $\dfrac{77}{160} = 0.48125$. Since these are the runs per inning, multiplying by nine gives "runs per nine innings" or the ERA. Thus, the formula for ERA is $ERA = \dfrac{ER}{IP} \times 9$.

	ER	IP	ERA
Ralph Branca	83	280	$\dfrac{83}{280} \times 9 = 2.67$
Joe Coleman	77	160	$\dfrac{77}{160} \times 9 = 4.33$

The standard way of displaying ERA is to show two places to the right of the decimal point.

Another indication of a pitcher's effectiveness is how many batters he allows to reach base. Obviously if men do not get on, they cannot score. There are two primary ways a pitcher can allow men to reach base—walks and hits. This has led to the statistics "walks per inning," "hits per inning" and "walks/hits per inning." Each of these, like ERA, are often looked at as per nine innings, giving "walks per nine innings," "hits per nine innings" and "walks/hits per nine innings." Unlike ERA, these are not standard statistics so sometimes you will see "per inning" and others will use "per nine innings." Strikeouts per inning or strikeouts per nine innings is another commonly used statistic. Here are these statistics for a few pitchers from the 1988 season.

Name	IP	H	H/IP	H/9IP	BB	BB/IP	BB/9IP	SO	SO/IP	SO/9IP	W + H	WH/IP	WH/9IP
Lee Smith	83.67	72	0.86	7.75	37	0.44	3.98	96	1.15	10.33	109	1.30	11.73
Jeff Sellers	85.67	89	1.04	9.35	56	0.65	5.88	70	0.82	7.35	145	1.69	15.23
John Franco	86	60	0.70	6.28	27	0.31	2.83	46	0.53	4.81	87	1.01	9.10

Name	IP	H	H/IP	H/9IP	BB	BB/IP	BB/9IP	SO	SO/IP	SO/9IP	W + H	WH/IP	WH/9IP
Terry Clark	94	120	1.28	11.49	31	0.33	2.97	39	0.41	3.73	151	1.61	14.46
Jeff Ballard	153.33	167	1.09	9.80	42	0.27	2.47	41	0.27	2.41	209	1.36	12.27
John Candelaria	157	150	0.96	8.60	23	0.15	1.32	121	0.77	6.94	173	1.10	9.92
Sid Fernandez	187	127	0.68	6.11	70	0.37	3.37	189	1.01	9.10	197	1.05	9.48
Pascual Perez	188	133	0.71	6.37	44	0.23	2.11	131	0.70	6.27	177	0.94	8.47
Nolan Ryan	220	186	0.85	7.61	87	0.40	3.56	228	1.04	9.33	273	1.24	11.17

During the season, fans are often interested in whether or not their team is in first place and, if not, how far from first their team is. The statistic **games behind** gives an indication of this. For example, suppose the following are the standings for the National League's Eastern Division

Team	W	L	PCT
Mets	85	60	.586
Phillies	80	65	.552
Nationals	77	70	.524
Marlins	68	80	.459
Braves	52	95	.354

Obviously the Mets are in first place, but how far ahead are they? Games behind can be calculated a number of ways. One way is to look at how many more games a team has won than it has lost. That is called "number of games above .500." For these standings, those numbers would be

Mets	25
Phillies	15
Nationals	7
Marlins	−12
Braves	−43

The Mets are in first place so they are no games behind. This is usually designated by one or more hyphens (−). The Mets are 10 more games above .500 than the Phillies. The number of games the Phillies are behind the Mets is thus 10/2 = 5. The Mets are 25 − −12 = 37 more games above .500 than the Marlins so the Marlins are 37/2 = 18.5 games behind. This gives the following standings.

Team	W	L	PCT	GB
Mets	85	60	.586	—
Phillies	80	65	.552	5
Nationals	77	70	.524	9
Marlins	68	80	.459	18.5
Braves	52	95	.354	34

One more statistic, which receives considerable attention late in the season is the **magic number**. That is the number of a team's wins and other teams losses that will guarantee the one team wins the division championship or wild card. In the standings above, the Mets have already eliminated the Marlins and Braves from any chance of winning the division. To see this, remember that each team is scheduled to play 162 games. Since the Braves have lost 95 games, the most they could win would be 67. That would get them nowhere near the Mets record. Likewise, the most the Marlins could win is 82, insufficient to catch the Mets. The Nationals and Phillies could conceivably catch the Mets. The Nationals could win 92 games. Thus, if the Mets win eight more games, the Nationals are out. But that assumes the Nationals win all their remaining games. The magic number for the Nationals to be eliminated is 8, but it is any combination of Mets wins and Nationals losses adding to 8. Similarly, any combination of Mets' wins and Phillies losses adding to 13 would eliminate the Phillies.

Section 4.6—Sabermetrics

The Society for American Baseball Research (SABR) is home to many people who like to analyze baseball statistics in all kinds of interesting ways. Bill James, Pete Palmer and many others have created all kinds of statistics to try to better describe what has happened, how it happened and which players are better than others.

One such statistic that is very popular among statistically-minded fans is OPS, On Base Plus Slugging. If we already have the OBP and SLG, it is simply a matter of adding them together to get OPS. OPS has the value of including OBP, thus rewarding hitters who get on by more than just base hits. It also rewards those who get a lot of extra base hits.

Following are the top 30 players (500 or more plate appearances) in OPS from 1947.

Rank	Name	OPS	AVG	SLG	OBA
1	Ted Williams	1.133	.343	.634	.499
2	Ralph Kiner	1.055	.313	.639	.417
3	Johnny Mize	.998	.302	.614	.384
4	Whitey Kurowski	.964	.310	.544	.420
5	Bob Elliott	.927	.317	.517	.410
6	Walker Cooper	.926	.305	.586	.339
7	Harry Walker	.924	.363	.487	.436
8	Joe DiMaggio	.913	.315	.522	.391
9	Stan Musial	.902	.312	.504	.398
10	Willard Marshall	.894	.291	.528	.366
11	Hank Greenberg	.885	.249	.478	.408
12	Tommy Henrich	.857	.287	.485	.372
13	Jeff Heath	.850	.251	.485	.366
14	Bobby Thomson	.844	.283	.508	.336
15	Joe Gordon	.842	.272	.496	.346
16	Dixie Walker	.842	.306	.427	.415
17	Pee Wee Reese	.841	.284	.426	.414
18	Ferris Fain	.837	.291	.423	.414
19	George McQuinn	.832	.304	.437	.395

Rank	Name	OPS	AVG	SLG	OBA
20	Bill Nicholson	.831	.244	.466	.364
21	Grady Hatton	.825	.281	.448	.377
22	Roy Cullenbine	.823	.224	.422	.401
23	Stan Spence	.819	.279	.441	.378
24	Enos Slaughter	.818	.294	.452	.366
25	Lou Boudreau	.811	.307	.424	.388
26	Jackie Robinson	.810	.297	.427	.383
27	Hoot Evers	.801	.296	.435	.366
28	Andy Pafko	.800	.302	.454	.346
29	George Kell	.798	.320	.412	.387
30	Luke Appling	.797	.306	.412	.386

Everyone in the top ten had a fairly high batting average but notice Hall of Famer Hank Greenberg at 11. His batting average was only .249 but he got on base over 40% of the time and had a fairly high slugging percentage, even though it was .127 below his career SLG in this, his last year as a player. Notice Roy Cullenbine at 22. His batting average was rather poor. As with Greenberg, this was Cullenbine's last season in the majors. Yet his OBP was over .400. He had 137 walks to go with only 104 hits. If the goal is to get on base, Cullenbine was a star. His slugging percentage was also fairly good.

Another, more complicated, statistic is Runs Created. Runs Created combines the OBP, total bases, stolen bases, caught stealing, grounding into double plays, batting average and homers with men in scoring position. The purpose is to try to determine the number of runs for which a player is responsible.

One of the most popular statistics for measuring the overall value of a player is Win Shares, also created by Bill James. We will not look at how to calculate Win Shares. A description can be seen at www.baseballgraphs.com/main/index.php/site/details/#winshares. Suffice it to say, the description takes nearly a page and a half in nine-point font. It involves, among other things, a team's runs scored, a team's runs allowed, a team's wins, runs created (and thus OBP, total bases, stolen bases, caught stealing, grounding into double plays, batting average and homers with men in scoring position), outs made, adjustments for the ballpark, and defense (home runs, walks and strikeouts for pitchers, passed balls, errors, double plays, etc.).

Other sabermetric statistics could include Isolated Slugging (percentage of extra bases on a player's hits), VORP (value over replacement player), Runs Created Above Average (how the player compares to an "average" player), Offensive Winning Percentage (what winning percentage would a team have if it was made of guys like the particular player), Bases Per Plate Appearance (calculated by $(TB + BB + HBP + SB - CS - GIDP)/(AB + BB + HBP + SF)$) and others.

Another interesting statistic is the team focused Pythagorean Formula.

Developed by Bill James, it looks at Runs Scored and Runs Allowed and does a remarkable job of predicting what a team's winning percentage should be. The formula is simple.

$$\frac{Team\ Wins}{Team\ Losses} = \frac{(Runs\ Scored)^2}{(Runs\ Allowed)^2}$$

Consider the 1969 Houston Astros. They scored 676 runs while allowing 668. Thus, their Pythagorean Rating would be $\frac{676^2}{668^2} = 1.024096$. So their wins divided by losses should be 1.024096. Using x to represent wins, this gives

$$\frac{x}{162 - x} = 1.024096$$

$$x = 1.024096 * 162 - 1.024096x$$

$$2.024096x = 1.024096 * 162$$

$$2.024096x = 165.9035$$

$$x = 81.96425$$

Thus, James' formula predicts they would win 81.96425 games. They actually won 81. Here are the results for the entire 1969 National League.

	Runs Scored	Actual Wins	Actual Losses	Runs Allowed	Pythagorean Rating	Predicted Wins	Predicted Losses
Eastern Division							
Cardinals	595	87	75	540	1.214078	88.83	73.17
Cubs	720	92	70	611	1.388617	94.18	67.82
Expos	582	52	110	791	0.541369	56.90	105.10
Mets	632	100	62	541	1.364708	93.49	68.51
Phillies	645	63	99	745	0.749561	69.41	92.59
Pirates	725	88	74	652	1.236462	89.56	72.44
Western Division							
Astros	676	81	81	668	1.024096	81.96	80.04
Braves	691	93	69	631	1.199216	88.34	73.66
Dodgers	645	85	77	561	1.321885	92.23	69.77
Giants	713	90	72	636	1.256796	90.22	71.78
Padres	468	52	110	746	0.393563	45.75	116.25
Reds	798	89	73	768	1.079651	84.10	77.90

This chart lists the difference between actual wins and predicted wins.

	Actual Wins	Predicted Wins	Difference
Eastern Division			
Cardinals	87	88.83	−1.83
Cubs	92	94.18	−2.18
Expos	52	56.90	−4.90
Mets	100	93.49	6.51
Phillies	63	69.41	−6.41
Pirates	88	89.56	−1.56

	Actual Wins	Predicted Wins	Difference
Western Division			
Astros	81	81.96	−0.96
Braves	93	88.34	4.66
Dodgers	85	92.23	−7.23
Giants	90	90.22	−0.22
Padres	52	45.75	6.25
Reds	89	84.10	4.90

Notice that eight of the 12 teams finished within 5 of their predicted wins total. Also, notice that the Mets, who won the Eastern Division and eventually won the World Series, significantly outperformed the Cubs who finished second in the Eastern Division. The Mets won the division by winning more games than they "should" have and the Cubs lost games they "should" have won. The Braves won the Western Division in large part due to the fact that they outperformed their Pythagorean Projection by more than any team in the division (except for the lowly Padres) instead of finishing third like their statistics predicted.

Section 4.7—Other Sports

While baseball makes greater use of more statistics, other sports do have their own statistics. All of them have some basic counting statistics. All also have some percentage statistics and some rate statistics. Some have some unique statistics as well.

FOOTBALL

Counting statistics in football are things like yards gained, first downs, passes attempted, interceptions, touchdowns scored, tackles and sacks. Tackles and sacks are, like innings pitched, able to include fractions.

Football has some basic percentage statistics. Unlike baseball, they are typically written as percentages rather than decimals. Third down success (100 * 3rd down success/3rd down attempts) and a quarterback's completion percentage (100 * completions/attempts) are two of them.

Football has several rate statistics. They are fairly straightforward. A running back's yards per carry, a receiver's yards per reception, a punter's yards per punt, a team's yards offense per game, etc., are simple averages. Each is the mean of the attempts, catches or game.

One football statistic that is a little different is the turnover margin. If a team has lost a fumble or thrown an interception (giveaways) 14 times but has recovered an opponent's fumble or intercepted an opponent's pass (takeaways) nine times, they have a −5 turnover margin. On the other hand, if they have lost a fumble or thrown an interception nine times but have recovered an opponent's fumble or intercepted an opponent's pass 14 times, they have a +5 turnover margin. The turnover margin is Takeaways minus Giveaways.

Quarterback ratings are the most complicated of the common football statistics. As with many statistics in baseball, the quarterback rating is not a good statistic to immediately use to compare players from different eras. The philosophy of the passing game is very different now than it was 40 years ago. Back in the 1960s, the majority of passes were thrown 15–20 yards down field. Relatively few passes were thrown within five yards of the line of scrimmage. Because of that, completion percentages are much higher now than they were then. Yards per reception were much higher then than they are now.

The quarterback rating is a complicated statistic. It is calculated using completions, attempts, touchdowns, interceptions and yards. The calculation goes as follows:

$$a = (((Comp/Att) * 100) - 30) / 20$$
$$b = ((TDs/Att) * 100) / 5$$
$$c = (9.5 - ((Int/Att) * 100)) / 4$$
$$d = ((Yards/Att) - 3) / 4$$

a, b, c and d cannot be greater than 2.375 or less than zero.

$$QB\ Rating = (a + b + c + d) / .06$$

Notice a is based on the completion percentage, b is based on the rate of touchdowns per attempt, c is based on interceptions per attempt and d is based on yards per attempt.

Example—Suppose a quarterback has thrown 97 passes, completing 56 for 720 yards, with seven touchdowns and four interceptions.

$$a = (((56/97) * 100) - 30) / 20 = 1.386597938$$
$$b = ((7/97) * 100) / 5 = 1.443298969$$
$$c = (9.5 - ((4/97) * 100)) / 4 = 1.344072165$$
$$d = ((720/97) - 3) / 4 = 1.105670103$$

$$QB\ Rating = (a + b + c + d) / .06$$
$$= (1.386597938 + 1.443298969 + 1.344072165 + 1.105670103)/ .06$$
$$= 87.99398625$$

Basketball

Counting statistics in basketball would include things like shots attempted, shots made, assists, rebounds, turnovers, etc. Shooting percentages (field goal or free throw) are examples of percentage statistics. Common rate statistics would be points, assists or rebounds per game. These again are means. A group of less common rate statistics would be assists, points or rebounds per 48 minutes. In other words, if a player played the entire game, scoring at the same rate he does during the times he is in the game, how many points would he score. For points per 48 minutes, the calculation would be $\dfrac{total\ points\ scored}{total\ minutes\ played} \times 48$.

An interesting rate statistic in basketball is the assist to turnover ratio. If a player has 45 assists and 12 turnovers, his assist to turnover ratio is $45/12 = 3.75$.

Basketball has turnovers, just like football, and thus has an identical turnover margin. A similar statistic would be the rebounding margin.

Volleyball

Counting statistics in volleyball would be digs, kills, assists, service errors, aces, etc. Percentage statistics would include serve success rate. The most interesting statistic in volleyball is a percentage statistic that has an interesting twist to it. When a player attempts a kill in volleyball, there are three possible results. It can be returned, it can be successful, or it can be an error (ball hit into net, blocked or hit out of bounds). The Kill Percentage $= \dfrac{kills - errors}{hits}$.

Note that this can be negative if a player has more errors than kills. It should be noted that not all people in volleyball calculate Kill Percentage the same way. The difference involves the definition of an "error." Some include kill attempts that are blocked as errors, some do not.

Golf

Golf has counting statistics like strokes, putts attempted, birdies, eagles, etc. Percentage statistics would include things like greens reached in regulation. Average drive and average score would be examples of means. Holes per eagle would be a rate statistic.

Par for a particular hole is an average of sorts. It is, in the estimation of the person supervising the course, how many strokes an average golfer should need to complete a hole.

A handicap in golf is a mechanism for making it possible for golfers of varying abilities to have a competitive match. Weaker golfers will have strokes removed from their scores to make the match competitive. The handicap index is probably the most complicated golf statistic.

Here is the process for establishing a handicap. In order to establish a handicap, a golfer must have played at least five rounds on rated courses. A maximum of 20 rounds is used.

1. differential calculations

    For each round played, we must calculate the "differential." To do that, we need the USGA course and slope ratings for the courses played.

    Differential = (Golfer's Score − Course Rating) * 113 / Slope Rating

2. choosing appropriate differentials

    Not all differentials are used.

Number of Rounds	Differentials Used
5–6	1 lowest
7–8	2 lowest
9–10	3 lowest
11–12	4 lowest
13–14	5 lowest
15–16	6 lowest
17	7 lowest
18	8 lowest
19	9 lowest
20	10 lowest

3. average differential

    Find the mean of the differentials. Multiply the result by .96, dropping (not rounding) everything to the right of the first decimal place. The resulting number is the handicap index.

Example—Consider the following rounds, with course and slope ratings shown.

Score	Course Rating	Slope Rating
98	71.8	128
104	72.5	135
87	71.8	128
93	72.2	131
89	71.8	128
93	72.5	135
90	72.1	134

Let's calculate the differential for the first round.

Differential = (98 − 71.8) * 113 / 128 = 23.1296875

The next table shows all of the differentials.

Score	Course Rating	Slope Rating	Differential
98	71.8	128	23.12969
104	72.5	135	26.36667
87	71.8	128	13.41875
93	72.2	131	17.94198
89	71.8	128	15.18438
93	72.5	135	17.15926
90	72.1	134	15.09478

With seven rounds played, we take the two lowest differentials, 13.41875 and 15.09478, add them and divide by 2, getting 14.25677. Multiply this by .96 and truncate after the tenths place to get 13.6. This is our golfer's handicap.

Now we calculate the golfer's "Course Handicap." To do that, we take his handicap index, multiply by the course's slope rating (not course rating) and divide by 113. Then round the result to the nearest whole number. For our golfer above, on a course with a slope rating of 138, that would be 13.6 * 138/113 = 16.60884956 which rounds to 17.

What this now means, is that, if our golfer plays a round at this course in 95 strokes, we would subtract 17 from his score to get a "net" score of 78.

Chapter 4—Exercises

4.1—PERCENTAGES

1. A coat that Mary wanted was priced at $344. She didn't want to pay that much. It was discounted 30%. She still didn't want to pay that much. A week later, after it was discounted another 20%, she bought it. How much did Mary pay for the coat?

2. In 1972, Nate Colbert had 24.5575221% of the San Diego Padres' team RBIs. If Colbert had 111 RBIs, how many did the whole team have?

3. In 1972, Colbert hit 38 of the Padres' 102 home runs. What percentage of the Padres' HRs did Colbert hit?

4. From 1974 to 1975, Gene Tenace's batting average went up 20.85308% to .255. What was his average in 1974?

5. Bob bought a jacket on sale for $170.85. The jacket had been discounted 15%. What was the original price? (Show all necessary work.)

6. Bob Caruthers pitched 445 innings for the Brooklyn Bridegrooms in 1889. The Bridegrooms' pitching staff had a total of 1212 innings pitched. What percentage of the total innings were pitched by Caruthers?

7. Bubba was working at the hardware store. A customer wanted to buy some tools totaling $165. The boss told Bubba to give the man a 15% discount. Bubba incorrectly charged the man $142.50. Did Bubba overcharge or undercharge the man and by how much? (Show all necessary work.)

8. The football team's coach had a goal of increasing the team's passing yardage from an average of 210 yards per game. He wanted to raise it 22%. After that they began to average 253 yards per game. Did the team reach the goal? By how much did they exceed their goal or fall short of their goal?

9. It 1955, the Cincinnati Reds drew 693,662 fans to their home games in Crosley Field. That was only 34.582% of the home attendance the Milwaukee Braves had in County Stadium. What was the Braves' home attendance in 1955?

10. In 1900, Bonanza, Arkansas, had a population of 906. By 1910, the population had dropped 10.49%. By 1920 it had dropped another 36.37%. What was the population of Bonanza in 1920?

11. In 1906, the Chicago Cubs won 76.3% of their 152 games. How many games did they win? (It is not possible to win a fraction of a game, so round off your answer.)

12. Babe Ruth hit 60 home runs in 1927. That was 13.667426% of the entire American League's home runs that year. How many home runs were hit in the American League that year?

13. In 2004, Bobby Abreu of the Philadelphia Phillies made a salary of $10,600,000. That was an increase of 16.4835% from his 2003 salary. What was Abreu's 2003 salary?

14. In 2004, the total payroll for the New York Yankees was $182,835,513. They paid Alex Rodriguez $21,726,881. What was Rodriguez' salary as a percentage of the total team payroll?

15. Will White pitched in the National League and American Association from 1877 to 1886. He threw 394 complete games. That was 97.7667494% of all of his pitching appearances. In home many games did White pitch?

16. Juan Pierre of the Florida Marlins was paid $600,000 in 2002. For 2003, his salary went up 66.6667%. For 2004, his salary went up 140%. What was his 2004 salary?

17. Suppose Bubbaville's population is 1,400. If it decreases 15% this year and goes up 12.5% next year, what will its population be then?

18. The top two in National Football League history for receiving yardage (through the 2013 season), are Jerry Rice and Terrell Owens. Rice had 143.6865% of the 15,934 yards that Owens had. How many yards did Rice have?

19. The White Sox home attendance went from 797,451 in 1958 to 1,423,144 in 1959. What was the percentage increase?

20. The population increased from 55,390 to 68,390. What was the percent change of the population?

4.2—MEAN, MEDIAN AND MODE AND "FIVE NUMBER SUMMARY"

1. The table below gives the number of base hits pitcher Jerry Koosman had in his first six full seasons in the major leagues.

Year	Hits
1968	7
1969	4
1970	6
1971	8
1972	4
1973	8

Find the mean, median and mode for this data set. Do this problem without using a calculator at all.

2. The following are the number of at-bats for each of the 1969 New York Mets.

365	353	362	400	395	565	483	327	303	247
215	211	202	177	169	93	74	40	15	10	1
91	84	74	47	37	29	24	17	12	4	1

Give the Five Number Summary, mean and mode for this set of data.

3. The following chart shows the number of times Alex Rodriguez has grounded into double plays over the past ten years.

Year	GIDP
1996	15
1997	14
1998	12
1999	12
2000	10
2001	17
2002	14
2003	16
2004	18
2005	8

Find the mean, median and mode for this data set.

4. The following chart gives the strikeout leaders from 1964.

Name	Strikeouts	Name	Strikeouts
Jim Bunning	219	Juan Marichal	206
Dean Chance	207	Sam McDowell	177

Name	Strikeouts	Name	Strikeouts
Tony Cloninger	163	Camilo Pascual	213
Al Downing	217	Orlando Pena	184
Don Drysdale	237	Gary Peters	205
Whitey Ford	172	Juan Pizarro	162
Bob Gibson	245	Dick Radatz	181
Jim Kaat	171	Chris Short	181
Sandy Koufax	223	Dick Stigman	159
Denny Lemaster	185	Bob Veale	250
Mickey Lolich	192	Dave Wickersham	164
Jim Maloney	214	Earl Wilson	166

Give the Five Number Summary, mean and mode for this set of data.

5. Consider the following data set which gives the major league leading home run totals from the years 1950–1969. (They have been placed in increasing order to make things easier for you so the first one is not from 1950, etc.)

37	41	42	44	44	44	45	46	47	47
47	49	49	49	49	49	51	52	52	61

Give the Five Number Summary, mean and mode for this set of data.

6. a. Explain why the median is sometimes a better indicator of general tendency than the mean.

   b. Define "outlier."

7. The following are the National and American League leading strike out totals from 1988 to 1997.

228	291	201	301	233	232	241	241	215	241
227	308	189	204	236	294	276	257	319	292

Give the Five Number Summary, mean and mode for this set of data.

8. The following are the major league leading triples totals from 1963 through 1968 (sorted into ascending order).

13	13	13	14	14	16

Find the mean, median and mode for this data set. Do it without using your calculator so you can be sure you really know how to do it.

9. The following are the major league leading doubles totals from 1950 through 1969 (sorted into ascending order).

37	38	39	39	40	40	41	41	41	41
43	43	44	44	45	46	47	51	53	56

Give the Five Number Summary, mean and mode for this set of data.

10. The following data are the major league leading doubles totals from 1950 through 1969.

56	41	43	53	41	38	40	39	39	47
37	41	51	43	44	45	40	44	46	41

Give the Five Number Summary, mean and mode for this set of data.

11. The following are the American and National League leading home run totals from 1971–1980. You may use your calculator.

48	41	48	45	40	46	52	39	38	32
38	36	36	32	44	32	40	37	48	33

Give the Five Number Summary, mean and mode for this set of data.

4.3—COUNTING STATISTICS

1. Go to baseball-reference.com and look at the 1895 National League and 2005 National League. Looking at the team statistics and the leaders table at the bottom of the page, note the differences between the two leagues in the following counting statistics.

   Team errors ("E" under "League Miscellaneous Stats")
   League leaders in at-bats
   League leaders in pitcher's strikeouts
   League leaders in home runs
   League leaders in saves
   League leaders in stolen bases
   League leaders in triples
   League leaders in innings pitched
   League leaders in games started by pitchers

   For each statistic, try to determine whether the difference is due to numbers of games played or changes in the way the game has been played.

2. In the text, we discussed the unusual concentration of pitchers from the 1880s in the single season pitcher's strikeouts leaders. Go to baseball-reference.com and look at the single season leaders in the following statistics and see if you see similar oddities. Try to explain those oddities.

   Saves   Home Runs   Stolen Bases   Complete Games

4.4—PERCENTAGE STATISTICS

1. Find the batting averages for each of the following players.

Name	Year	At-bats	Hits	AVG
Maury Wills	1966	594	162	
Garry Templeton	1977	621	200	
Lou Brock	1977	489	133	
Frank Taveras	1978	654	182	
Bill North	1979	460	119	
Lonnie Smith	1982	592	182	
Omar Moreno	1982	645	158	
Rickey Henderson	1982	536	143	
Steve Sax	1983	623	175	
Harold Reynolds	1988	598	169	
Vince Coleman	1988	616	160	

Name	Year	At-bats	Hits	AVG
Gerald Young	1989	533	124	
Eric Yelding	1990	511	130	
Brett Butler	1991	615	182	
Ray Lankford	1992	598	175	
Chad Curtis	1993	583	166	
Luis Polonia	1993	576	156	

2. Find the winning percentage for each of the following players.

Name	Year	Wins	Losses	PCT
Pete Donohue	1926	20	14	
Carl Mays	1927	3	7	
Grover C Alexander	1927	21	10	
Herb Pennock	1930	11	7	
Eppa Rixey	1932	5	5	
Hi Bell	1932	8	4	
Bill Swift	1932	14	10	
Leo Mangum	1933	4	3	
Bob Smith	1933	8	7	
Red Lucas	1933	10	16	
Carl Hubbell	1934	21	12	
Leon Chagnon	1935	0	2	
Watty Clark	1935	13	8	
Syl Johnson	1938	2	7	
Dizzy Dean	1938	7	1	
Paul Derringer	1939	25	7	
Johnny Podgajny	1940	1	3	
Tot Pressnell	1942	1	1	
Harry Eisenstat	1942	2	1	
Dutch Leonard	1942	2	2	
Ted Lyons	1942	14	6	
Tiny Bonham	1942	21	5	
Schoolboy Rowe	1943	14	8	
Curt Davis	1945	10	10	

4.5—OTHER BASEBALL STATISTICS

1. Find the Earned Run Average for each of the following players. Recall that 35.1 innings pitched really means 35⅓.

Name	Year	Innings Pitched	Earned Runs	ERA
Jim Barr	1971	35.1	14	
Terry Forster	1975	37	9	
Eddie Watt	1974	38	17	
Danny McDevitt	1961	39.2	18	
Greg Thayer	1978	45	19	
Bobby Bolin	1961	48	17	
Aubrey Gatewood	1964	60	15	
Elias Sosa	1977	63.2	14	
Ray Washburn	1970	66	51	
Ron Taylor	1971	69	28	

Name	Year	Innings Pitched	Earned Runs	ERA
Wayne Twitchell	1979	78	45	
Pascual Perez	1982	79.1	27	
Orlando Pena	1973	107	35	
Dick Hall	1962	118	30	
Lary Sorensen	1981	140.1	51	
Curt Simmons	1962	154	60	
Ferguson Jenkins	1977	193	79	
Dennis Eckersley	1982	224.1	93	
Mudcat Grant	1966	249	90	
Ron Reed	1975	250.1	98	
Claude Osteen	1967	288	103	
Dean Chance	1968	292	82	

2. The following are the National League East standings at the close of play on September 10, 1969. For each team, find the Winning Percentage, Games Behind, and Magic Number for them to be eliminated by the Mets.

Team Name	Wins	Losses	PCT	GB	Magic Number
New York Mets	84	57			
Chicago Cubs	84	59			
St. Louis Cardinals	77	65			
Pittsburgh Pirates	75	64			
Philadelphia Phillies	56	84			
Montreal Expos	44	99			

4.6—SABERMETRICS

1. Fill in all of the blanks in the chart, where "TB" is Total Bases, "AVG" is Batting Average, "OBP" is On Base Percentage, "SLG" is Slugging Average and "OPS" is On Base Plus Slugging.

Name	Year	AB	H	2B	3B	HR	TB	BB	HBP	SF	AVG	OBP	SLG	OPS
Lon Warneke	1941	77	9	0	0	0		11	0	0				
Glenn Myatt	1936	78	17	1	0	0		9	0	0				
Johnny Sain	1950	102	21	2	0	1		6	1	0				
George Dickey	1942	116	27	3	0	1		9	0	0				
Ed McGhee	1954	128	28	3	0	2		16	0	1				
Skeeter Kell	1952	213	47	8	3	0		14	2	0				
Hal Smith	1956	227	64	12	0	5		15	0	0				
Marv Blaylock	1956	460	117	14	8	10		50	2	5				
Arky Vaughan	1935	499	192	34	10	19		97	7	0				
Wally Moon	1957	516	152	28	5	24		62	1	7				

4.7—OTHER SPORTS

1. For the following members of the 2008 Cincinnati Bengals, find the average yards per rushing attempt.

Player	Att	Yds	Yds/Att
Cedric Benson	214	747	
Chris Perry	104	269	
Ryan Fitzpatrick	60	304	
Kenny Watson	13	55	
James Johnson	9	29	
Carson Palmer	6	38	
Andre Caldwell	5	53	
DeDe Dorsey	5	8	
Antonio Chatman	2	4	
T.J. Houshmandzadeh	1	9	
Jordan Palmer	1	4	

2. For the following quarterbacks, again from the 2008 Bengals, calculate the quarterback rating.

Player	Att	Comp	Yds	TD	INT	Rating
Ryan Fitzpatrick	372	221	1905	8	9	
Carson Palmer	129	75	731	3	4	
Jordan Palmer	12	7	41	0	2	

3. For the following members of the 1971–1972 Lakers (who had a 33-game winning streak), fill in all the blanks. "G" = Games, "Min" = Minutes Played, "FG" = Field Goals Made, "FGA" = Field Goals Attempted, "FG%" = Field Goal Percentage, "Reb" = Rebounds, "R/G" = Rebounds per game, "PTS" = Points Scored, "P/G" = Points per game, "P/48" = Points per 48 minutes.

Player	G	Min	FG	FGA	FG%	Reb	R/G	PTS	P/G	P/48
Gail Goodrich	82	3040	826	1695		295		2127		
Jerry West	77	2973	735	1540		327		1985		
Jim McMillian	80	3050	642	1331		522		1503		
Wilt Chamberlain	82	3469	496	764		1572		1213		
Happy Hairston	80	2748	368	798		1045		1047		
Flynn Robinson	64	1007	262	535		115		635		
Pat Riley	67	926	197	441		127		449		
Leroy Ellis	74	1081	138	300		310		342		
John Trapp	58	759	139	314		180		329		
Elgin Baylor	9	239	42	97		57		106		
Jim Cleamons	38	201	35	100		39		98		
Keith Erickson	15	262	40	83		39		86		

4. Fill in the blanks in this chart for the leading hitting percentages in 2008 NCAA Division 2 volleyball.

Name, Team	Kills	Errors	Total Attacks	PCT
Stacey Borgia, Lock Haven	402	74	685	
Rhe-Ann Niles, New Haven	400	80	685	
Ludmila Amaral, California (Pa.)	511	91	991	
Maria Broslawsky, West Va. Wesleyan	358	90	658	
Jordan Kent, West Ala.	240	52	466	

Name, Team	Kills	Errors	Total Attacks	PCT
Racey Bartley, Mount Olive	439	102	843	
Kaitlin McKenna, St. Leo	388	95	736	
Sara Rice, Cal St. San B'dino	257	55	512	
Enobong Shammah, Queens (N.Y.)	516	139	966	
Amanda Luedtke, West Virginia St.	270	52	566	

5. Suppose a golfer has played the following rounds at course with the indicated ratings. Calculate the golfer's handicap.

Score	Course Rating	Slope Rating
98	72.2	123
104	71.4	134
87	73.0	127
93	74.1	129
89	72.4	125
93	71.8	131
90	72.4	124
85	73.2	129
106	72.4	124

5—Statistics: Display

"The greatest moments are those when you see the result pop up in a graph or in your statistics analysis—that moment you realize you know something no one else does and you get the pleasure of thinking about how to tell them."—Emily Oster

"Do we need to have 280 brands of breakfast cereal? No, probably not. But we have them for a reason—because some people like them. It's the same with baseball statistics."—Bill James

Statistics and data are interesting and important. However, in order to use them to their greatest advantage, we must be able to express them in a way that other people can understand and interpret. As we will see, there are many ways to present statistics. Some are very simple. Some are more complicated. Some are visually plain. Some are visually appealing. Each method has advantages. Each has limitations and disadvantages. As we look at the various means of displaying data we will consider those advantages and limitations.

Section 5.1—Lists and Tables

The simplest way to represent data is listing the data. For example, the following is the number of strikeouts for each year of Dennis Ribant's major league pitching career.

35	13	84	75	27	7

An advantage to simply listing the data is that there is no way the data are being misrepresented. One disadvantage, in this case, is that no context is given. Unless you happen to know who Ribant was, and when he played, you do not have enough information to make much use of these data.

Year	Team(s)	SO
1964	Mets	35
1965	Mets	13

Year	Team(s)	SO
1966	Mets	84
1967	Pirates	75
1968	Tigers—White Sox	27
1969	Cardinals—Reds	7

When we give more information like this, we will typically call it a table rather than a list. However, it is really just a list with some detail and context.

One distinct limitation for lists is if there are more data values. Consider the following example. This list gives the number of times members of the 2005 Arizona Diamondbacks were hit by pitches.

1	0	0	0	0	0	8	4	0	1	8
0	0	0	1	0	0	0	11	6	0	0
0	1	1	0	0	0	5	0	1	7	

This list definitely has a problem. It has no context. But aside from that, there is too much data for a list to be of help. We can do something about that by changing the list a little and creating what we call a **frequency table**.

Hit by Pitch	Number of Players
0	19
1	6
4	1
5	1
6	1
7	1
8	2
11	1

The frequency table helps us make more sense out of the data. We can do a bit more by extending the frequency table and adding percentages. This helps us see the percentage of each occurrence.

Hit by Pitch	Number of Players	PCT
0	19	59.4
1	6	18.8
4	1	3.1
5	1	3.1
6	1	3.1
7	1	3.1
8	2	6.3
11	1	3.1

Such charts can still have limitations. Consider the following data.

647	633	620	615	611	605	604	602	600	599	582	581	580
573	571	563	559	558	556	555	550	546	535	528	523	521
500	500	498	490	489	484	472	467	460	456	454	446	446
444	439	438	435	435	426	422	421	421	417	405	402	385
384	383	383	369	359	358	358	347	343	337	332	320	307

304	302	301	300	296	289	283	281	279	278	277	267	265
261	253	237	192	192	190	187	177	175	166	166	121	118
117	117	116	113	106	105	102	97	96	95	95	93	92
89	88	88	85	84	84	84	83	82	79	79	76	75
75	74	74	72	72	70	70	70	69	68	67	66	66
64	59	56	55	55	54	54	54	54	52	50	49	47
46	46	43	43	43	43	43	42	41	40	39	39	39
36	36	32	30	29	29	29	28	28	28	26	25	25
24	24	22	22	21	21	21	19	19	19	19	18	18
17	17	17	16	15	14	14	14	14	13	13	12	10
10	9	9	8	7	7	7	7	7	7	7	6	6
6	6	5	5	4	4	4	3	3	3	2	2	2
2	1	1	1	1	1	1	1	1	1	1	1	

This gives the number of at-bats for everyone (with at least one AB) in the National League in 1934. Even with the data in order, this list is not of much value. There is just too much data. A frequency table is not much better.

AB	Freq	AB	Freq	AB	Freq	AB	Freq	AB	Freq
647	1	472	1	300	1	92	1	40	1
633	1	467	1	296	1	89	1	39	3
620	1	460	1	289	1	88	2	36	2
615	1	456	1	283	1	85	1	32	1
611	1	454	1	281	1	84	3	30	1
605	1	446	2	279	1	83	1	29	3
604	1	444	1	278	1	82	1	28	3
602	1	439	1	277	1	79	2	26	1
600	1	438	1	267	1	76	1	25	2
599	1	435	2	265	1	75	2	24	2
582	1	426	1	261	1	74	2	22	2
581	1	422	1	253	1	72	2	21	3
580	1	421	2	237	1	70	3	19	4
573	1	417	1	192	2	69	1	18	2
571	1	405	1	190	1	68	1	17	3
563	1	402	1	187	1	67	1	16	1
559	1	385	1	177	1	66	2	15	1
558	1	384	1	175	1	64	1	14	4
556	1	383	2	166	2	59	1	13	2
555	1	369	1	121	1	56	1	12	1
550	1	359	1	118	1	55	2	10	2
546	1	358	2	117	2	54	4	9	2
535	1	347	1	116	1	52	1	8	1
528	1	343	1	113	1	50	1	7	7
523	1	337	1	106	1	49	1	6	4
521	1	332	1	105	1	47	1	5	2
500	2	320	1	102	1	46	2	4	3
498	1	307	1	97	1	43	5	3	3
490	1	304	1	96	1	42	1	2	4
489	1	302	1	95	2	41	1	1	11
484	1	301	1	93	1				

There are 153 different at-bat totals here. That is too many categories for a frequency table to be of much value. In cases like this, it is helpful to use a variation on the frequency table called **binned data** or **grouped data**.

AB	Freq
641–680	1
601–640	8
561–600	7
521–560	10
481–520	6
441–480	8
401–440	11
361–400	5
321–360	7
281–320	10
241–280	7
201–240	1
161–200	8
121–160	1
81–120	23
41–80	39
1–40	81

When grouping or binning data, we gain by having fewer categories. We lose some information, however. For example, in the above chart, we cannot tell how many players had 192 at-bats. We only know that eight players had from 161 to 200 at-bats. Maybe all eight had 192. Maybe none had 192. We cannot tell.

There are a few guidelines when binning data.

1. Do not have overlap. Do not have one bin for 1–40 and another for 31–70.

2. Do not have gaps. Do not have a bin for 1–40 and then the next bin for 51–90.

3. Keep bins the same size. Do not have a bin for 1–5 and then another for 6–100.

4. Do not have too few bins. In the above chart, we would have very little usefulness if we had bins 1–340 and 341–680.

5. Do not have too many bins. If we had 1–2, 3–4, 5–6, etc., we would be no better off than when we listed each number separately.

Though we used 17 bins in the above chart, it is customary to try to have from six to 12. The number of bins we use depends on various things such as how spread out the data are, the number of data values in each bin, etc.

Section 5.2—Charts

There are times that we use a more visual approach to displaying data. Each of the following kinds of charts can be used to serve the same purpose as a frequency table.

A **bar graph** uses rectangles of various lengths to display the frequency of occurrence of the various categories of data. (Bar graphs and histograms are technically different methods of displaying data. They are sufficiently similar that we will not differentiate between them. For our purposes, they will be considered the same thing.) Consider the following example that shows the top ten National League home run hitters from 1965. We'll start off with a chart.

Rank	Name	HR
1	Willie Mays	52
2	Willie McCovey	39
3	Billy Williams	34
T4	Ron Santo	33
T4	Frank Robinson	33
T6	Johnny Callison	32
T6	Hank Aaron	32
T6	Eddie Mathews	32
T6	Deron Johnson	32
10	Mack Jones	31

The same data are now displayed in this bar graph.

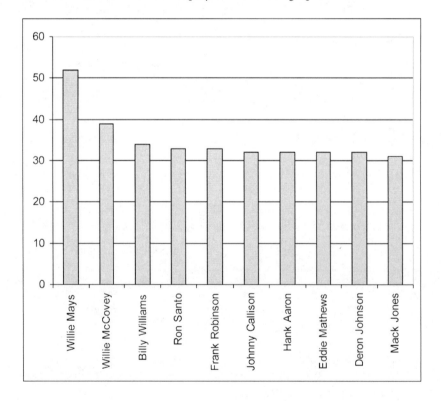

People who are more visually-oriented thinkers are likely to prefer bar graphs to tables. Such methods of displaying data are easier for some people to interpret. A difficulty of bar graphs, however, is that precision is lost. For example, it is not easy to tell if Billy Williams hit 33 or 34 home runs in 1965. Looking at the table above makes it clear he hit 34 but the bar graph is not as clear.

Another problem with bar graphs is that they are open to misrepresentation, intentional or not. Consider the following example.

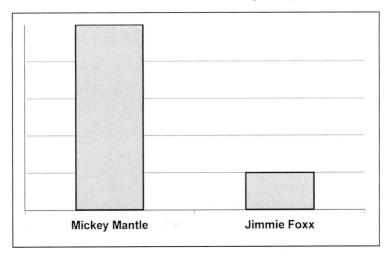

This chart shows the career home run totals for Mickey Mantle and Jimmie Foxx. From the chart, it seems obvious that Mantle hit many more home runs than Foxx. However, that is not the case. Notice that the vertical axis, which is used to represent the quantities, has no labels. Let us look at the graph again, but with labels.

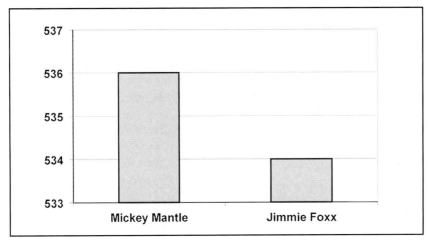

The labels make it clear that these two players hit almost exactly the same number of homers. However, the chart still gives the appearance of a distinct advantage for Mantle. If we only rely on the visual aspect, we can be misled. Ideally, the chart would have its vertical axis start at 0. Unfortunately, in this case, as we will see below, that would make the chart again misleading.

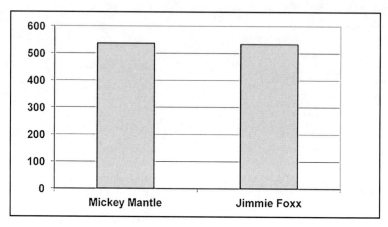

Generally we like to have our vertical axis start at 0, but in this case it makes it very difficult to see any difference between the two players' totals. A general rule, then, would be to start the vertical axis at 0 unless the numbers are large enough and close enough to make it difficult to discern differences between them.

A **line graph** is more or less the same thing as a bar graph. The only difference is that instead of a rectangle, each data value is denoted by a dot, which appears at the top of where the rectangle would be. Additionally, the various dots are then connected with line segments. Here is a repeat of our 1965 NL home run leader chart, this time as a line graph (top of following page).

Line graphs are generally preferable to bar graphs when several different quantities are being represented.

In our next chart, we are going to show Willie Mays' double, triple, home run and stolen base totals from 1954 to 1962 (middle of following page).

When a number of categories of data are being displayed in a line graph over a period of time, we typically call it a **time series plot**.

It is not hard to see how this can be preferable to the same data shown in a series of bar graphs (bottom of following page).

This shows the same data but it is cluttered and not as easy to read.

We also need to be careful is in making sure we don't try to answer questions a given statistical display cannot answer. For example, suppose we asked, "What is the most home runs Mays ever hit in a season?" From the chart, we

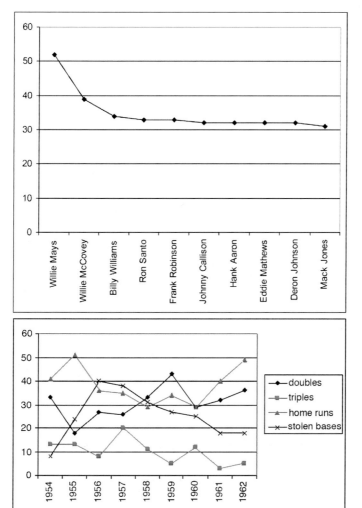

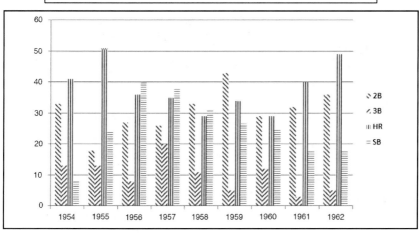

might say 51 in 1955. But that would be wrong since he hit 52 in 1965. The problem is that the chart only gives his data for a subset of his career. So occasionally the best answer we can give to a question may be "Based on the information given we cannot answer that question."

Another kind of chart that is useful when we are showing relative frequencies is a **pie chart**.

Consider the following chart. It shows the division of pitching wins among pitchers for the 1969 Mets.

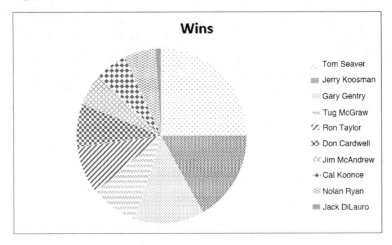

As shown, the chart is not as useful as it could be. We can tell which pitchers had the most wins. Clearly Tom Seaver had the most, followed by Jerry Koosman and Gary Gentry. However, it is hard to tell who had more, Tug McGraw or Ron Taylor. Based on the fact that it appears the quantities are going down as we go clockwise around the chart, we might guess Taylor won fewer than McGraw. But perhaps they were tied. So there may be times that the best answer we can give for a question about a chart is "We don't know for sure."

The best charts are the ones that give the most information without being too cluttered. Here is our chart again (top of following page).

Now we can easily tell that McGraw and Taylor had the same number of wins. Often pie charts will be used to show percentages, rather than actual quantities (second chart on following page).

This is not as useful for this particular type of data since we are usually more concerned with the number of wins a pitcher has rather than what percentage of a team's wins the pitcher has. You might, however, notice something about the last two charts. The percentage numbers and win numbers are identical. This is because the 1969 Mets won exactly 100 games. Thus, Seaver winning 25 games means he won 25% of the team's wins.

Let's talk now about the angles of the pieces of the pie.

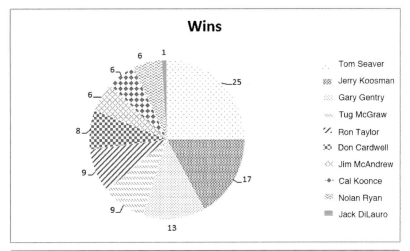

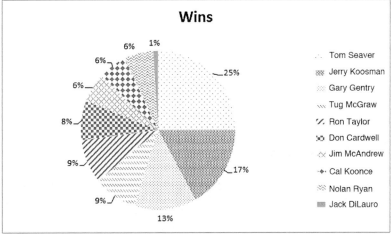

Example—Let's calculate the angle of the piece of the pie representing Tug McGraw's wins. McGraw had 9% of the wins so he should have 9% of the pie. "All the way around" a circle is 360°. So we need to figure out what 9% of 360° would be. Recall how we calculated percentages.

$$\frac{PART}{WHOLE} = \frac{part}{whole}$$

For the percentage side, the "PART" is 9 and the "WHOLE" is 100. For the degrees of the circle, the "part" is unknown and the "whole" is 360.

$$\frac{9}{100} = \frac{x}{360}$$

Multiplying both sides by 360 gives us $x = 9 * 360/100 = 32.4$. So McGraw's piece of the pie would be 32.4°.

The pie chart was popularized by Florence Nightingale, the famous British nurse. She invented the chart as a way to convince military command of the wisdom of getting medical treatment closer to the front lines during wars. Her pie charts were a bit different than the ones we use. We use the same radius for all pieces of the pie and vary the angle. She used the same angle for all pieces and varied the radius. Therefore, her chart might look like this.

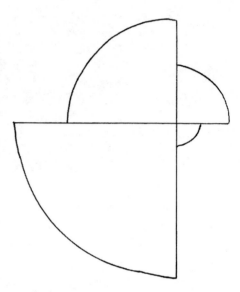

This is actually a bit deceptive, though I make no claim the deception was intentional on Nightingale's part. The area of a portion of the circle varies with the square of the radius. That means that if the radius doubles, the area will be four times as large. If the radius is three times as large, the area will be nine times as large. So the larger regions are much larger than their relative percentages would merit. Areas of portions of circles increase in a linear fashion as the angle increases. Thus, if we double the angle, we double the area. If the angle is three times as large, the area is three times as large. Therefore, keeping the same radius and varying the angle is a more accurate method of representing the data.

Section 5.3—Scatter Plots

A **scatter plot** is a kind of chart that is typically used when looking at relationships between two sets of quantitative data. In Chapter 6, we will look at correlation, an important concept when comparing two such sets.

The top of the following page is a chart showing a scatter plot with the comparison between walks and strikeouts for the 77 leading strikeout pitchers for 1965.

Section 5.4—Contour Plots

The last kind of graph we will discuss is the **contour plot**. This is particularly useful when the categories under consideration are geographic in

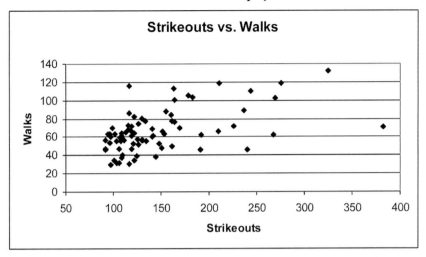

nature. One example of a contour plot that you have surely seen at some point is a weather map. The map is marked with lines or shading that indicate regions with certain temperatures or levels of rainfall. Consider the example below.

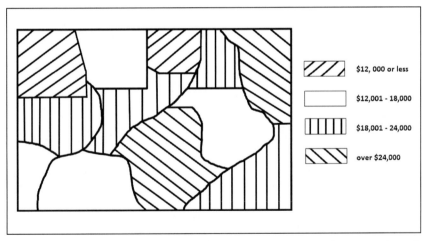

This chart shows the per capita income for a mythical state with each shaded region representing one of the twelve counties in the state.

Another type of contour plot is a weather map. Consider the map of Arkansas (top of following page).

This map would indicate that the areas between the curves for 70° and 75° will have temperatures between 70° and 75°. Similar predictions would be made for the other regions.

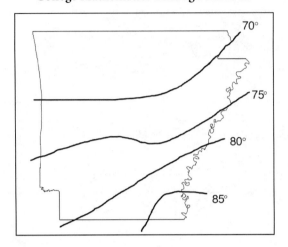

5—Exercises

1. The following chart gives historic population data for Russellville, Arkansas.

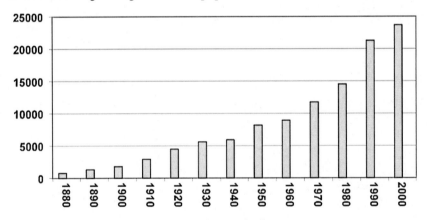

  a. What was the population of Russellville in 1950?
  b. Which decade saw the greatest population change?
  c. How many decades saw the population decrease?
  d. What was the population of Russellville in 1963?

2. The following table gives some career statistics for Willie Mays, the best all-around player in baseball history.

Year	Team	G	AB	R	H	2B	3B	HR	RBI	BB	SO	AVG
1951	Giants	121	464	59	127	22	5	20	68	57	60	.274
1952	Giants	34	127	17	30	2	4	4	23	16	17	.236
1954	Giants	151	565	119	195	33	13	41	110	66	57	.345
1955	Giants	152	580	123	185	18	13	51	127	79	60	.319
1956	Giants	152	578	101	171	27	8	36	84	68	65	.296

Year	Team	G	AB	R	H	2B	3B	HR	RBI	BB	SO	AVG
1957	Giants	152	585	112	195	26	20	35	97	76	62	.333
1958	Giants	152	600	121	208	33	11	29	96	78	56	.347
1959	Giants	151	575	125	180	43	5	34	104	65	58	.313
1960	Giants	153	595	107	190	29	12	29	103	61	70	.319
1961	Giants	154	572	129	176	32	3	40	123	81	77	.308
1962	Giants	162	621	130	189	36	5	49	141	78	85	.304
1963	Giants	157	596	115	187	32	7	38	103	66	83	.314
1964	Giants	157	578	121	171	21	9	47	111	82	72	.296
1965	Giants	157	558	118	177	21	3	52	112	76	71	.317
1966	Giants	152	552	99	159	29	4	37	103	70	81	.288
1967	Giants	141	486	83	128	22	2	22	70	51	92	.263
1968	Giants	148	498	84	144	20	5	23	79	67	81	.289
1969	Giants	117	403	64	114	17	3	13	58	49	71	.283
1970	Giants	139	478	94	139	15	2	28	83	79	90	.291
1971	Giants	136	417	82	113	24	5	18	61	112	123	.271
1972	Giants	19	49	8	9	2	0	0	3	17	5	.184
1972	Mets	69	195	27	52	9	1	8	19	43	43	.267
1973	Mets	66	209	24	44	10	0	6	25	27	47	.211

    a. What is the most home runs (HR) he hit in one season? What year?

    b. In how many seasons did he have a batting average (AVG) above .300?

    c. What is the most consecutive seasons in which he hit at least 30 home runs (HR)?

    d. In how many seasons did he exceed both 100 runs scored (denoted R) AND runs batted in (denoted RBI)?

3. The only major league players to have at least 20 doubles, 20 triples, 20 homeruns and 10 stolen bases in a single season are Willie Mays (1957), Wildfire Schulte (1911), Jeff Heath (1941), George Brett (1979), Jimmy Rollins (2007), Curtis Granderson (2007) and Jim Bottomley (1928). This chart shows the data for those players in those years (Sabermetric Encyclopedia) (on top of following page).

    a. Which player(s) had exactly 20 triples (denoted 3B)?

    b. Which player hit the most home runs (denoted HR)?

    c. Which player had the fewest stolen bases (denoted SB)?

    d. How many stolen bases did Willie Mays have?

4. The following chart shows the number of wins each year from 1961 to 1970 for the National League Champion and the American League Champion (www.baseball-reference.com) (second chart on following page).

    a. How many games did the National League champion win in 1969?

    b. How many times did the National League champion win more games than the American League champion?

    c. How many times did BOTH league champions finish with fewer than 100 wins?

    d. Who won more games in 1961, and by how many?

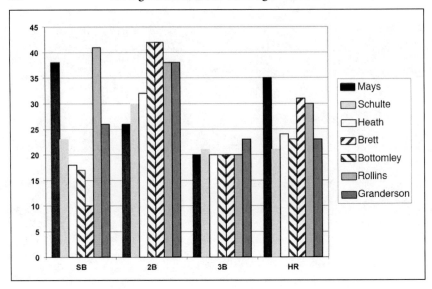

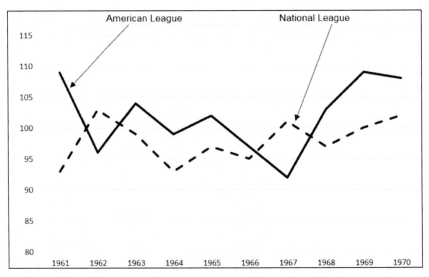

5. The following chart shows the number of times Alex Rodriguez grounded into double plays from 1996 to 2005. Draw a line graph to illustrate these data.

Year	GIDP	Year	GIDP
1996	15	2001	17
1997	14	2002	14
1998	12	2003	16
1999	12	2004	18
2000	10	2005	8

6. The Angels, Astros, Blue Jays, Devil Rays, Diamondbacks, Expos/Nationals, Mariners, Marlins, Mets, Padres, Pilots/Brewers, Rockies, and Royals are Major League Baseball's expansion teams. The following chart shows the number of games won by each of these teams from 1969 through 2005.

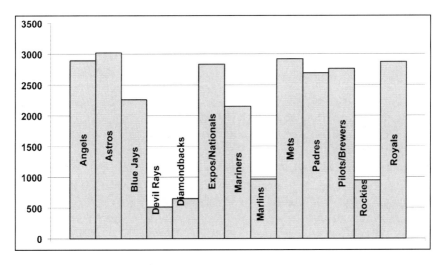

a. Which of these team has won the most games?
b. How many games have the Mets won?
c. Not all of these teams started play during the same year. Based on what the chart shows, which four teams have probably played the fewest seasons?
d. How many of these teams won more than 2000 games during this time period?

7. The following chart gives some of Babe Ruth's career statistics.

Team	G	AB	R	H	2B	3B	HR	RBI	AVG	OBP	SLG
1914 Red Sox	5	10	1	2	1	0	0	2	.200	.200	.300
1915 Red Sox	42	92	16	29	10	1	4	21	.315	.376	.576
1916 Red Sox	67	136	18	37	5	3	3	15	.272	.322	.419
1917 Red Sox	52	123	14	40	6	3	2	12	.325	.385	.472
1918 Red Sox	95	317	50	95	26	11	11	66	.300	.411	.555
1919 Red Sox	130	432	103	139	34	12	29	114	.322	.456	.657
1920 Yankees	142	458	158	172	36	9	54	137	.376	.532	.847
1921 Yankees	152	540	177	204	44	16	59	171	.378	.512	.846
1922 Yankees	110	406	94	128	24	8	35	99	.315	.434	.672
1923 Yankees	152	522	151	205	45	13	41	131	.393	.545	.764
1924 Yankees	153	529	143	200	39	7	46	121	.378	.513	.739
1925 Yankees	98	359	61	104	12	2	25	66	.290	.393	.543
1926 Yankees	152	495	139	184	30	5	47	146	.372	.516	.737
1927 Yankees	151	540	158	192	29	8	60	164	.356	.486	.772

Team	G	AB	R	H	2B	3B	HR	RBI	AVG	OBP	SLG
1928 Yankees	154	536	163	173	29	8	54	142	.323	.463	.709
1929 Yankees	135	499	121	172	26	6	46	154	.345	.430	.697
1930 Yankees	145	518	150	186	28	9	49	153	.359	.493	.732
1931 Yankees	145	534	149	199	31	3	46	163	.373	.495	.700
1932 Yankees	133	457	120	156	13	5	41	137	.341	.489	.661
1933 Yankees	137	459	97	138	21	3	34	103	.301	.442	.582
1934 Yankees	125	365	78	105	17	4	22	84	.288	.448	.537
1935 Braves	28	72	13	13	0	0	6	12	.181	.359	.431
TOTAL	2,503	8,399	2,174	2,873	506	136	714	2,213	.342	.474	.690

a. In how many seasons did Ruth hit at least 40 home runs (denoted HR)?

b. What was Ruth's highest batting average (denoted AVG)?

c. How many times did Ruth get MORE than 200 hits (denoted H)?

d. In which seasons did Ruth have more than 160 runs batted in (denoted RBI)?

8. In 1988, the New York Mets hit 152 home runs as a team. The following chart shows the distribution of home runs broken down by home runs hit by Lenny Dykstra, Mookie Wilson, Kevin Elster, Gary Carter, Keith Hernandez, Howard Johnson, Kevin McReynolds, Darryl Strawberry and "other" players.

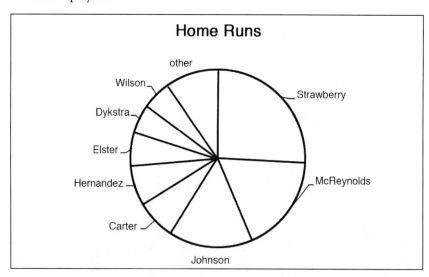

a. The portion of the pie for Darryl Strawberry has an angle of 92.36842°. How many home runs did he hit?

b. Three players hit more than 20 home runs. Who were they?

c. How many home runs did Wally Backman hit?

d. Who hit more home runs, Kevin McReynolds or Keith Hernandez?

9. The following chart gives some population data for Clark County, Arizona.

Age	Persons
45 to 49 years	1052
50 to 54 years	931
55 to 59 years	911
60 to 61 years	409
62 to 64 years	545
65 to 69 years	970
70 to 74 years	887
75 to 79 years	771
80 to 84 years	520
85 years and over	427

   a. How many people were in their 70's?

   b. How many people were 74 years old?

10. Draw a bar graph representing the given data. Keep the people in the order given. These are all the players who hit triples for the 1880 Troy Trojans.

Player	Triples
Ed Caskin	4
John Cassidy	8
Ed Cogswell	3
Roger Connor	8
Buttercup Dickerson	2
Jake Evans	1
Pete Gillespie	5
Bill Harbidge	1
Bill Holbert	1
Mickey Welch	3
Bill Tobin	1

11. Draw a line graph representing the given data.

Year	National League Leading Home Run Total
1961	46
1962	49
1963	44
1964	47
1965	52
1966	44

12. The following table describes the age distribution of players from the 1962 Mets.

Age	35–39	30–34	25–29	20–24	15–19
Number	4	11	23	5	1

   a. Which region of this pie chart represents the number of players between 30 and 34?

   b. What is the angle for the region representing players who were from 15–19?
   c. How many players were from 20 to 24 years old?
   d. How many players were 17 years old?

13. The following chart gives population data for several Arkansas counties from 1940 to 1990.

	1940	1950	1960	1970	1980	1990
Baxter	10,281	11,683	9,943	15,319	27,409	31,186
Benton	36,148	38,076	36,272	50,476	78,115	97,499
Chicot	27,452	22,306	18,990	18,164	17,793	15,713
Clark	24,402	22,998	20,950	21,537	23,326	21,437
Mississippi	80,217	82,375	70,174	62,060	59,517	57,525

   a. Which county had the largest population in 1950?
   b. Which county had the largest INCREASE in population from 1940 to 1990?
   c. Which county had the largest PERCENTAGE INCREASE in population from 1940 to 1990?
   d. Which county had the largest DECREASE in population from 1940 to 1990?

14. The following chart lists the home runs hit each year from 1959 through 1965 by Willie Mays, the best all-around player in baseball history. Draw a line graph illustrating the data. Use "Years" as your horizontal axis.

Year	Home Runs
1959	34
1960	29
1961	40
1962	49
1963	38
1964	47
1965	52

15. The following chart gives the National and American League home run leaders from 1955 through 1965.

Year	National League	Team	HR	American League	Team	HR
1965	Willie Mays	Giants	52	Tony Conigliaro	Red Sox	32
1964	Willie Mays	Giants	47	Harmon Killebrew	Twins	49
1963	Willie McCovey AND Hank Aaron	Giants Braves	44	Harmon Killebrew	Twins	45
1962	Willie Mays	Giants	49	Harmon Killebrew	Twins	48
1961	Orlando Cepeda	Giants	46	Roger Maris	Yankees	61
1960	Ernie Banks	Cubs	41	Mickey Mantle	Yankees	40
1959	Eddie Mathews	Braves	46	Harmon Killebrew AND Rocky Colavito	Senators Indians	42

Year	National League	Team	HR	American League	Team	HR
1958	Ernie Banks	Cubs	47	Mickey Mantle	Yankees	42
1957	Hank Aaron	Braves	44	Roy Sievers	Senators	42
1956	Duke Snider	Dodgers	43	Mickey Mantle	Yankees	52
1955	Willie Mays	Giants	51	Mickey Mantle	Yankees	37

    a. What was the most home runs hit in any one year by any player?

    b. What was the most home runs hit in any one year by any National League player?

    c. Which player(s) led the National League the most times? (counting ties)

    d. Which player(s) led the American League the most times? (counting ties)

    e. Which team had a player lead a league the most times?

    f. In which year did one league's leading number exceed the other league's leading number by the most?

16. The following table gives the number of pitching wins by Sandy Koufax for the years from 1958 to 1966. Draw a line graph to illustrate the data.

Year	Wins
1958	11
1959	8
1960	8
1961	18
1962	14
1963	25
1964	19
1965	26
1966	27

17. In 1927, Babe Ruth hit 60 home runs. The whole American League (including Babe Ruth) hit only 439. If a pie chart were to be drawn giving each player a slice of pie representing his home runs, what would the angle be for Babe Ruth's piece of the pie?

18. The chart below shows the number of home runs hit by Willie Mays (the best all-around player in baseball history), Hank Aaron and Mickey Mantle from 1954 through 1965 (top of following page).

    a. Which player hit the most home runs in 1965? How many did he hit?

    b. Which player had the most home runs in any one of these seasons? How many home runs did he hit and in what year?

    c. Which player(s) hit more than 50 home runs in a season?

    d. How many times did Willie Mays have the most home runs of these three players?

    e. How many times did Hank Aaron have the fewest home runs of these three players?

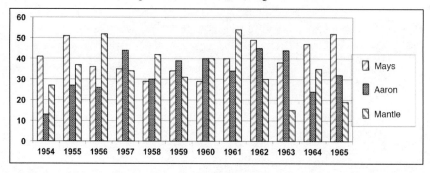

19. The following chart shows the National League and American League leading home run totals from 1941 through 1946. Draw a time series plot of the data, with one line representing the National League total and one representing the American League total. Be sure to label your graph.

Year	National League	American League
1941	34	37
1942	30	36
1943	29	34
1944	33	22
1945	28	24
1946	23	44

20. The following chart gives the National and American League home run leaders from 1918 through 1927. Answer the questions below.

Year	National League	HRs	American League	HRs
1918	Gavvy Cravath (Phillies)	8	TIE between Babe Ruth (Red Sox) and Tilly Walker(Athletics)	11
1919	Gavvy Cravath (Phillies)	12	Babe Ruth (Red Sox)	29
1920	Cy Williams (Philies)	15	Babe Ruth (Yankees)	54
1921	George Kelly (Giants)	23	Babe Ruth (Yankees)	59
1922	Rogers Hornsby (Cardinals)	42	Ken Williams (Browns)	39
1923	Cy Williams (Phillies)	41	Babe Ruth (Yankees)	41
1924	Jack Fournier (Dodgers)	27	Babe Ruth (Yankees)	46
1925	Rogers Hornsby (Cardinals)	39	Bob Meusel (Yankees)	33
1926	Hack Wilson (Cubs)	21	Babe Ruth (Yankees)	47
1927	TIE between Cy Williams (Phillies) and Hack Wilson (Cubs)	30	Babe Ruth (Yankees)	60

   a. Which player led his league in home runs the most times?

   b. List any year(s) in which the National League leader had more home runs than the American League leader.

   c. What was the most home runs hit in a season by a league leader who was not named Babe Ruth? What was that hitter's name?

21. The following chart shows the number of doubles (denoted by diamonds), triples (denoted by triangles) and home runs (denoted by

squares) for Willie Mays (the greatest all-around player in history) in each year of his career. (The quantity is represented by the middle of the shape.)

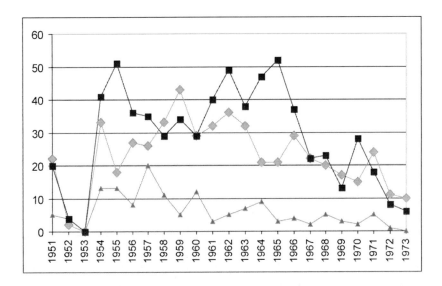

a. How many doubles did Mays hit in 1966?
b. In what year did Mays hit the most triples?
c. How many triples did Mays hit the year he hit the most?
d. How many times did Mays have more doubles than home runs?
e. How many times did Mays exceed 30 in both doubles AND home runs?
f. How many times did Mays have at least 10 triples?
g. What is the most consecutive years Mays hit at least 30 home runs?
h. Did Mays ever have a season when he had at least 20 of each kind of hit?

6—Uses of Statistics

"Statistics are used much like a drunk uses a lamppost: for support, not illumination."—Vin Scully

"Awards mean a lot, but they don't say it all. The people in baseball mean more to me than statistics."—Ernie Banks

"If the statistics are boring, then you've got the wrong numbers."—Edward R. Tufte

We mentioned earlier that people often use statistics incorrectly. It can be intentional or unintentional. In this chapter we will discuss ways that statistics can be used properly. We will look at putting statistics in their proper context so that they support what we claim they support.

One thing to keep in mind, however, is that many statistical arguments are actually subjective arguments. It can simply come down to a matter of opinion. For instance, it is not hard to argue that Willie Mays was a better all-around ball player than Hank Aaron. There are good statistical arguments to support that conclusion. However, there are also good statistical arguments to support the opposite conclusion, that Hank Aaron was a better all-around player than Willie Mays. Sometimes the best we can hope for is giving good data to support our opinion and hope people will agree with us.

Section 6.1—Leaders

Who led the American League in triples in 2008? Who has the most doubles of all time?

If you said Curtis Granderson and Tris Speaker you are right.

Who led the National League in batting average in 2008? Who has the highest batting average of all time?

If you answered Chipper Jones and Ty Cobb, you are wrong. You are wrong because eighteen National Leaguers had higher batting averages than

Chipper Jones. In fact, Charlie Haeger, Tim Dillard and Tyler Clippard each batted 1.000. You are wrong because 378 players have higher lifetime averages than Ty Cobb. In fact, through 2013, 83 players have career averages of 1.000.

At the same time, you are right if you said Chipper Jones and Ty Cobb. How can you be both right and wrong? Why was there no such confusion on the first two questions? Triples and doubles are counting statistics. Whoever has the most has the most. Batting average is a percentage statistic. For percentage and rate statistics, players who play very little can have an advantage over players who play more. Because of that, there are **qualifying levels** for being eligible to be a leader in such statistics. For batting average, the qualifying level is 502 plate appearances (not at-bats). If the season is not completed, however, it is lower. It is 3.1 plate appearances for each game a player's team had scheduled. So in 1981, Bill Madlock led the National League in batting even though he only had 320 plate appearances. The Pirates only had 102 scheduled games due to a player strike so Madlock only needed 316 plate appearances to qualify. In earlier years, some number of at-bats was required. Ted Williams did not lead the league in batting in 1954 even though he had over 3.1 plate appearances per game and had the highest average of those who did. In 1954, the requirement was 400 at-bats. Williams only had 386 at-bats due to his 136 walks.

For career leadership, the qualifying level is not standard. For batting average, SABR uses a cutoff of 1500 hits. Elias Sports Bureau uses 5000 at-bats. Cobb ends up being the all-time leader as long as we require at least 87 plate appearances (PA). Interestingly, if we only require 86 plate appearances, the all-time leader, at .397, is Terry Forster, a pitcher. If we drop to 40 PA, it is Glenn Williams at .425. If we go down to 20 PA Dan O'Connor and Vince Sherlock tie at .462. Ten PA as a minimum gives Luis Silverio at .545. Dropping to five gives the unbeatable John Paciorek at 1.000.

For ERA, the current qualifying level is one innings pitched (IP) per team's scheduled games. So, if the season goes full length, that is 162 IP. That has also changed over the years. At times it was based on games pitched.

Section 6.2—*Rating Players*

There are a number of times when players are rated and compared. When managers decide which players to keep on the team and which players to cut. When fans vote for the All-Star teams. When awards, like the Most Valuable Player, Cy Young award or Gold Gloves are decided. When the Baseball Writers Association of America votes for membership in the Hall of Fame.

Each of those decisions and comparisons has unique issues.

When a manager is trying to decide who to keep on his team and who to send to the minors, he has a number of things to consider. He has some statistics on which to base his decision. He can look at what each player did the previous year. But that is not as simple as it sounds. Suppose, for simplicity, that the manager is trying to decide which of two catchers to keep on the 25-man roster and which to send to the minor leagues. It may be that one of the players was in the major leagues last year and the other is a rookie, having never played in the majors. A straight comparison of statistics would be unreasonable due to the differing levels of competition. Perhaps the player who was in the major leagues last year is 35 years old and the rookie is 22 years old. Even if the veteran performed well last year, is he likely to be declining in his performance due to age? If the rookie did not perform as well, is he likely to be improving? Is he possibly not quite ready yet? The manager has some statistics on which to base a decision but those statistics cannot easily answer all of those questions.

Voting for the All-Star teams is done by the fans. Many of the fans pay attention to one thing—"I like this guy" or "I don't like this guy." Many fans pay no attention to how a player is performing that particular year. In fact, it is not uncommon for a player to be elected, or come close to being elected, while having hardly played all season due to injuries.

Assuming, however, that a fan has actually paid attention to how the players are playing, the comparisons are a lot easier than the manager's decision in our previous example. Consider, for example, the following players who played at least 100 games at third base in the 1964 American League.

	AVG	HR	RBI	OBA	Fielding PCT
Brooks Robinson	.317	28	118	.368	.972
Clete Boyer	.218	8	52	.269	.968
Don Wert	.257	9	55	.325	.965
Ed Charles	.241	16	63	.321	.954
Frank Malzone	.264	13	56	.312	.959
John Kennedy	.230	7	35	.280	.938
Max Alvis	.252	18	53	.313	.955
Pete Ward	.282	23	94	.348	.958
Rich Rollins	.270	12	68	.334	.947

In this case, it is not hard to decide who the best player is. Brooks Robinson is the leader in every single one of these statistics. So clearly a fan voting based on these data would choose Robinson. (Robinson received the American League Most Valuable Player award that year.)

Let us now look at the National League third basemen in the same season.

	AVG	HR	RBI	OBA	Fielding PCT
Bob Aspromonte	.280	12	69	.329	.973
Bob Bailey	.281	11	51	.336	.943
Dick Allen	.318	29	91	.382	.921
Eddie Mathews	.233	23	74	.344	.962

	AVG	HR	RBI	OBA	Fielding PCT
Jim Ray Hart	.286	31	81	.342	.937
Ken Boyer	.295	24	119	.365	.951
Ron Santo	.313	30	114	.398	.963
Steve Boros	.257	2	31	.342	.961

This decision is much less clear. Aspromonte is the fielding leader. Allen leads in batting average. Santo leads in on base percentage. Hart leads in homers. Boyer leads in RBIs. We could look at the ranks in each category.

	AVG	HR	RBI	OBA	Fielding PCT	Total Rank Points
Ron Santo	2	2	2	1	2	9
Ken Boyer	3	4	1	3	5	16
Dick Allen	1	3	3	2	8	17
Jim Ray Hart	4	1	4	5	7	21
Eddie Mathews	8	5	5	4	3	25
Bob Aspromonte	6	6	6	8	1	27
Bob Bailey	5	7	7	7	6	32
Steve Boros	7	8	8	6	4	33

Based on this, it wouldn't be hard to make a case for voting for Santo. This does, of course, get more complicated. Different players play their games in different ballparks. Santo may have benefitted from playing in Wrigley Field, generally regarded as a hitter's ballpark. Allen suffered since the Phillies' ballpark was more of a pitcher's park. Hart had the same problem in Candlestick Park. Boyer also benefited from playing in a hitter's park. Does that matter? Which statistics are more important? About the only thing that is clear here is that we wouldn't be voting for Boros, Bailey or Aspromonte.

The problems in comparing players for the Most Valuable Player are very similar, with one more complicating factor thrown in. In the All-Star discussion, we are considering players who play the same position. For Most Valuable Player, any position is a possibility. Suppose we were looking at the Most Valuable Player voting in the 1964 National League. For the purposes of this discussion, we will look at the following group of players.

	AVG	HR	RBI	OBA	OPS	POS	Place
Roberto Clemente	.339	12	87	.388	.872	OF	7
Rico Carty	.330	22	88	.388	.942	OF	5
Hank Aaron	.328	24	95	.393	.907	OF	5
Joe Torre	.321	20	109	.365	.863	C	5
Dick Allen	.318	29	91	.382	.939	3B	T2
Lou Brock	.315	14	58	.358	.821	OF	1
Ron Santo	.313	30	114	.398	.962	3B	8
Billy Williams	.312	33	98	.370	.901	OF	8
Curt Flood	.311	5	46	.356	.734	OF	1
Frank Robinson	.306	29	96	.396	.943	OF	T2
Lee Maye	.304	10	74	.346	.793	OF	5
Orlando Cepeda	.304	31	97	.361	.900	1B	4
Bill White	.303	21	102	.355	.829	1B	1
Ron Hunt	.303	6	42	.357	.763	2B	10

	AVG	HR	RBI	OBA	OPS	POS	Place
Joe Christopher	.300	16	76	.360	.826	OF	10
Willie Mays	.296	47	111	.383	.990	OF	4
Ken Boyer	.295	24	119	.365	.854	3B	1
Willie Davis	.294	12	77	.316	.729	OF	6
Dick Groat	.292	1	70	.335	.706	SS	1
Tim McCarver	.288	9	52	.343	.743	C	1
Jim Ray Hart	.286	31	81	.342	.840	3B	4
Denis Menke	.283	20	65	.368	.847	SS	5
Johnny Callison	.274	31	104	.316	.809	OF	T2
Deron Johnson	.273	21	79	.326	.798	1B	T2
Vada Pinson	.266	23	84	.316	.764	OF	T2

Which one is deserving? Some people would want to consider defense as well. Some also believe that the Most Valuable Player should be someone whose team did well, so the table includes "Place," representing where in the 10-team league the player's team finished. (It should be noted that of AVG, OBA and OPS, AVG was considered most important in 1964. In fact, OPS didn't even exist yet. Most statistically savvy people would now put OPS as most important of the three, AVG least.) While it seems obvious to the author that Willie Mays should have won the award, Ken Boyer was the winner.

The Cy Young award is given each year to the pitcher chosen as the best in each league. This is a little less complicated than the Most Valuable Player award since this involves only one position. It is still complicated in making comparisons because some pitchers are starters and some are relievers. For starters, ERA, wins, winning percentage, strikeouts, and Hits-Walks/9 IP are some of the more important statistics. For relievers, ERA, saves, and blown saves are some of the more important statistics. As we have previously mentioned, the way the game has been played has changed a lot. For years, relievers were generally viewed as pitchers who weren't good enough to be starters. There were often good relief pitchers, even in those days. Men like Firpo Marberry, Joe Page, Jim Konstanty, Johnny Murphy and Ted Wilks were respected relief pitchers before the 1960s, when relief pitching became far more respectable. But until the 1970s, relief pitchers were not given any consideration for the Cy Young award. That began to change, and in 1974, Mike Marshall (who for a time was the Henderson State University baseball coach) became the first reliever to win the Cy Young award. Since then others have won it.

Golden Glove awards may be the easiest comparison. The Gold Glove is awarded to the best fielder in each league at each position. Since it looks at only one position at a time and only looks at fielding, it is a comparatively straightforward competition. Still the voters need to decide what is most important. Is it flashy fielding? Is it a high fielding percentage? Is it the number of plays made? Is it the number of assists? Some infielders may get comparatively few chances because their teams have primarily strikeout pitchers or pitchers who allow a lot of fly balls rather than ground balls.

The most difficult rating to consider is whether or not players belong in the Hall of Fame. The reason this is difficult is that it involves players at all positions during every era of baseball. In 2008, a hitter with 20 home runs is not considered a particularly powerful hitter. In 1908, he would be considered a superstar. In 1888, a pitcher who won 18 games would have been considered mediocre. In 2008, he is likely in the running for the Cy Young award.

Section 6.3—Correlation

Certain quantitative data sets are related to each other. When one quantity goes up, the other goes up, or when one goes up, the other goes down. For example, height and weight for adults are related. Though there are short people who are heavy and tall people who are light, in general, taller people are heavier, shorter people are lighter. When such a relationship exists, we say the two data sets have a **correlation**.

If the two quantities go up at the same time, we say they have a **positive correlation**.

If one of the quantities goes up while the other goes down, we say they have a **negative correlation**.

If the points in the scatter plot fit a fairly tight pattern, we say the two quantities have a **strong correlation**.

If the points in the scatter plot do not fit a fairly tight pattern, we say the two quantities have a **weak correlation**.

If the points fit no pattern, we say there is **no correlation**.

Here are some scatter plots that illustrate various types and strengths of correlations.

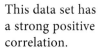

This data set has a strong positive correlation.

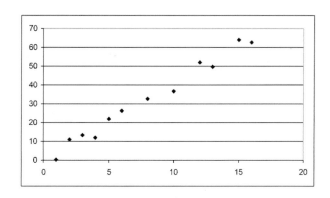

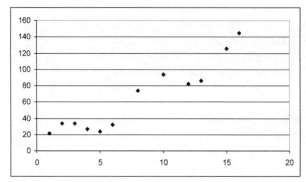

This data set has a weak positive correlation.

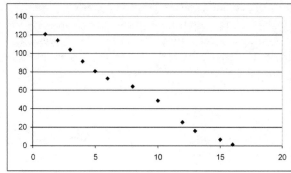

This data set has a strong negative correlation.

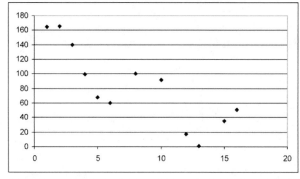

This data set has a weak negative correlation.

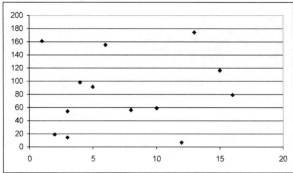

This data set has no correlation.

There is a tedious numerical formula that produces a number called the **correlation coefficient**. That number helps us tell if there is a strong correlation, a weak correlation or no correlation. It tells us if any correlation is positive or negative.

Your calculator can give you that number. If you have two sets of data, put one of them in L1 as you were shown in Chapter 5. Then put the other set of data in L2. Go back to the home screen. Choose <STAT> "CALC" "LinReg ax + b." Then press <ENTER>. You will see several numbers. The correlation coefficient is given by r. (If you do not see r, talk to your instructor.)

The correlation coefficient will always be between −1 and 1.

If the correlation coefficient is very close to 1 then we have a strong positive correlation.

If the correlation coefficient is positive and sort of close to 1 then we have a weaker positive correlation.

If the correlation coefficient is very close to −1 then we have a strong negative correlation.

If the correlation coefficient is negative and sort of close to −1 then we have a weaker negative correlation.

If the correlation coefficient is not at all close to 1 or −1 then we have no correlation.

An important question here is what is "close"? That is fairly subjective. Obviously .993 is close to 1. And .1 is not close to 1. Is .7 close to 1? Sort of. A lot depends what decisions may be made based on any perception of correlation. If costly decisions are going to be made, then we might say .7 is NOT close to 1. If the consequences of an error are not too severe, then perhaps we will say .7 IS close to 1.

I did an analysis of pitchers from 1984 and 1985 who had at least 100 IP. I compared their base runners per nine innings and their ERA. Not surprisingly, there is a fairly strong correlation between those two quantities. The correlation coefficient was 0.8062.

For all teams from 1970 to 1990, I compared various offensive statistics with the team winning percentage. Here are the correlations.

Winning PCT and Batting AVG	.48569
Winning PCT and Slugging AVG	.50472
Winning PCT and On Base AVG	.58127

Obviously a higher batting average is better than a lower batting average but this shows that Slugging AVG and On Base AVG are both more important to winning than batting AVG.

The following chart is the same one we looked at when discussing scatter plots in Chapter 5.

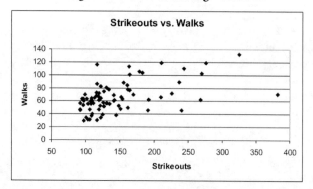

There is a general pattern to the data. For the most part, when strikeouts go up, walks go up. This could be due to the number of innings pitched (if a pitcher pitches more, he will have more BB and SO) and the fact that pitchers who throw harder may be more likely to have more BB and SO. Here is the chart again, with a line included that shows the pattern that "most" of the data fits.

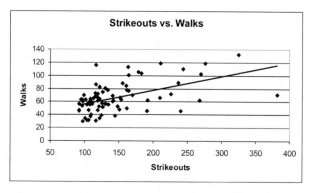

Notice that most of the data points are near the line. But you will notice that there are some pitchers who do not fit the pattern well. Such data points are called **outliers**.

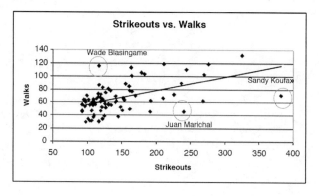

I have circled and labeled three outliers.

Exercise—Figure out who three other data points represent using www.baseball-reference.com.

This is not a very strong correlation. The correlation coefficient is .52279. We will revisit this example again in the chapter on modeling.

For a while I had noticed what appeared to me to be a correlation in the NBA. It appeared that the team that had more rebounds tended to win the game. I also thought I noticed some correlation between assists and wins. During the latter part of December 2008, I looked at 46 NBA games to see if that was the case. The following two charts show the plots of rebounding margin vs. scoring margin and assist margin vs. scoring margin. I always took the home team's value minus the visiting team's value.

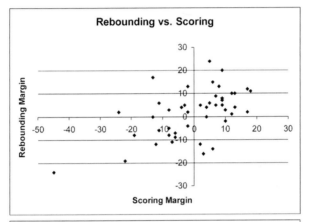

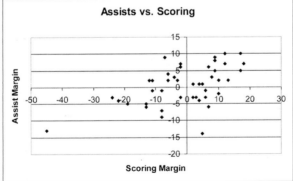

There ended up being a correlation in each set of data, though not a very strong one. For rebounding, the correlation coefficient was .56063. For assists, the correlation coefficient was .54767.

One other issue that comes up when there is a correlation between two events is determining whether or not there is **causation**. If I hold a ball in my hand, and then rapidly move my hand out from under the ball, the ball will fall to the ground. There is clearly a cause (my hand being moved) and a result (the ball falling to the ground).

However, suppose there is a ball and a pencil in my hand. If I move my hand rapidly out of the way, the ball and pencil will fall. There is a correlation between the ball falling and the pencil falling. But the ball falling does not cause the pencil to fall. Neither does the pencil falling cause the ball to fall.

So we see there are two possibilities when a correlation exists. It is possible that one event causes the other. But it is possible that neither event causes the other but, instead, some third event causes both of the other two.

There is still one other possibility. Consider the following example from football and politics. Steve Hirdt, of the Elias Sports Bureau, found that when the Washington Redskins win their last home game of the season during an election year, then the party of the current president will win that year's presidential election. If they lose, the challenging party will take the election. I think it is hard to argue that the Redskins cause a certain party to win the presidency or that the election affects whether the Redskins win a game. So we end up with a third possibility.

If two events, A and B, are correlated, there are three possible explanations.

1. Either A causes B or B causes A (hand moves, ball falls).
2. Some third event, C, causes both A and B (hand moves, ball and pencil fall).
3. The correlation is merely a coincidence (Redskins and politics).

It is not always easy to determine which of the three is the case. Consider, for example, the statement "healthy people exercise." It certainly seems like "exercise" and "good health" would be correlated. But what causes what? Are people healthy because they exercise? Or is it that healthy people are more likely to exercise?

Section 6.4—Comparisons of Eras and Different Ballparks

The following chart shows the National League stolen bases leaders from 1886 to 2008.

1886	Ed Andrews	56	1948	Richie Ashburn	32
1887	Monte Ward	111	1949	Jackie Robinson	37
1888	Dummy Hoy	82	1950	Sam Jethroe	35
1889	Jim Fogarty	99	1951	Sam Jethroe	35
1890	Billy Hamilton	102	1952	Pee Wee Reese	30
1891	Billy Hamilton	111	1953	Bill Bruton	26
1892	Monte Ward	88	1954	Bill Bruton	34

1893	Tom Brown	66	1955	Bill Bruton	25
1894	Billy Hamilton	98	1956	Willie Mays	40
1895	Billy Hamilton	97	1957	Willie Mays	38
1896	Joe Kelley	87	1958	Willie Mays	31
1897	Bill Lange	73	1959	Willie Mays	27
1898	Ed Delahanty	58	1960	Maury Wills	50
1899	Jimmy Sheckard	77	1961	Maury Wills	35
1900	Patsy Donovan/George Van Haltren	45	1962	Maury Wills	104
1901	Honus Wagner	49	1963	Maury Wills	40
1902	Honus Wagner	43	1964	Maury Wills	53
1903	Frank Chance/ Jimmy Sheckard	67	1965	Maury Wills	94
1904	Honus Wagner	53	1966	Lou Brock	74
1905	Art Devlin/Billy Maloney	59	1967	Lou Brock	52
1906	Frank Chance	57	1968	Lou Brock	62
1907	Honus Wagner	61	1969	Lou Brock	53
1908	Honus Wagner	53	1970	Bobby Tolan	57
1909	Bob Bescher	54	1971	Lou Brock	64
1910	Bob Bescher	70	1972	Lou Brock	63
1911	Bob Bescher	80	1973	Lou Brock	70
1912	Bob Bescher	67	1974	Lou Brock	118
1913	Max Carey	61	1975	Davey Lopes	77
1914	George Burns	62	1976	Davey Lopes	63
1915	Max Carey	36	1977	Frank Taveras	70
1916	Max Carey	63	1978	Omar Moreno	71
1917	Max Carey	46	1979	Omar Moreno	77
1918	Max Carey	58	1980	Ron LeFlore	97
1919	George Burns	40	1981	Tim Raines	71
1920	Max Carey	52	1982	Tim Raines	78
1921	Frankie Frisch	49	1983	Tim Raines	90
1922	Max Carey	51	1984	Tim Raines	75
1923	Max Carey	51	1985	Vince Coleman	110
1924	Max Carey	49	1986	Vince Coleman	107
1925	Max Carey	46	1987	Vince Coleman	109
1926	Kiki Cuyler	35	1988	Vince Coleman	81
1927	Frankie Frisch	48	1989	Vince Coleman	65
1928	Kiki Cuyler	37	1990	Vince Coleman	77
1929	Kiki Cuyler	43	1991	Marquis Grissom	76
1930	Kiki Cuyler	37	1992	Marquis Grissom	78
1931	Frankie Frisch	28	1993	Chuck Carr	58
1932	Chuck Klein	20	1994	Craig Biggio	39
1933	Pepper Martin	26	1995	Quilvio Veras	56
1934	Pepper Martin	23	1996	Eric Young	53
1935	Augie Galan	22	1997	Tony Womack	60
1936	Pepper Martin	23	1998	Tony Womack	58
1937	Augie Galan	23	1999	Tony Womack	72
1938	Stan Hack	16	2000	Luis Castillo	62
1939	Stan Hack/Lee Handley	17	2001	Juan Pierre/ Jimmy Rollins	46
1940	Lonny Frey	22	2002	Luis Castillo	48
1941	Danny Murtaugh	18	2003	Juan Pierre	65
1942	Pete Reiser	20	2004	Scott Podsednik	70
1943	Arky Vaughan	20	2005	Jose Reyes	60

1944	Johnny Barrett	28		2006	Jose Reyes	64
1945	Red Schoendienst	26		2007	Jose Reyes	78
1946	Pete Reiser	34		2008	Willy Taveras	68
1947	Jackie Robinson	29				

As you look at these data, it is easy to see that the numbers are not consistent. From 1886 to 1930, the lowest total is 35. From 1931 to 1948, the highest total is 34. What explains the difference? Were players from 1886 to 1930 just so much faster than in the 1930s and 1940s? Did catchers suddenly figure out how to throw out base stealers more effectively? Did the National League start playing fewer games so players had fewer opportunities to steal? In the 1920s, baseball saw the rise of Babe Ruth, Lou Gehrig, Jimmie Foxx and other big home run hitters. With that change in the game, the stolen base, once a necessary part of the offensive strategy in a game, fell into disfavor. There was not much need to steal bases. Because of that, the stolen base became less common. In the 1960s, there was a resurgence of pitching dominance because of changes in the strike zone and the height of the mound. The stolen base returned to favor.

From 1876 to 1920, there were only 25 major league pitchers who allowed 20 or more home runs in a single season. Only three of those pitchers threw less than 300 innings, with the least being 263 innings pitched. In 1998, there were 87 pitchers who allowed 20 or more home runs. Only one of those pitchers pitched MORE than 263 innings. Six of them pitched less than 120 innings. What was the difference? Were the pitchers back in the 1800s and early 1900s that much better? In 1998, more teams played more games. The lively ball is used instead of the dead ball of the earlier era. Balls are replaced if they hit the dirt once. In the early days, the entire game might have been played with just two or three balls. That meant the ball would get soft and not travel so far. Many old ballparks had very distant outfield fences.

Different eras in baseball produce drastically different sets of statistics. As we have mentioned, changes in equipment, rules, strategies, ballpark design and other things have made the game, and thus its numbers, change drastically over time. Though a player from the 1880s would recognize today's game, he would be amazed at many of those changes. Because of these changes, comparisons of statistical data are difficult.

One way to compare players from different eras is to look at how they performed compared to the rest of the players of that time. Consider Carl Yastrzemski in 1968 and Earl Webb from 1930. Both played outfield for the Boston Red Sox. Both hit over .300. Yastrzemski hit .301, Webb hit .323. That sounds like Webb was better than Yastrzemski. Webb's .323 average was good for 20th in the American League among players who had at least 300 plate appearances. He was one of 33 players who hit at least .300 that year. Yastrzemski, on the other hand, was the ONLY American Leaguer who qualified for the batting title to hit .300 that year. In fact, he was the only one to hit at least .291. The league batting average in 1930 was .288. The league batting average in 1968 was .230. That means that Webb hit 12.15% better than the league average while Yastrzemski hit an amazing 30.87% above the league average. Al Simmons led the American League in batting in 1930, with an average of .381. He was 32.29% above the league average, producing a result similar to that of Yastrzemski.

Different eras produce different results.

In 1908, Howie Camnitz had an ERA of 1.56. In 1994, Greg Maddux had an ERA of 1.56. But not all 1.56 ERAs are created equal. In 1908, the major league ERA was 2.37, so Camnitz was 34.18% below the average ERA. In 1994, the major league ERA was 4.51. That means Maddux was 65.41% below average. So Maddux' ERA was considerably more impressive than Camnitz'.

Different eras produce different results.

Ned Williamson played back in the 1880s. The following chart show's Ned Williamson's year-by-year home run data during his 11 seasons with the Chicago White Stockings. (White Stockings is an early name of the team now known as the Cubs.)

Year	Team	HR
1878	Browns	1
1879	White Stockings	1
1880	White Stockings	0
1881	White Stockings	1
1882	White Stockings	3
1883	White Stockings	2
1884	White Stockings	27
1885	White Stockings	3
1886	White Stockings	6
1887	White Stockings	9
1888	White Stockings	8
1889	White Stockings	1
1890	Pirates	2
Career	Total	64

Something seems a bit odd.

Here are the league leaders in home runs in the 1884 National League.

Rank	Name	Team	HR
1	Ned Williamson	Chicago White Stockings	27
2	Fred Pfeffer	Chicago White Stockings	25
3	Abner Dalrymple	Chicago White Stockings	22
4	Cap Anson	Chicago White Stockings	21
5	Dan Brouthers	Buffalo Bisons	14
6	King Kelly	Chicago White Stockings	13
7	Silver Flint	Chicago White Stockings	9
8	George Wood	Detroit Wolverines	8
T9	Joe Hornung	Boston Beaneaters	7
T9	Tom Burns	Chicago White Stockings	7

Something seems a bit odd.

Let's look at the career home run data for three of Williamson's team-mates.

	Fred Pfeffer	Cap Anson	Abner Dalrymple
1876	—	2	—
1877	—	0	—
1878	—	0	0
1879	—	0	0
1880	—	1	0
1881	—	1	1
1882	1	1	1
1883	1	0	2
1884	25	21	22
1885	5	7	11
1886	7	10	3
1887	16	7	2
1888	8	12	0
1889	7	7	1
1890	5	7	—
1891	7	8	—
1892	2	1	—
1893	3	0	—
1894	5	5	—
1895	0	2	—
1896	2	2	—
1897	0	3	—
career	94	97	43

Something seems a bit odd.

Here are the home run totals in 1884 by team.

Team	HR
White Stockings	142
Bisons	39
Gothams	23
Beaneaters	36
Grays	21
Quakers	14
Blues	16
Wolverines	31
TOTALS	322

Something seems a bit odd.

So what was going on? In Lakefront Park, the White Stockings ballpark, the right field fence was so short (less than 200 feet) that balls hit over it were considered doubles. Except in 1884. For that one year, they were considered homers.

Different ballparks produce different results.

Many ballparks have had what we would consider odd dimensions. (The following data come from *Take Me Out to the Ballpark* by Josh Leventhal.)

Ballpark	City	Teams	Left	Center	Right
South End Grounds	Boston	Braves	250 ft	440 ft	250 ft
Washington Park	Brooklyn	Dodgers	335 ft	445 ft	215 ft
Polo Grounds	New York	Giants, Mets	277 ft	500 ft	258 ft
Exposition Park	Pittsburgh	Pirates	400 ft	450 ft	400 ft
Huntington Avenue Grounds	Boston	Red Sox	350 ft	635 ft	280 ft
Hilltop Park	New York	Yankees	365 ft	542 ft	400 ft
Griffith Stadium	Washington	Senators	407 ft	421 ft	320 ft
Fenway Park	Boston	Red Sox	321 ft	488 ft	314 ft

It is not hard to see why some of these parks did not have a lot of home runs. Many parks had dimensions change several times so these distances are not necessarily what they were at the end of the park's use or, in the case of Fenway, how they are now.

Odd dimensions also provided opportunity for some unusual statistical situations. Mel Ott hit 511 home runs in his career with the New York Giants. He hit 323 of them at home, while on the road, he hit only 188. Looking above at the Polo Grounds dimensions help us see why. Ott, a left-handed hitter, had a very short right field to attack.

Over the course of baseball history, many teams or individuals have had significantly different levels of success at home and on the road. A modern example of this is in Colorado. The unusually high elevation creates a thinner atmosphere in Denver. Because of that, balls tend to travel farther and, it has been alleged, that curveballs do not curve as much. Because of that, the Rockies have regularly been one of the more productive teams offensively while being one of the weaker teams in pitching. Consider 1995–1997. In each year, the Rockies led the league in runs, home runs and batting average. In most cases they led by considerable margins. The following chart shows how the Rockies compared to the average for the rest of the teams in the league.

Year	Team	R	HR	AVG
1995	Rockies	785	200	.282
1995	league average	657	132	.262
1996	Rockies	961	221	.287
1996	league average	743	153	.261
1997	Rockies	923	239	.288
1997	league average	732	148	.261

During the same period, the Rockies were always the worst in the league in ERA.

Year	Team	ERA
1995	Rockies	4.97
1995	league average	4.12
1996	Rockies	5.60
1996	league average	4.12
1997	Rockies	5.25
1997	league average	4.13

Section 6.5—Situational Statistics and Statistical Breakdowns

Many decisions in baseball are based on statistics. Every team has at least one person in charge of accumulating and analyzing statistics. He will break player statistics down into widely varied "situational statistics." He will compare a player's performance on grass vs. artificial turf. He will look at differences in games at home and away. Batting average with men on base, vs. left handed pitchers and right handed pitchers. Batting average with two outs and men in scoring position. Batting average in late innings. Batting average on different counts, on different days of the week ... you get the idea.

Baseball is not unique in statistics needing to be looked at in various ways. On February 8, 2007, *USA Today* reported a study (source reported as "Centers for Disease and Prevention, USA Today research") that said suicide was more common among police officers than in the general population. Police were committing suicide at a rate of about 18 per 100,000 while the general population rate was about 11.1 per 100,000. Since police tend to be in the 25–50 year age bracket, the suicide rate for that group, which was 14.6 per 100,000, was also reported. Considerable concern was expressed over this problem. James Taranto, author of the blog "Best of the Web Today" on OpinionJournal.com, using data from the Centers for Disease Control, pointed out a serious problem with this study. Breaking the issue down into different categories helped shed more light on the subject. Males make up 88.8% of law enforcement officers. The rate of suicide among males is about 18.4 per 100,000. The rate of suicide among females is 4.2 per 100,000. Since most police are male, it is not surprising if the suicide rate is higher than in the general population since police are disproportionately found in a demographic group where the suicide rate is considerably higher. Further, the suicide rate for males aged 25–44 is 22.2%. Again, police will have disproportionately many people from that category. Combining all that data, it would appear that police may be committing suicide at a rate LOWER than would be predicted by the kinds of people in the ranks of law enforcement.

Section 6.6—Abuses of Statistics

Statistics are a valuable way to convey information and to compare players and other things. Sometimes, though, people do not use statistics correctly. We have already seen some examples of this in other sections but we will now look at a few more examples.

Example—In 2008, United Press International reported "U.S. Media Jobs Slashed 88 Percent." An 88% cut in jobs would mean only 12% of those in these jobs were still employed. The problem is that was not true. What was true was that 88% more media jobs were cut in 2007 than in 2006.

Example—In 2008, the *New York Times* reported that 51% of the women in the United States are living without a husband. That statistic is very deceptive since the Times was using "woman" to mean any female over age 15. Including females age 15–17, who will rarely be married, inflates the numbers of women living without a husband.

Example—In 2004, the *New York Times* reported that one-third of the people killed by recent earthquakes and tidal waves in Asia were children. It called that "an exceptionally high number of children." However, it went on to note that "children make up at least half the population of Asia." If a group makes up half the population but only suffers one-third of the fatalities, then it has suffered a surprisingly SMALL number of deaths.

Example—The *Arkansas Democrat-Gazette* once reported on a particularly hot summer by pointing out that heat waves in other years had been worse. It mentioned that, in 1954, Arkansas suffered through 115 days of 90 degrees or more between June 7 and September 9. There is a problem with that. June 7 through September 9 is only 95 days.

Example—In 1999, *USA Today* reported some statistical data that appeared to be wrong but could indeed be correct. It printed a table showing the most common names given to boys and girls who were born in each state in 1998. It also showed the ten most common names nationally. For girls names, Emily was the most common in 26 states. Hannah was the most common in 10 states. Other most common names were Alexis (two states), Ashley (two states), Jessica (two states), Madison (five states), Samantha (two states) and Taylor (one state). The most common name nationally was Kaitlyn. How is that possible? An error is possible but it could also have been correct. It could be that Kaitlyn was the second most common name in every state while Emily and the other names may have been far down the list in states where they were not first.

Example—It is common for newspapers to report that a parent who serves as a cook, financial manager, psychologist, bus driver, etc., should receive a huge salary. One such report said the amount was $508,700 per year. Such a claim is silly. The way the salary is produced by taking the average annual salaries for the cook, financial manager, psychologist, bus driver, etc., and adding them together. This ignores that each of those people work at their jobs for at least 40 hours per week and no parent does all of those jobs 40 hours each week.

Example—In 1999, the "Ripley's Believe It or Not" newspaper feature claimed that there are 31,556,925.51 seconds, 525,948.75 minutes and 21,914.531 hours in one year. While the seconds and minutes are correct, the hours claim is wrong. In doing their calculations, Ripley's erroneously used 60 hours in a day and 24 minutes in an hour.

Chapter 6—Exercises

SECTION 6.1—LEADERS

1. Go to baseball-reference.com. For each of the following statistics, find the people who led their league the most consecutive years in
   a. batting average.
   b. home runs.
   c. pitcher's strikeouts.
   d. stolen bases.

2. Go to baseball-reference.com. For each of the following statistics, find the all-time leader in
   a. batting average.
   b. home runs.
   c. pitcher's strikeouts.
   d. stolen bases.

3. Go to http://www.baseball-reference.com/leagues/AL/2012-standard-batting.shtml and scroll down to "Player Standard Batting." Sort by batting average by clicking on BA at the top of that table.
   a. Who was the league leader in batting average?
   b. Notice "Hide non-qualifiers for rate stats" is checked so non-qualifiers for the batting title are not included. Uncheck that box so that all batters will be included. How many players had higher averages than the league leader but didn't have enough plate appearances to qualify for the title?

4. Go to http://www.baseball-reference.com/leagues/AL/2012-standard-pitching.shtml and do the same thing as in #3 for Earned Run Average (ERA, not ERA+).

SECTION 6.2—RATING PLAYERS

1. The following chart gives all 1965 National League outfielders with at least 502 plate appearances. Determine which three should be All-Stars for 1965. Give reasons for your choices.

	AVG	HR	RBI	SB	OBA	OPS
Bill Virdon	.279	4	24	4	.322	.692
Billy Williams	.315	34	108	10	.377	.929
Curt Flood	.310	11	83	9	.366	.788
Frank Robinson	.296	33	113	13	.386	.925
Hank Aaron	.318	32	89	24	.379	.938
Jesus Alou	.298	9	52	8	.317	.715
Jimmy Wynn	.275	22	73	43	.371	.841
Johnny Callison	.262	32	101	6	.328	.836
Johnny Lewis	.245	15	45	4	.331	.715
Lou Brock	.288	16	69	63	.345	.791
Lou Johnson	.259	12	58	15	.315	.706
Mack Jones	.262	31	75	8	.313	.822
Roberto Clemente	.329	10	65	8	.378	.842
Ron Fairly	.274	9	70	2	.361	.738
Tommy Harper	.257	18	64	35	.340	.733
Vada Pinson	.305	22	94	21	.352	.836
Willie Davis	.238	10	57	25	.263	.609
Willie Mays	.317	52	112	9	.398	1.043
Willie Stargell	.272	27	107	1	.328	.829

2. Go to baseball-reference.com. Look up Ken Boyer and Ron Santo. Look at their statistics for 1964.

    a. Give reasons why Ken Boyer was more valuable than Ron Santo in 1964.

    b. Give reasons why Ron Santo was more valuable than Ken Boyer in 1964.

    c. Which of your arguments in (a) and (b) is more persuasive and why?

    d. Who was named the National League most valuable player in 1964?

3. The following chart gives the players from the 1965 American League who had at least 502 plate appearances.

    a. Determine who should be the Most Valuable Player. Feel free to look at baseball-reference.com or other sites for additional information that might be helpful.

    b. Find out who was voted the Most Valuable Player in the American League in 1965. Explain why this was a good choice. Explain why this was a bad choice.

	AVG	HR	RBI	SB	OBA	OPS
Bert Campaneris	.270	6	42	51	.326	.709
Bill Skowron	.274	18	78	1	.316	.740
Bob Allison	.233	23	78	10	.342	.787
Bobby Knoop	.269	7	43	3	.313	.696
Bobby Richardson	.247	6	47	7	.287	.609
Boog Powell	.248	17	72	1	.347	.754
Brooks Robinson	.297	18	80	3	.351	.797
Carl Yastrzemski	.312	20	72	7	.395	.932
Clete Boyer	.251	18	58	4	.304	.728
Curt Blefary	.260	22	70	4	.381	.851

	AVG	HR	RBI	SB	OBA	OPS
Danny Cater	.270	14	55	3	.316	.719
Dick Green	.232	15	55	0	.308	.671
Don Buford	.283	10	47	17	.358	.747
Don Wert	.261	12	54	5	.341	.704
Ed Charles	.269	8	56	13	.332	.720
Felix Mantilla	.275	18	92	7	.374	.790
Floyd Robinson	.265	14	66	4	.352	.737
Frank Howard	.289	21	84	0	.358	.835
Jerry Adair	.259	7	66	6	.303	.653
Jerry Lumpe	.257	4	39	7	.333	.655
Jim Fregosi	.277	15	64	13	.337	.744
Jimmie Hall	.285	20	86	14	.347	.810
Joe Pepitone	.247	18	62	4	.305	.699
Jose Cardenal	.250	11	57	37	.287	.654
Ken Berry	.218	12	42	4	.268	.615
Ken Harrelson	.238	23	66	9	.329	.758
Ken McMullen	.263	18	54	2	.323	.737
Lee Thomas	.271	22	75	6	.361	.826
Leon Wagner	.294	28	79	12	.369	.864
Luis Aparicio	.225	8	40	26	.286	.625
Max Alvis	.247	21	61	12	.308	.706
Mike Hershberger	.231	5	48	7	.289	.601
Norm Cash	.266	30	82	6	.371	.883
Paul Schaal	.224	9	45	6	.310	.622
Pete Ward	.247	10	57	2	.327	.694
Rich Rollins	.249	5	32	4	.309	.641
Rocky Colavito	.287	26	108	1	.383	.851
Ron Hansen	.235	11	66	1	.304	.649
Tom Tresh	.279	26	74	5	.348	.825
Tony Conigliaro	.269	32	82	4	.338	.850
Tony Oliva	.321	16	98	19	.378	.870
Vic Davalillo	.301	5	40	26	.344	.716
Wayne Causey	.261	3	34	1	.341	.684
Willie Horton	.273	29	104	5	.340	.831
Zoilo Versalles	.273	19	77	27	.319	.781

4. The following chart gives all pitchers from the 1938 National League with at least 154 innings pitched. The Cy Young award was not instituted until 1956. If it had been given in the National League in 1938, who should have won it? Give reasons for your answer.

	ERA	W	L	IP	BB	SO
Bill Lee	2.66	22	9	291	74	121
Charlie Root	2.85	8	7	161	30	70
Paul Derringer	2.93	21	14	307	49	132
Danny MacFayden	2.95	14	9	220	64	58
Bob Klinger	3.00	12	5	159	42	58
Freddie Fitzsimmons	3.01	11	8	203	43	38
Carl Hubbell	3.07	13	10	179	33	104
Russ Bauers	3.07	13	14	243	99	117
Clay Bryant	3.10	19	11	270	125	135
Johnny Vander Meer	3.12	15	10	225	103	125

	ERA	W	L	IP	BB	SO
Lou Fette	3.15	11	13	240	79	83
Bill McGee	3.21	7	12	216	78	104
Jim Turner	3.46	14	18	268	54	71
Jim Tobin	3.47	14	12	241	66	70
Hal Schumacher	3.50	13	8	185	50	54
Tot Pressnell	3.56	11	14	192	56	57
Bob Weiland	3.59	16	11	228	67	117
Curt Davis	3.64	12	8	173	27	36
Luke Hamlin	3.68	12	15	237	65	97
Cy Blanton	3.69	11	7	173	46	80
Larry French	3.81	10	19	201	62	83
Vito Tamulis	3.83	12	6	160	40	70
Cliff Melton	3.89	14	14	243	61	101
Peaches Davis	3.96	7	12	168	40	28
Lon Warneke	3.97	13	8	197	64	89
Harry Gumbert	4.00	15	13	236	84	84
Bucky Walters	4.20	15	14	251	108	93
Al Hollingsworth	4.37	7	18	208	89	93
Max Butcher	4.47	9	12	171	70	50
Claude Passeau	4.52	11	18	239	93	100
Hugh Mulcahy	4.62	10	20	267	120	90
Tex Carleton	5.41	10	9	168	74	80

5. Go to baseball-reference.com and find out the players who have won at least ten Golden Glove awards.

Section 6.3—Correlation

In numbers 1–4, for each chart, discuss whether or not there is a correlation between the two data sets. If so, is it strong or weak, positive or negative? Identify any outliers.

1. 1972, National League, Winning Percentage vs. Earned Run Average, minimum 100 innings pitched

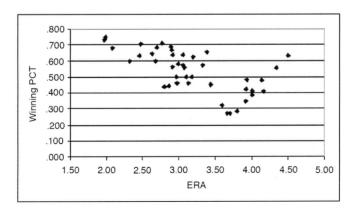

2. 1952, Major League, Batting average vs. On base percentage, minimum 450 plate appearances

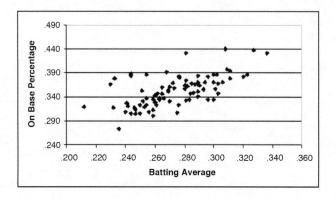

3. 1969, Major League, Winning Percentage vs. Hits per 9 Innings Pitched, minimum 120 innings pitched

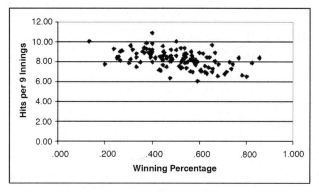

4. 1948, Major League, Innings Pitched vs. Winning Percentage, minimum one inning pitched

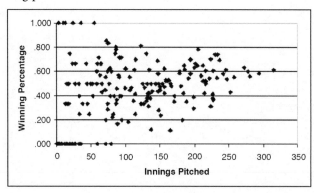

For #5–7, find the correlation coefficient for the pairs of data sets. Determine whether or not there is a correlation, whether it is strong or weak, positive or negative.

5. 1967, Cincinnati Reds, Putouts vs. Fielding Percentage, minimum 30 games played

Fielding Percentage	Putouts	Fielding Percentage	Putouts
1.000	1	.976	12
1.000	13	.974	249
.995	208	.972	287
.994	606	.971	190
.992	703	.968	131
.990	454	.967	264
.986	341	.947	9
.985	414	.941	15
.984	59	.913	4
.981	53	.892	8
.976	146	.882	1

6. 1887, American Association, At-bats vs. Batting average, minimum 580 plate appearances

Batting Average	At-bats	Batting Average	At-bats
.402	547	.278	544
.367	570	.275	524
.341	551	.267	580
.316	627	.266	533
.309	551	.266	526
.301	532	.265	486
.290	559	.265	585
.289	540	.264	534
.288	598	.263	548
.286	539	.258	520
.281	569	.250	567

7. 1948, Major League, Batting Average vs. weight, minimum 625 plate appearances

Batting Average	Weight	Batting Average	Weight
.376	175	.289	215
.369	205	.286	175
.355	185	.285	168
.336	195	.283	185
.325	180	.281	168
.321	170	.281	180
.321	180	.280	180
.320	193	.274	160
.310	174	.269	185
.308	180	.265	195
.297	190	.250	173
.296	180	.250	175
.296	195	.249	170
.290	195	.246	185
.290	170		

8. The chart below shows each state's (along with the District of Columbia) population plotted against the number of major league baseball players who were born in that state (as of 2006).

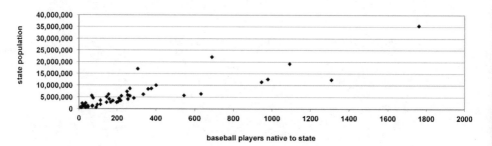

a. Is there a correlation between the two sets of data? Why or why not?
   (i) If so, is the correlation positive or negative?
   (ii) If so, is the correlation strong or weak?
   (iii) If so, do you think there is a causal relationship between the two data sets, or some third event that causes both, or the correlation is a coincidence? Why?
b. On the graph above, circle an outlier.

Section 6.4—Comparisons of Eras and Different Ballparks

1. Paleontologist Steven Jay Gould was a SABR member and huge baseball fan. He made some comments regarding changes in the variation in abilities of ballplayers over time making it unlikely we would ever see another .400 hitter in the major leagues. Find out what Gould said and write a short summary of your response.

2. Go to baseball-reference.com. Look at Luis Tiant's ERA from 1968 and Lefty Grove's ERA from 1931. Which is more impressive? Something that may help is the statistic *ERA+. You'll see it a couple columns to the right of ERA. Go to the "glossary" (right next to the word "Pitching" just above their statistics) to see what *ERA+ is.

3. Look at the league batting statistics for several seasons in the 1890s and for several seasons in the 1910s.
   a. Do you notice significant differences in batting averages or runs scored?
   b. The 1910s are the second half of an era in baseball that has a special name related to offensive production. Find that name. What in your answer to (a) explains that name?

SECTION 6.6—ABUSES OF STATISTICS

1. The following list shows the ten highest grossing films of all time (as reported on www.movieweb.com on August 7, 2011). Notice the dates on the films listed and explain why these statistics may not tell the whole story.

Rank	Title	Year
1	Avatar	2009
2	Titanic	1997
3	Marvel's The Avengers	2012
4	Harry Potter and the Deathly Hallows—Part 2	2011
5	Frozen film currently playing	2013
6	Iron Man 3	2013
7	Transformers: Dark of the Moon	2011
8	The Lord of the Rings: The Return of the King	2003
9	Skyfall	2012
10	The Dark Knight Rises	2012

2. Suppose the county health department reported that incidents of rabies increased 200% over last year. Explain why this is not necessarily an emergency.
3. Statistics show that the fewest accidents occur when people are driving above 60 miles per hour or below 20 miles per hour. Does that mean that we are safest when driving above 60 mph or below 20 mph?
4. In 2012, Derek Jeter committed fewer errors than Yunel Escobar. Both played shortstop. Explain why this does not necessarily mean Jeter was better defensively than Escobar.
5. In 1945, visiting players hit six times as many home runs as home team players at Griffith Stadium, the home of the Washington Senators. Discuss the possible explanations and statistical issues that may have been involved in this. Then go to http://www.baseball-almanac.com/players/player.php?p=kuheljo01 and see some discussion on the topic.

7—Probability and Combinatorics

"Never underestimate a theorem that counts something."—John Fraleigh

"But to us, probability is the very guide of life."—Joseph Butler

We all have an intuitive concept of probability. When certain things happen, we are not shocked because it is a common occurrence. No one is shocked if Miguel Cabrera hits a home run. He does it with a high level of frequency. But if Prince Fielder steals a base, we are surprised. Cabrera's probability of hitting a home run is high. Fielder's probability of stealing a base is poor. In this chapter will try to turn from the intuitive understanding of probability and arrive at a more mathematically rigorous understanding.

Section 7.1—Basic Probabilities

What is the probability of getting heads when flipping a coin? Most people have a good enough intuitive understanding of probability to answer that question. The answer may take several forms. You might say "50–50." You might say 50%. Both of those answers are correct. When answering most of the kinds of questions we will consider in probability, the answer comes down to a simple fraction.

$$P(our\ event) = \frac{number\ of\ ways\ our\ event\ can\ happen}{total\ number\ of\ ways\ the\ event\ can\ happen}$$

We would read the left side of the above equation as "the probability of our event." For this equation to work, each event must have the same probability of happening. That is, the events must be "equally likely."

It is important to notice that if the particular event CANNOT happen, then the probability is 0. If an event MUST happen, then it has a probability of 1. For example, if you roll a standard six-sided die, the probability you roll a 9 is 0. It cannot happen because the only possibilities are 1, 2, 3, 4, 5 or 6. On the other hand, the probability of rolling a number less than 9 is 1.

If you are doing a probability problem and get a negative number for your answer then *you are wrong!*

If you are doing a probability problem and get an answer bigger than 1 for your answer then *you are wrong!*

Example—Roll a standard six-sided die. What is the probability of rolling a four? There are six results possible. Only one of them is a four, so

$$P(4) = \frac{number\ of\ ways\ of\ getting\ a\ 4}{total\ number\ of\ ways\ the\ die\ can\ land} = \frac{1}{6}.$$

Sometimes we have to work a little bit in order to look at the problem.

Example—Roll two standard six-sided dice. Add up the numbers. What is the probability of rolling a four? How many events are possible? The sum can come up as a 2, 3, 4, 5, 6, 7, 8, 9, 10, 11 or 12. But these eleven results are not equally likely. There is only one way to roll a 2 (both dice coming up 1). There are two ways to roll a 3 (the first die is a 1 and the second is a 2, or the first die is a 2 and the second is a 1). We can use a table to help us see how to approach this problem.

First Die

		1	2	3	4	5	6
Second Die	1	2	3	4	5	6	7
	2	3	4	5	6	7	8
	3	4	5	6	7	8	9
	4	5	6	7	8	9	10
	5	6	7	8	9	10	11
	6	7	8	9	10	11	12

From this table we see that there are 36 different ways the two dice can land. Those 36 are equally likely. So P(4) = 3/36 = 1/12.

Example—The 1962 Mets had nine players who had at least 200 at-bats. Some of them batted right-handed, some batted left-handed.

Player	Batted	Player	Batted
Frank Thomas	R	Elio Chacon	R
Charlie Neal	R	Marv Throneberry	L
Felix Mantilla	R	Rod Kanehl	R
Richie Ashburn	L	Joe Christopher	R
Jim Hickman	R		

If we choose a player at random, what is the probability he is left-handed? Again, there are two events possible, R or L. But those are not equally likely. But if we view our "event" as an individual player, each is equally likely. P(L) = 2/9.

Some probabilities are not easy to calculate unless we think of a helpful way to look at them.

Example—You flip three coins. What is the probability you get two heads and one tail? The best way to answer this question is by drawing a tree diagram.

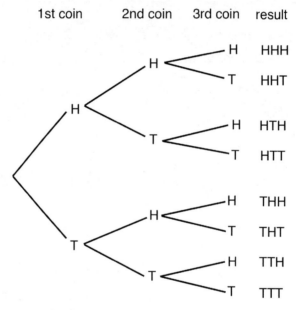

From the chart, we see that eight results are possible and that two heads, one tail can happen three ways so P(2H, 1T) = 3/8.

There are a number of baseball computer or board games that use real players and real statistics. Strat-o-matic is one of these. It has each player perform at roughly the skill level he actually plays. Such games do this using probabilities. If we consider all possible results of an at-bat, it can be fairly complicated. So let us look at a simple case. In 1979, Ron LeFlore had a batting average of exactly .300. That can be viewed as a probability. The probability that LeFlore got a base hit in a given official at-bat was .3. Board games of this nature will typically use dice to produce a result. The possible outcomes for the dice are assigned results such that the probability of the dice roll matches the probability of a given event. We can do the same thing using the random number generator in a spread sheet or on a calculator.

Example—Using a random number generator, have the 1979 Ron LeFlore "bat" 12 times and see how many hits he gets.

Using a spreadsheet's random number generator, I get the following numbers (obviously you will get different numbers).

.6449619 .0959125 .0849503 .2673045 .8788334 .6231493
.7913608 .8076177 .1149601 .0664810 .3530857 .9097904

Five of those numbers fall below .3. We can view each of those results as a "hit" and each of the others as an "out." So, in these 12 "at-bats," LeFlore went 5 for 12.

Since these are probabilities and random numbers, we will get different results each time we do this. Doing the same experiment a second time, I get these numbers.

0.2989769 0.1281831 0.0878777 0.6448103 0.5845381 0.7922997
0.6998449 0.9645948 0.6573619 0.5568468 0.7628610 0.3449517

This time LeFlore went 3 for 12, with hits in his first three at-bats and then outs in his last nine.

Consider another example in which more events are possible.

Example—In 1903, Homer Smoot had 500 official at-bats. He had 114 singles, 22 doubles, eight triples and four homers. We can consider the following probabilities.

$$P(double) = \frac{22}{500} = .044 \quad P(single) = \frac{114}{500} = .228$$

$$P(homer) = \frac{4}{500} = .008 \quad P(triple) = \frac{8}{500} = .016$$

To simulate Smoot's at-bats, we can again use a random number generator. If we get less than or equal to .228, we will say he hit a single. If we get greater than .228 but less than or equal to .272 (.228 + .044), we will say he hit a double. If we get greater than .272 but less than or equal to .288 (.272 + .016), we will say he hit a triple. If we get greater than .288 but less than or equal to .296 (.288 + .008) we will say he hit a homer. Anything above .296 we will call an out.

Let's have Smoot bat 10 times.

.2196117 .5923954 .0907369 .1915428 .0115618
.1663543 .5937129 .9428797 .8242674 .7700127

In these 10 "at-bats," Smoot has five singles and no other hits. That is not very close to the actual expected numbers.

Consider the following 100 "at-bats."

.0918485 .9831997 .0162790 .3628187 .2901831 .8272169 .5904153 .5731404 .3580236 .3317300
.2026024 .6933004 .2728938 .9444693 .5008784 .6748821 .0915023 .8658349 .4212199 .1480500
.5378171 .6219339 .3837685 .5610492 .4708424 .7386350 .4720524 .6329877 .8997063 .7792649
.4380414 .7643812 .8683156 .6929671 .7543775 .5967461 .8273296 .0229036 .6004921 .8323661
.4854464 .3212357 .5789609 .7005707 .5835592 .0643520 .4890958 .0318864 .6028691 .5283447
.0430272 .5838401 .4733573 .0896523 .4785671 .2387816 .9030780 .9511026 .5884812 .3029411
.6496971 .8396206 .9719991 .1651357 .0124240 .4942590 .7081239 .1048671 .8106770 .9406938
.0927099 .8470286 .7331226 .9505233 .6253803 .3286182 .9330718 .1271507 .3855933 .7273824
.6310121 .4676396 .0208364 .3212814 .7082308 .2700621 .2205664 .3831468 .2150724 .9138536
.2859628 .7157515 .7647044 .6182235 .1894670 .8544654 .0422238 .7865718 .2695606 .5500723

With these results, we have Smoot getting 20 singles, three doubles, two triples and one homer. That would be a batting average of .260.

Note that our 100 at-bat simulation of Homer Smoot did not have the same batting average as the real player did. Based on the probabilities, he should have had 22.8 singles, 4.4 doubles, 1.6 triples and .8 homers. (Note that, since these numbers are not whole numbers, we will never actually see 22.8 singles or .8 homers.) These 100 at-bats gave results much closer, however, than did our first trial with 10 at-bats. The important thing to remember is that "probabilities" deal with PROBABLE results, not CERTAIN results. There are also some other things going on when we repeat experiments more and more. We will talk about that in section 7.6.

Section 7.2—Averages as Probabilities

Certain percentage statistics have an interesting application. They can be viewed as probabilities. As with many other mathematical applications, there are some limitations, but it can be useful to view them in this way.

Consider a batter with a .300 batting average. That-batting average means that, all things being equal, he has a .3 probability of getting a hit in a particular at-bat. That is essentially what we did in the previous section with Homer Smoot. We treated his hitting performance, broken down into singles, doubles, triples, home runs and outs, as probabilities.

What are the limitations here? Not all at-bats are created equal. Mickey Mantle was a .298 lifetime hitter. But he was typically a poor hitter when Dick Radatz was pitching. Tommy Hutton was a .248 lifetime hitter. But until the last year or two of his career, he had a batting average of over .400 against

Hall of Famer Tom Seaver. As we discussed in the last chapter, players perform differently in different situations. Some batters do better against right-handed pitchers than left-handers. Some batters hit better in day games than they do in night games. Some batters did much better on artificial turf than on natural grass. Until they started keeping baseballs in a humidor, almost every hitter did much better in Colorado. So treating a player as though every at-bat in every situation in every ballpark against every pitcher is the same creates an overly simplistic picture. However, over a long period of time, it ends up being a fairly realistic approach.

Section 7.3—Combined Probabilities; At Least Once Rule

Suppose we flip a coin and roll a die. What is the probability that the coin comes up heads and the die comes up a 5? We can draw a tree diagram that can help us answer that question.

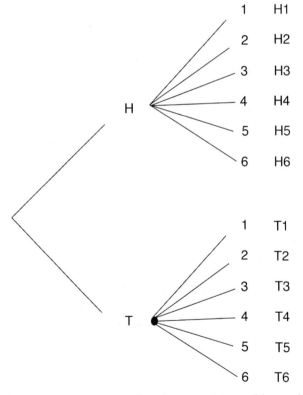

From the picture, we can see that there are 12 possible results, with all of them equally likely. Only one of them satisfies our condition so the probability is 1/12. Consider the individual pieces of the event. The probability of getting heads on the coin is 1/2. The probability of getting a 5 on the die is 1/6. Is there some way to use a 1/2 and a 1/6 to get a 1/12? Of course. $\dfrac{1}{2} * \dfrac{1}{6} = \dfrac{1}{12}$.

This suggests a way of working problems of combined probabilities. What it suggests is P(event A and B) = P(event A) * P(event B). This will always be true when events A and B are **independent events**. An intuitive definition of independent events will work for our purposes. If the outcome of event A does not influence the outcome of event B, then events A and B are independent events. The formal definition is a good bit more complicated but this will work for us.

Example—Suppose we have a box of marbles. In that box are eight red marbles, 10 blue marbles and six plaid marbles.

You reach into the box and pull out two marbles. What is the probability both marbles are red?

The problem does not change if we act as though you pulled out one marble and then pulled out a second marble. The probability the first marble is red is 8/24 = 1/3. If the first marble was red, what is the probability the second is red? It would be 7/23 since one red marble is gone from the box. Now what is P(1st is red and 2nd is red)? Are these independent events? The answer is yes. Though the first marble being red changes the arrangement of marbles in the box, no individual marble in the box is more or less likely to be chosen because the first marble was red. So P(1st is red and 2nd is red) = P(1st is red) * P(2nd is red) = $\dfrac{1}{3} * \dfrac{7}{23} = \dfrac{7}{69}$.

You reach into the box and pull out a marble, noting its color. You put it back, shake the box to mix the marbles up, and pull out another marble. What is the probability that both marbles are red?

This time, P(red) is the same both times we reach into the box. So P(both red) = P(1st red) * P(2nd red) = $\dfrac{1}{3} * \dfrac{1}{3} = \dfrac{1}{9}$.

You reach into the box, pull out a marble, put it back, shake the box and pull out another marble. What is the probability the first marble is plaid and the second is blue?

P(1st plaid, 2nd blue) = P(1st plaid) * P(2nd blue) = $\dfrac{6}{24} * \dfrac{10}{24} = \dfrac{1}{4} * \dfrac{5}{12} = \dfrac{5}{48}$.

You reach into the box, pull out a marble, put it back, shake the box and pull out another marble. What is the probability one marble is plaid and the other is blue?

At first this seems like the same problem. But there is a distinct difference. This time we are not specifying the order. Last time, if we got blue first and plaid second, we would not have satisfied our condition. This time we would. We will need to look at another idea before we can do this problem.

Suppose we roll a die. What is the probability that we roll a 3 or a 5? Obviously the answer is 2/6 = 1/3. The probability of rolling a 3 is 1/6. The probability of rolling a 5 is 1/6. Notice that $\frac{1}{6} + \frac{1}{6} = \frac{2}{6} = \frac{1}{3}$. This looks promising. When two events were connected with an "and" we multiply the probabilities (as long as the events are independent). And now it looks like we add the probabilities when two events are connected with an "or." Unfortunately that is not always the case.

Suppose we roll a die. What is the probability we roll an even number or a number less than 5? Looking at the two parts separately, we see P(even) = 3/6 and P(< 5) = 4/6. And $\frac{3}{6} + \frac{4}{6} = \frac{7}{6}$. But something is wrong. Remember, if we do a probability and get an answer larger than 1, we are wrong. Why is this wrong? Let's look at the ways the two events can be satisfied. The die comes up even if we get a 2, 4 or 6. It comes up less than 5 if we get a 1, 2, 3 or 4. Notice, 2 and 4 satisfied both conditions. So when we added the probabilities, we counted each of 2 and 4 twice.

Two events are **mutually exclusive** if they cannot happen simultaneously. Rolling a 3 on the die and rolling a 5 on the die are mutually exclusive. Rolling an even number and rolling a number less than 5 are not.

If events A and B are mutually exclusive, then P(A or B) = P(A) + P(B).

That is why adding worked for P(3 or 5). For the case when events are not mutually exclusive, things get more complicated.

If events A and B are not mutually exclusive, then P(A or B) = P(A) + P(B) − P(A and B).

So, P(even or < 5) = P(even) + P(< 5) P(even and < 5) = $\frac{3}{6} + \frac{4}{6} - \frac{2}{6} = \frac{5}{6}$. Sometimes we may work with more than two events.

If every pair of A, B and C are mutually exclusive, then P(A or B or C) = P(A) + P(B) + P(C).

If the events are not mutually exclusive, things get messy. If something can satisfy both A and B, we need to subtract off P(A and B) to eliminate duplication. But suppose something satisfies A and B and C. Then when we do P(A) + P(B) + P(C) we have counted it three times. Since it satisfies both A and B, we have to subtract off P(A and B). Since it satisfies both A and C, we have to subtract off P(A and C). Since it satisfies both B and C, we have to subtract off P(B and C). So now we have added it in three times and subtracted it off three times. To fix that, we have to add back P(A and B and C). In other words, we have this.

If A, B and C are not mutually exclusive, then P(A or B or C) = P(A) + P(B) + P(C) − P(A and B) − P(A and C) − P(B and C) + P(A and B and C).

But wait. It can get worse.

If A, B, C and D are not mutually exclusive, then P(A or B or C or D) = P(A) + P(B) + P(C) + P(D) − P(A and B) − P(A and C) − P(A and D) − P(B and C) − P(B and D) − P(C and D) + P(A and B and C) + P(A and B and D) + P(A and C and D) + P(B and C and D) − P(A and B and C and D).

Mercifully, we will never consider more than two events unless all pairs of events are mutually exclusive.

If every pair of A, B and C are mutually exclusive, then P(A or B or C) = P(A) + P(B) + P(C).

Now let's go back to the problem we looked at before.

Example—You reach into the box, pull out a marble, put it back, shake the box and pull out another marble. What is the probability one marble is plaid and the other is blue?

We have an "or" problem here. We are looking at getting "plaid first, blue second" OR "blue first, plaid second." Fortunately these are mutually exclusive. You cannot get a plaid marble first at the same time you are getting a blue marble first.

P(one plaid, one blue) = P((plaid first and blue second) OR (blue first and plaid second)) = P(plaid first and blue second) + P(blue first and plaid second) = P(plaid first) * P(blue second) + P(blue first) * P(plaid second) =

$$\frac{6}{24}*\frac{10}{24}+\frac{10}{24}*\frac{6}{24}=\frac{1}{4}*\frac{5}{12}+\frac{5}{12}*\frac{1}{4}=\frac{5}{48}+\frac{5}{48}=\frac{10}{48}=\frac{5}{24}.$$

Example—In 1927, Babe Ruth batted .356 and Lou Gehrig batted .373. If Ruth and Gehrig follow each other, what is the probability that both of them get hits? What is the probability that Ruth or Gehrig gets a hit? Assume the events are independent.

P(both get a hit) = P(Ruth hits) * P(Gehrig hits) = .356 * .373 = .133.

P(Ruth hits or Gehrig hits) = P(Ruth hits) + P(Gehrig hits) − P(both hit) = .356 + .373 − .133 = .596.

Sometimes it is easier to figure out the probability of an event NOT happening, rather than the event happening. Suppose you roll two dice. What is the probability of getting a number less than 10? There are a lot of sums less than 10. It is easier to count the ones that are NOT less than 10. Let us see why that is helpful.

Consider an event, E. Suppose we want to calculate P(E or NOT E). Obviously E and NOT E are mutually exclusive events. So P(E or NOT E) = P(E) + P(NOT E). But also, note that E happens or doesn't happen. So P(E or NOT E) = 1 since it must happen. So, we have P(E) + P(NOT E) = 1. Or P(E) = 1 − P(NOT E). Now let us go back to the problem we were considering.

$$P(<10) = 1 - P(\text{NOT} < 10) = 1 - P(\text{at least } 10) = 1 - \frac{6}{36} = 1 - \frac{1}{6} = \frac{6}{6} - \frac{1}{6} = \frac{5}{6}.$$

Example—Suppose you are rolling a die four times. What is the probability that you roll a 2 at least once?

"At least once" means we could roll it once, twice, three times or all four times. It would be easier to look at the opposite of the event.

P(at least one 2) = 1 − P(no 2s in four rolls)

= 1 − P(no 2 on 1st roll and no 2 on 2nd roll and no 2 on 3rd roll and no 2 on 4th roll)

= 1 − P(no 2 on 1st roll) * P(no 2 on 2nd roll) * P(no 2 on 3rd roll) * P(no 2 on 4th roll)

= 1 − P(no 2 on a given roll) * P(no 2 on a given roll) * P(no 2 on a given roll) * P(no 2 on a given roll)

= 1 − (P(no 2 on a given roll))^4

$$= 1 - \left(\frac{5}{6}\right)^4 = 1 - \frac{625}{1296} = \frac{671}{1296} = .5177$$

The probability that an event, E, happens **at least once** in n independent trials is P(E happens at least once) $1 - (P(\text{not } E))^n$.

Example—A .270 hitter bats 10 times. What is the probability he gets at least one hit in those ten ABs? Assume at-bats are independent events.

P(at least one hit) = 1 − (P(no hit in a given AB))^{10} = 1 − $.730^{10}$ = .957. So there is roughly a 1/25 probability that he will go 0 for 10.

Many baseball people consider Joe DiMaggio's 56-game hitting streak to be one of baseball's unbreakable records. Let us consider the probability of a .345 hitter coming up with a 57-game hitting streak.

Example—To calculate the probability of a .345 hitter having a 57-game hitting streak, we are going to have to make some assumptions in order to make the problem reasonably doable. We will assume that the player has

4 at-bats each game. We will also assume all at-bats in all games are independent events. We will also only consider the probability he gets a hit in each of a certain set of 57 games, not that he does it at some point in the season.

For one game, we need the probability that he gets "at least one hit."

P(at least one hit in a given game) = 1 − P(no hit in four at-bats)
$$= 1 - (P(\text{no hit in an at-bat}))^4$$
$$= 1 - .655^4$$
$$= 0.8159$$

P(57-game hitting streak) = P(hit in game 1 AND hit in game 2 AND ... AND hit in game 57)
$$= P(\text{hit in game 1}) * P(\text{hit in game 2}) * ... * P(\text{hit in game 57})$$
$$= (.8159)^{57}$$
$$= 0.000009190$$

That would mean that we might expect that player to get a 57-game hitting streak once in 1/0.000009214 = 108,530 sets of 57 games. In other words, it is not likely.

A **conditional probability** measures the probability of an event given that another event has occurred. For example, consider the following statistics for Sam Rice, the Hall of Fame Senators outfielder from the early part of the 20th century.

Year	AB	H	2B	3B	HR	AVG
1922	633	187	37	13	6	.295

Example—As we discussed above, for a given at-bat, Rice had a .295 probability of getting a hit. His probability of hitting a home run would be 6/633 = 0.0095. But suppose we know Rice had a hit. The probability that he hit a home run, given that he got a hit would be 6/187 = 0.0321. The probability that he hit a home run, given that he had an extra-base hit (2B, 3B or HR) would be 6/56 = 0.1071.

Section 7.4—Counting

Let's learn to count. Obviously I mean something other than 1, 2, 3, 4, ... What I mean is trying to count how many different ways certain things can happen.

Example—Suppose a restaurant has only two kinds of items on its menu, sandwiches and drinks. Under "drinks," the only three choices are water, cola and diet cola. Under "sandwich," the only two choices are hamburger and bologna. How many different meals can you order if you order one of each type of item?

A tree diagram will help here.

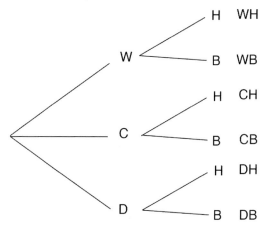

So there are six choices. It is not hard to see why. There are two events happening, choosing a drink and choosing a sandwich. The two are separate events, meaning there is nothing that is both a drink and a sandwich. The first event can happen three different ways. For each of the three ways the first event can happen, the second can happen two ways. Since 3 * 2 = 6, we have 6 different meals possible.

Multiplication Principle—If two separate events, E_1 and E_2, will be occurring, and E_1 can happen n_1 ways while E_2 can happen n_2 different ways, then the combined event can happen $n_1 * n_2$ ways.

Example—Suppose a restaurant's menu has eight cold appetizers, nine hot appetizers, four soups, five breads, eight salads, 47 entrees, 12 beverages, 10 vegetables, and 11 desserts. If you order one of each type of item, how many different meals could you order?

We have nine different "events" happening. They are separate events since they are "coming out of different groups of stuff." So the total number of ways the nine events can happen is 8 * 9 * 4 * 5 * 8 * 47 * 12 * 10 * 11 = 714,700,800. So we can order 714,700,800 different meals.

Assume the restaurant has the same menu for breakfast, lunch and dinner. You eat there three meals a day. How many years would it take to get to where you had to order the same meal twice?

Accounting for leap year by using 365.25 days per year, we have 365.25 * 3 = 1095.75 meals per year so 714,700,800/1095.75 = 652248.0493 years before you would have to order the same meal twice.

Example—Suppose Billy Bob got in trouble and ends up in prison making license plates. The license plates consist of three letters followed by three numbers. How many license plates are possible?

There are 26 choices for each letter and 10 choices for each number. Looking at each letter and each number as independent events, we have 26 * 26 * 26 * 10 * 10 * 10 = 17,576,000 different license plates.

Suppose no letters may be repeated. How many license plates are possible?

There are 26 choices for the first letter, 25 for the second, and 24 for the third. So we have 26 * 25 * 24 * 10 * 10 * 10 = 15,600,000 different license plates.

Suppose no letters may be repeated and no numbers may be repeated. How many license plates are possible?

There are 26 choices for the first letter, 25 for the second, and 24 for the third. There are 10 choices for the first number, nine for the second and eight for the third. So we have 26 * 25 * 24 * 10 * 9 * 8 = 11,232,000 different license plates.

So far we have looked at problems where the events are separate events, that is, where the choices are coming out of different "sets of stuff." Now we will consider problems where they come out of the same "set of stuff." In a sense, we already did that in the last two parts of the last example when we did not allow repetitions in parts of the license plates.

Suppose you have a group of five students. In how many different lines can the students stand? There are five choices for the first student, four for the second, and so on. So there are 5 * 4 * 3 * 2 * 1 = 120 different lines in which the students can stand. Suppose we ask the same question but 12 students are involved. It will be 12 * 11 * 10 * 9 * 8 * 7 * 6 * 5 * 4 * 3 * 2 * 1 = 479,001,600. That is a lot of button-pushing on the calculator. There is a standard mathematical shorthand that we can use to help us here. We write 5! to represent 5 * 4 * 3 * 2 * 1. We write 12! to represent 12 * 11 * 10 * 9 * 8 * 7 * 6 * 5 * 4 * 3 * 2 * 1. We read 12! as "12 factorial." There is a built in command on your calculator for this. To do 12!, you would type 12, then press <MATH>, choose "PROB" and then choose "!" which is option 4.

Example—Suppose you have a group of 25 students and nine of them are going to play baseball. You have a pitcher, catcher, etc. How many different arrangements would there be?

Pitcher	25 choices
1st base	24 choices
2nd base	23 choices
Shortstop	22 choices

3rd base	21 choices
Catcher	20 choices
Left field	19 choices
Center field	18 choices
Right field	17 choices

So that would be 25 * 24 * 23 * 22 * 21 * 20 * 19 * 18 * 17. Before we do the arithmetic, let us review what is going on mathematically. We have 25 objects. We are choosing nine objects. All nine objects are coming out of the same group of 25 objects. Repetitions are not allowed. Notice that this is like the factorial idea we did above. The only problem is we are not going all the way down to one. But there is still a notational and mathematical shorthand. This is called permutations. Our notation is 25 P 9 since we are looking at the "number of permutations of 25 objects chosen 9 at a time." On your calculator, type 25, then <MATH> "PROB" "nPr," and then type 9. We get $7.41354768 \times 10^{11} = 741,354,768,000$.

One note here. If you have n objects and order matters, if you choose all n, you can use n nPr n or n!. When all objects are chosen, nPr and n! give the same answer.

Suppose we had a similar problem as the last example except we did not have an order involved.

Example—Suppose you have 25 students and you are choosing nine of them to go with you to pick up some supplies. How many different groups of nine could you choose?

This problem has a similar setting as the last one. You are choosing nine objects. All nine objects are coming out of the same group of 25 objects. Repetitions are not allowed. The difference is that in the last example, order mattered. In this one order does not matter. Again, there is a notational and mathematical shorthand. This is called combinations. Our notation is 25 C 9 since we are looking at the "number of combinations of 25 objects chosen 9 at a time." On your calculator, type 25, then <MATH> "PROB" "nCr," and then type 9. We get 2,042,975 different groups of nine.

Let us summarize what we have learned.

If you are taking objects out of different "groups of stuff" then use the **multiplication principle**.

If the objects are coming out of the "same group of stuff" and repetitions ARE allowed, then use the **multiplication principle**.

If the objects are coming out of the "same group of stuff" and repetitions ARE NOT allowed, if ORDER MATTERS then use **permutations (nPr)**.

If the objects are coming out of the "same group of stuff" and repetitions

ARE NOT allowed, if ORDER DOES NOT MATTER then use **combinations (nCr)**.

Example—Suppose the 2008 Mets were going to be playing a game. The players playing were as follows:

Jose Reyes	SS
David Wright	3B
Carlos Beltran	CF
Carlos Delgado	1B
Brian Schneider	C
Luis Castillo	2B
Ryan Church	RF
Fernando Tatis	LF
Johan Santana	P

If we just say "how many different lineups are possible" it will be 9! = 362,880. But Santana is going to bat ninth and Reyes is going to bat first. With those restrictions, how many lineups are possible?

Reyes   ?   ?   ?   ?   ?   ?   ?   Santana

There are seven people to fill the seven slots, order matters, repetitions are not allowed so it is 7 nPr 7 or 7! = 5040.

Suppose we specify that Beltran, Wright and Delgado, in some order, will be the third, fourth and fifth hitters. Reyes is still batting first and Santana is still batting ninth. This ends up being a combination of the multiplication principle and permutations.

We actually have four different events. Once we find out how many ways each event can happen, we will multiply those numbers together.

Event	Ways It Can Happen
Reyes bats first	1
Santana bats ninth	1
Beltran, Wright and Delgado, in some order, will bat third, fourth and fifth	3! = 6
Schneider, Castillo, Church, Tatis, in some order, will bat second, sixth, seventh and eighth	4! = 24

So, with the given restrictions, there are still 1 * 1 * 6 * 24 = 144 different possible lineups.

Section 7.5—Streaks and Slumps

We often hear discussion of players who are "hot" or "cold." Many cases of "hot streaks" or "slumps" are really nothing more than random fluctuations due to the simple probabilities involved.

Suppose we are talking about a .300 hitter. We will assume at-bats are independent events. For him, P(at least one hit in 10 ABs) = 1 – (P(no hit in given AB))^{10} = 1 – .7^{10} = .9718. So it is unlikely he will go 10 consecutive ABs without a hit. But it is a long season. Suppose he has 600 ABs. We will look at the 600 ABs as 60 distinct groups of 10 ABs. P(none of our 60 ten AB blocks in which he goes 0 for 10) = 1 – (P(at least one hit in 10 AB block))^{60} = 1 – .9718^{60} = .8203. So there is better than an 82% chance that he will have at least one ten AB stretch with no hits. It would actually be higher if we realize that there would really be 591 groups of 10 ABs. 1–10, 2–11, 3–12, ..., 590–599, 591–600. This would be a harder problem though since these blocks overlap.

Consider the same batter. What is the probability that he would have a stretch in which he had hits in four straight ABs? Again, we will look at the 600 ABs as 150 groups of four. The probability of four straight hits in a given set of at-bats is .300^4 = .0081. So the probability that he does not get four straight hits in that given set of at-bats would be .9919.

P(at least one string of four straight hits in 150 sets of four ABs) = 1 – P(no string of four straight hits in 150 sets of 4 ABs) = 1 – (P(doesn't have four straight hits in given set of four ABs))^{150} = 1 – .9919^{150} = .7048. So there is a fairly good chance that he will have a string of four straight hits. Again, our simplification of the problem (150 separate sets of four ABs) lowers what the probability would really be.

Section 7.6—Law of Large Numbers

Suppose you roll a die six times. Would you be surprised if you rolled no fives? Of course not. Suppose you roll a die 600 times. Would you be surprised if you rolled no fives? Absolutely. Would you be surprised if you rolled only 20 fives. Of course. How many fives would you expect? Probably about 100. If that is the case, then you have an intuitive idea of the law of large numbers.

The Law of Large Numbers says that as an experiment is repeated (assuming trials are independent) more and more times, each possible outcome will come to occur at roughly the rate indicated by its probability.

Example—If you roll a die hundreds of times, you would expect that approximately 1/6 of the rolls will be ones, approximately 1/6 of the rolls will be two, approximately 1/6 of the rolls will be threes, approximately 1/6 of the rolls will be fours, approximately 1/6 of the rolls will be fives, and approximately 1/6 of the rolls will be sixes.

Example—If you flip a coin hundreds of times, you would expect to get about half heads and about half tails.

Example—If a player is a .250 hitter, as he gets more and more at-bats, his batting average should go to .250.

Example—In section 7.1, we looked at Homer Smoot, a .296 hitter. Let's look at him again. As before, I used a random number generator to produce 1000 ABs for Smoot. After four ABs, he was hitting .750. After 10, he was hitting .500. Being a manager, we would hope it would continue. Being realistic, we would not expect that to continue. After 25 ABs, he was still hitting .400. Even after 58 ABs, Smoot was hitting .397. By 115 ABs, he was down to .304. After 166 ABs, he was back up to .325. Here is a table showing some of his averages.

AB	AVG
183	.301
184	.299
202	.277
250	.280
300	.283
350	.280
400	.283
450	.278
500	.282
600	.280
700	.280
800	.289
900	.286
950	.292
1000	.298

The following chart shows the progression. Notice the behavior is more erratic at the beginning but ultimately levels off in the expected region.

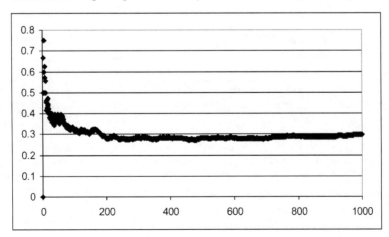

This chart shows the expected number of Smoot's different types of hits based on his actual hits of those types. The last column shows how many of those he had in our randomly generated at-bats.

Expected	Type	Actual
228	single	225
44	double	48
16	triple	17
8	homer	8

An idea that formalizes some of the concepts involved in the law of large numbers is the **expected value** of an experiment. The term "expected value" is a deceptive one. It seems to imply the idea of a value that we "expect." While that is, in a sense, true, it is NOT a value that we would expect on a single occurrence of the experiment.

Example—Consider what happens when we roll a standard six-sided die. There are six events, each with a probability of 1/6. This can be viewed in the following way. One-sixth of the time, we would expect to get a one. Likewise, 1/6 of the time we would expect to get a two, and so on. If we did our experiment 6 times, getting what we would "expect" would give us a 1, a 2, a 3, a 4, a 5 and a 6 in some order. (Note: It is actually not likely that a single sequence of 6 rolls would actually do that but that is what the probabilities would cause us to expect. If we were to perform the experiment over and over, we would expect about 1/6 of the occurrences to be a 1, 1/6 to be a 2, etc.)

Event	Probability	Product of Event and Probability
1	1/6	1/6
2	1/6	2/6
3	1/6	3/6
4	1/6	4/6
5	1/6	5/6
6	1/6	6/6
Expected Value = Total		21/6 = 7/2 = 3.5

The **expected value** of an experiment is obtained by multiplying each outcome by its probability and adding the resulting numbers.

Expected Value = (event 1) (probability of event 1) + (event 2) (probability of event 2) + ... + (event n) (probability of event n).

Example—A game involves putting the following pieces of paper in a hat and pulling out a piece of paper. Find the expected value of the following:

1	2	2	3	3
4	4	6	8	10

Event	Probability	Product
1	1/10	1/10
2	2/10	4/10
3	2/10	6/10
4	2/10	8/10
6	1/10	6/10
8	1/10	8/10
10	1/10	10/10
Expected Value		43/10 = 4.3

The gambling industry functions entirely on the idea of expected value. For example, if a casino were running a game like the example above, it might charge $5 to play, giving the player the number of dollars corresponding to the result of the piece of paper. Then the person would expect, on average over a large number of games, to win $4.30. However, since the player had to pay $5 to play, the player would expect to lose $0.70 every time he played. Since the casino designs the games, the casino controls the probabilities and thus the chances of winning. And since the casino is in business to make money, the casino will, in the long run, win more often and in larger amounts. The casino will try to make a large payoff seem possible, tempting players to risk losing frequently in the hopes of eventually winning "the big one." Since the casino controls how often "the big one" is won, it happens rarely enough that the casino makes large amounts of money. The casino hopes the players do not understand probabilities and expected values.

Chapter 7—Exercises

SECTION 7.1—BASIC PROBABILITIES

1. Suppose you flip a coin twice.
    a. What is the probability that you get heads both times?
    b. What is the probability that you get different results?
    c. What is the probability that you get the same results?
    d. What is the probability that you get heads at least once?
2. Draw a tree diagram to illustrate flipping three coins. Use your tree diagram to determine the probability of
    a. getting three heads.
    b. getting two heads and one tail.
    c. getting at least two heads.
    d. getting an odd number of tails.
    e. not having all coins the same.
    f. getting exactly two tails.
3. You roll a standard six-sided die. Find the probability of

   a. getting a five.

   b. getting an even number.

   c. getting a number less than three.

   d. getting a number less than or equal to three.

   e. getting a seven.

   f. getting a number less than seven.

4. You roll two standard six-sided dice. Find the probability that

   a. the sum of the two dice is seven.

   b. the sum of the two dice is two.

   c. the sum of the two dice is greater than 10.

   d. the sum of the two dice is odd and less than six.

   e. the sum of the two dice is greater than or equal to 10.

   f. the sum of the two dice is less than 10.

   g. the product of the two dice is greater than 17.

   h. the product of the two dice is 11.

   i. the product of the two dice is less than 30.

   j. the product of the two dice is odd and less than 12.

   k. the product of the two dice is twelve.

   l. the product of the two dice is four.

5. You roll three standard six-sided dice. What is the probability that

   a. the sum of the numbers on the dice is five?

   b. the sum of the numbers is at least 14?

   c. the product of the three numbers is at least 100?

SECTION 7.2—AVERAGES AS PROBABILITIES AND SECTION 7.3—COMBINED PROBABILITIES; AT LEAST ONCE RULE; CONDITIONAL PROBABILITIES

For problems 1–13, we will use the following chart which gives Willie Mays' career statistics.

Year	Team	AB	H	2B	3B	HR	SO	AVG
1951	Giants	464	127	22	5	20	60	.274
1952	Giants	127	30	2	4	4	17	.236
1954	Giants	565	195	33	13	41	57	.345
1955	Giants	580	185	18	13	51	60	.319
1956	Giants	578	171	27	8	36	65	.296
1957	Giants	585	195	26	20	35	62	.333
1958	Giants	600	208	33	11	29	56	.347
1959	Giants	575	180	43	5	34	58	.313
1960	Giants	595	190	29	12	29	70	.319
1961	Giants	572	176	32	3	40	77	.308
1962	Giants	621	189	36	5	49	85	.304
1963	Giants	596	187	32	7	38	83	.314
1964	Giants	578	171	21	9	47	72	.296

Year	Team	AB	H	2B	3B	HR	SO	AVG
1965	Giants	558	177	21	3	52	71	.317
1966	Giants	552	159	29	4	37	81	.288
1967	Giants	486	128	22	2	22	92	.263
1968	Giants	498	144	20	5	23	81	.289
1969	Giants	403	114	17	3	13	71	.283
1970	Giants	478	139	15	2	28	90	.291
1971	Giants	417	113	24	5	18	123	.271
1972	Giants/Mets	244	61	11	1	8	48	.250
1973	Mets	209	44	10	0	6	47	.211
career totals		10881	3283	523	140	660	1526	.302

For all of these questions, assume we are interested in official at-bats (AB), not plate appearances.

1. For his career, what is the probability that Mays got a hit (H)?
2. In 1954, what is the probability that he got a home run (HR) given that he got a hit?
3. For his career, what is the probability that he hit a home run?
4. In 1965, what is the probability that he hit a home run?
5. In 1958, what is the probability that he struck out (SO)?
6. In 1963, what is the probability that he got a hit?
7. In 1957, what is the probability that he got a triple (3B)?
8. For his career, what is the probability he got an extra base hit?
9. In 1962, what is the probability he got a double (2B)
10. In 1959, what is the probability he hit a home run or double?
11. In 1966, what is the probability that it was a single given that he got a hit?
12. For his career, if he got a hit, what is the probability it was an extra base hit?
13. Using Mays' career batting average, if Mays had 10 at-bats, what would be the probability that he got at least one hit?
14. You roll a die four times. What is the probability that you roll a two at least once?
15. A box contains eight cats, seven slugs and five water buffaloes. You reach into the box and pull out a creature at random. You note the kind of creature, return it to the box, and pull out another creature. What is the probability that you pull out two slugs?
16. The following chart gives a breakdown of some people in a class. Answer the following questions based on the chart.

	Male	Female	Totals
Freshmen	12	10	22
Sophomores	13	12	25

	Male	Female	Totals
Juniors	5	9	14
Seniors	1	4	5
Totals	31	35	66

a. If a student is chosen at random, what is the probability that the student is male?

b. If a student is chosen at random, what is the probability that the student is a male junior?

c. If a female is chosen at random, what is the probability that she is a sophomore?

d. If a student is chosen at random, what is the probability that the student is a male or a junior?

17. The following chart gives the pitchers on the New York Mets' roster between the 2005 and 2006 season.

	Name	Height	Weight	Birth Date
1	Brian Bannister	6-2	200	02/28/81
2	Heath Bell	6-3	225	09/29/77
3	Kris Benson	6-4	205	11/07/74
4	Bartolome Fortunato	6-1	195	08/24/74
5	Anderson Garcia	6-2	170	03/23/81
6	Tom Glavine	6-0	185	03/25/66
7	Tim Hamulack	6-4	220	11/14/76
8	Aaron Heilman	6-5	220	11/12/78
9	Philip Humber	6-4	210	12/21/82
10	Matt Lindstrom	6-4	210	02/11/80
11	Pedro Martinez	5-11	180	10/25/71
12	Henry Owens	6-3	230	04/23/79
13	Juan Padilla	6-0	200	02/17/77
14	Juan Perez	6-1	170	09/03/78
15	Royce Ring	6-0	220	12/21/80
16	Jae Seo	6-1	215	05/24/77
17	Steve Trachsel	6-4	205	10/31/70
18	Billy Wagner	5-11	200	07/25/71
19	Mitch Wylie	6-3	190	01/14/77
20	Tyler Yates	6-4	240	08/07/77
21	Victor Zambrano	6-0	205	08/06/75

Based on this chart, answer the questions below.

a. If a player is chosen at random, what is the probability he is under six feet tall?

b. If a player is chosen at random, what is the probability he was born since January 1, 1980?

c. If a player is chosen at random, what is the probability that he weighs at least 200 pounds?

d. If a player is chosen at random, what is the probability that he weighs at least 200 pounds or is under 6 feet tall?

18. You have a box. In the box are eight red marbles, five blue marbles, and 11 plaid marbles.

   a. If you reach into the box and pull out a marble, what is the probability the marble is plaid?
   b. If you pull out a marble, note its color, put it back and pull out another marble, what is the probability both marbles are blue?
   c. If you pull out a marble, note its color and pull out another marble, what is the probability both marbles are blue?

SECTION 7.4—COUNTING

1. Suppose the Astros clubhouse manager decides to give the players some unusual snack options during games. He puts two baskets by the clubhouse door. The first basket contains an apple, an orange, a pear, a peach and a jar of pickled pigs' feet. The second basket contains a package of M & M's, a Kit Kat, a Snickers bar, a package of cupcakes, and a habanero pepper. When a player leaves the clubhouse, without looking he grabs two items from the first basket and one from the second basket. How many different three item snacks could he have?

2. From the 25-player roster, the Astros decide to choose five for a committee to choose a new clubhouse manager. How many different committees are possible?

3. Tampa Bay Rays manager Joe Maddon is taking six books with him on a road-trip. He will be taking them from a stack of 34 books. How many different combinations of books are possible?

4. The University of Oregon is famous for its variety of football uniform combinations. Suppose they have five different uniform pants, six different shirts, four different helmets, six different pairs of socks and four different pairs of shoes. Assuming all the combinations actually match, how many different ways can they dress?

5. The Braves lineup for a game will include the following players: Chris Johnson (third base), Andrelton Simmons (shortstop), Tommy La Stella (second base), Freddie Freeman (first base), Justin Upton (left field), Gerald Laird (catcher), Ervin Santana (pitcher), Jason Heyward (right field), BJ Upton (center field).

   a. How many different batting lineups are possible?
   b. How many different batting lineups are possible if Santana is going to bat ninth?
   c. How many different batting lineups are possible if Santana is going to bat ninth and Heyward is going to lead off?

    d. How many different batting lineups are possible if Santana is going to bat ninth and Simmons is NOT going to bat fourth?

    e. How many different batting lineups are possible if Santana is going to bat ninth, Heyward is going to bat first, the Uptons and Freeman are going to bat second, third or fourth, and Simmons, La Stella and Laird are going to bat sixth, seventh or eighth?

6. Give the number of possible license plates under each of the following conditions.

    a. there are three letters and three numbers

    b. there are three letters and three numbers but letters cannot be repeated

    c. there are three letters and three numbers but letters and numbers cannot be repeated

    d. six characters (either letters or numbers) are used

    e. six characters (either letters or numbers) are used but none may be repeated

    f. there are four letters and three numbers

    g. there are four letters and three numbers but no letter or number may be repeated

7. The online menu for a major league team's stadium concession stands shows at least ten kinds of sandwiches, 15 other kinds of entrees, 28 different beverages, 13 side dishes and 7 desserts. If you order one of each kind of item, how many meals could you order?

8. You go to a restaurant where the menu consists of seven types of salads, eight types of hot appetizers, seven types of cold appetizers, 21 types of entrees, nine types of drinks, five types of bread, 12 types of pasta, eight types of soup and seven types of desserts.

    a. If you order one of each kind of item, how many different meals could you order?

    b. How many meals can you order if you get a hot appetizer or a cold appetizer but not both and one of each other type of item?

9. One of the items on Olive Garden's online menu is the Sampler Italiano. From calamari, stuffed mushrooms, fried zucchini, chicken fingers, fried mozzarella or toasted meat ravioli you can choose any three for $8.25. How many different Sampler Italianos are possible?

10. Fifteen people have formed a baseball team. We are interested in the number of nine player batting orders that can be created from the fifteen players.

    a. Is this a combination problem or a permutation problem?

    b. How many different lineups are possible?

11. A class has 14 boys and 12 girls.

   a. You are going to take four boys and three girls to help you with something. In how many different orders (walking in single file) could the seven children walk if the boys go first and the girls follow?

   b. A committee of five people is going to be chosen. How many different committees are possible?

12. In 1969, Tommie Agee, Cleon Jones, Ron Swoboda, Art Shamsky, Rod Gaspar, and Amos Otis were the main outfielders for the New York Mets. They needed to have a right fielder, a left fielder and a center fielder. Assuming each player can play each position, we are interested in how many different arrangements of these players they could have had. How many different arrangements were possible?

13. Suppose the 2008 Mets were going to be playing a game. The players playing were as follows.

Jose Reyes	SS
David Wright	3B
Carlos Beltran	CF
Carlos Delgado	1B
Brian Schneider	C
Luis Castillo	2B
Ryan Church	RF
Fernando Tatis	LF
Johan Santana	P

   a. How many different lineups are possible?

   b. How many different lineups are possible if Santana bats last?

   c. How many different lineups are possible if Santana bats last and Reyes bats first?

   d. How many different lineups are possible if Santana bats last, Reyes bats first and Beltran, Wright and Delgado will bat third through fifth (but not necessarily in that order?

Section 7.5—Streaks and Slumps

1. A basketball player is a 75% free throw shooter. If he shoots five free throws, what is the probability he makes all of them? If he shoots five free throws, what is the probability that he misses all five?

2. In 1941, Ted Williams batted .401. In a given game, if he had four official at-bats, what is the probability he got at least three hits?

Section 7.6—Law of Large Numbers

1. A game involves rolling a die. You get three points for rolling a one. You get five points for rolling a two or a three. You get ten points for rolling

a four, a five or a six. What is the expected value of the number of points you would get?

2. A game involves rolling a die. If you roll a 1 or 2, you receive $3. If you roll a 3, 4 or 5, you receive $6. If you roll a 6, you receive $10. If you have to pay $5 to play the game, what would be your expected gain or loss (include the cost of playing)?

3. The following ten sheets of paper are in a hat.

| 1 | 3 | 3 | 6 | 6 | 6 | 9 | 9 | 9 | 9 |

If one piece of paper is pulled out of the hat at random, what is the expected value of the number on the paper? (Hint: "Expected value" does NOT mean the number that has the greatest probability of being chosen.)

4. Eight pieces of paper, number 1 through 8 are in a bowl. You draw one piece at random. What is the expected value of the number?

5. Explain the Law of Averages (law of large numbers). Use an example to illustrate your explanation.

6. Use the random number generator on your calculator (set it to choose an integer from 1–20). Use that to model at-bats for a baseball player. For each number, the table below shows his result.

Number	Result	Number	Result
1	single	11	out
2	single	12	out
3	single	13	out
4	double	14	out
5	double	15	out
6	home run	16	out
7	walk	17	out
8	out	18	out
9	out	19	out
10	out	20	out

a. Based on the table, what should the players batting average be?

b. Model 20 at-bats using the above table. What was the player's average in those 20 at-bats?

c. Using the 20 from (b), continue and model 50 at-bats using the above table. What was the player's average in those 50 at-bats?

d. Using the 50 from (c), continue and model 100 at-bats using the above table. What was the player's average in those 100 at-bats?

8—Finance

"I believe that through knowledge and discipline, financial peace is possible for all of us."—Dave Ramsey

"Don't gamble; take all your savings and buy some good stock and hold it till it goes up, then sell it. If it don't go up, don't buy it."—Will Rogers

We are now going to discuss some financial topics. We will begin with financial topics that are of interest to all people, not just those interested in sports. These include issues like savings accounts, retirement funds and loans. After all, whether you play sports or not, you're going to want to buy a house and have enough money to live on once you retire. Admittedly, the numbers we will be dealing with will be somewhat different depending on whether we will be considering major league athletes or non-athletes. In some ways, the athlete's issues are easier; in some ways they are harder.

We will then conclude with a couple of issues that are specific to the world of sports.

Section 8.1—Simple Savings

Most people, particularly college students, do not just put money in a savings or checking account and leave it there for a long period of time. The typical college student puts some money in the account, takes some out, takes some out, takes some out, takes some out, takes some out, takes some out, takes some out, takes some out, and, hopefully before the checks start bouncing, puts some more money in.

Savings accounts and many checking accounts make money for the account holder by accumulating interest. Interest is money the bank pays to the account holder for the privilege of holding the money in that bank. The bank, in turn, uses the money to invest and make money, hopefully at higher rates of interest than the bank pays.

There are two kinds of interest, simple and compound. Simple interest pays money on the original investment and only on the original investment. Compound interest pays money on the original investment and also on any previously paid interest.

Compound interest is handled a variety of ways. It can be compounded annually, monthly, quarterly, weekly, daily, or every 37 seconds. It can also be compounded continuously, which can be viewed as being compounded infinitely often. If an account pays 5%, compounded annually, then it will receive 5% interest once a year. If an account pays 5%, compounded quarterly (that is, four times a year), then it will receive 1.25% (5% divided by 4) four times a year. If an account pays 5%, compounded monthly, then it will receive .41667% (5% divided by 12) 12 times a year.

In EVERY formula we use in this chapter, whenever we use a percentage we must put the percentage in decimal form. That means we move the decimal point two places to the left.

4% would be .04

3.5% would be .035

10.4% would be .104

If you are working with 4% interest and put it into the formula as a 4, instead of .04, then you are effectively working with 400% interest.

One kind of account that is typically treated in the "put money in then leave it alone" way is a certificate of deposit (CD).

Suppose we put P dollars in a CD that pays an annual interest rate of r (assume r is already in decimal form), with the interest compounded n times a year. Then n times per year the account will earn interest at a rate of r/n. The amount of interest earned would be $P * \frac{r}{n}$. Thus, since we have the original amount of money plus the interest, we now have $P + P * \frac{r}{n} = P * \left(1 + \frac{r}{n}\right)$ in the account. The next time the interest is compounded, the interest earned would be $\frac{r}{n} * P * \left(1 + \frac{r}{n}\right)$. Since we already had $P * \left(1 + \frac{r}{n}\right)$ in the account, we now have

$$P * \left(1 + \frac{r}{n}\right) + \frac{r}{n} * P * \left(1 + \frac{r}{n}\right) = P * \left(1 + \frac{r}{n}\right) * \left(1 + \frac{r}{n}\right) = P * \left(1 + \frac{r}{n}\right)^2$$ in the account.

The pattern will continue so that we will always have $A = P * \left(1 + \frac{r}{n}\right)^m$ in the account, where m is the number of compoundings that have occurred. And that number of compoundings will be n times the number of years the money is in the account.

If money is put in an account where the only money added or subtracted is interest, with the interest compounded any ways EXCEPT continuously, the amount of money in the account will be given by the following formula.

$$A = P*\left(1+\frac{r}{n}\right)^{(n*t)}$$

A = amount of money in the account
P = original amount of money in the account
r = annual interest rate IN DECIMAL FORM
n = number of compoundings of interest per year
t = number of years the money is in the account

As mentioned above, interest can be compounded continuously. The derivation of the formula for this case is beyond the scope of this course. However, there is a number involved in the formula that we need to discuss briefly. Recall, from mathematics you have done previously, that there is a number that is approximately 3.14. It is not 3.14. It is more like 3.14159265359140397848 25424142192796639198932348258351990748479774631213467319607687311770 2027606580198567877822933137487565529317947017 5082. Actually, though, the decimal expansion for that number never ends. Because of that, we use a symbol that will always mean that number for us. That symbol, is, of course, the Greek letter, π. There is another number that comes up in many kinds of applications. Like π its decimal expansion never ends. It is approximately equal to 2.718281828458563411. As with π, we want to use a symbol that will always mean that number. This one, however, is represented by an English letter, not a Greek one. We use e.

If money is put in an account where the only money added or subtracted is interest, with the interest compounded continuously, the amount of money in the account will be given by the following formula.

$$A = P*e^{(r*t)}$$

A = amount of money in the account
P = original amount of money in the account
r = annual interest rate IN DECIMAL FORM
t = number of years the money is in the account

Example 1—Suppose you put $2,000 in an account that earns 3.5% compounded quarterly. How much money will be in the account after five years if the only money added to or subtracted from the account is the interest?

This is not a continuous compounding problem so the formula we use is

$A = P*(1 + \dfrac{r}{n})^{(n*t)}$. For this problem, then, we have

$A = 2000*\left(1 + \dfrac{.035}{4}\right)^{(4*5)} = \$2,380.68.$

Note: Let your calculator do the work for you. You will avoid round off error or careless errors if you simply type the entire formula into your calculator exactly as it is written. Once you type it, proofread it to assure you do not have any typographical errors. But do not do any preliminary calculations, like .035/4 = .00875 and type that in instead.

Example 2—Suppose you have the same account as in the previous problem except that the interested is compounded continuously. How much money will you have after five years?

The formula we use is $A = P*e^{(r*t)}$. For this problem, then, we have
$A = 2000*e^{(.035*5)} = \$2382.49.$

Example 3—Jose Reyes' first full season in the major leagues was 2005. That year, he was paid $332,000. Suppose he took $100,000 of that money and put it in a CD earning 3.87% compounded quarterly and left it there until 2014. How much money would the CD be worth? If he continued to leave the money in the account, how long would it take to be worth $1,000,000?

The formula we will use is $A = P*(1 + \dfrac{r}{n})^{(n*t)}$. For this problem, then,

we have $A = 100,000*\left(1 + \dfrac{.0387}{4}\right)^{(4*9)} = \$141,428.75.$

To solve the second question easily we would need logarithms, which we will not consider in this book. But we can come up with a good approximation by simply increasing the value for t until we get A = $1,000,000. A value of t = 59 years gives A = $970,193.42. A value of t = 60 years gives A = $1,008,288.32. So, to become a millionaire, Reyes could leave the money in the account for almost 60 years or wait until 2007 when his salary jumped from $401,500 to $2,875,000.

Section 8.2—Savings Plans

Another kind of savings plan is one in which a certain amount of money is regularly deposited in an account that is designated for a particular purpose.

Retirement funds, college funds, etc., are examples of this kind of savings plan. Again we are going to keep the problem fairly simple by making a couple of restrictions. In a retirement account, the amount deposited is often based on a percentage of one's income. We will simplify the problem by assuming the amount deposited is always the same. Another simplification is with the interest rate. In many retirement funds, the interest rate is not fixed. Rather, it is dependent on the investments made by the company running the plan. Sometimes the interest rate may be high. Sometimes it may be lower. Sometimes it may even lose money. We will simplify the problem by assuming the interest rate stays fixed.

This particular kind of savings plan, or other kinds of investments, are particularly important for major league ballplayers. The average ballplayer, or any professional athlete for that matter, has a much shorter earning career than the average accountant. So, while players have years of very high earnings, those years of high income are relatively few.

In 1986, Barry Bonds earned $60,000 as a rookie. By 1991, he was being paid $2.3 million. When he retired after 2007, he had eight years in which he was paid more than $10 million and finished with a career income of over $188 million. Many athletes make significant additional income through endorsements. However, Barry Bonds' situation was not the typical ballplayer career path.

Consider Hall of Famer Al Kaline. He played from 1953 to 1974. Like Bonds', his is a 22-year career. But Kaline's highest single season salary was $110,000. His career earnings total was $1,184,000. Obviously things cost less during Kaline's career than during Bonds' career but there was also a significant jump in income for players and teams as television contracts and other income sources greatly increased during the 1980s and 1990s.

Robby Hammock played for the Diamondbacks for parts of six seasons from 2003 to 2011. His total salary for the three years for which baseball-refer ence.com has data was $1,114,000. To most of us that still sounds like a lot of money. But had Hammock not continued in baseball in coaching and managing (minor league level), he would need to have done something to prepare for his post-baseball income. Many players do not have skills or training that bring large incomes in the non-sports world. Some kind of savings plan is wise for anyone, particularly for the athlete who can reasonably expect to have relatively few peak income years.

If a fixed amount of money is regularly deposited in an account with a fixed rate of interest, the amount of money in the account will be given by the following formula.

$$A = PMT * \frac{\left((1 + \frac{r}{n})^{(n*t)} - 1 \right)}{\left(\frac{r}{n} \right)}$$

A = amount of money in the account
PMT = amount of money deposited each time the interest is compounded
r = annual interest rate IN DECIMAL FORM
n = number of compoundings of interest per year
t = number of years the money is in the account

Example 1—Mickey Morandini made it to the major leagues in 1990. His salary that year was $100,000. Assuming that was broken into monthly payments of $8,333.33, suppose he put $1,200 of each month's check into a retirement fund earning 6.47% compounded monthly until he retired following the 2000 season (an 11-season career). How much money would be in that fund? How much of that was put in by Morandini? How much of that was interest?

A = amount of money in the account = unknown
PMT = amount of money deposited each time the interest is compounded = 1200
r = annual interest rate IN DECIMAL FORM = .0647
n = number of compoundings of interest per year = 12
t = number of years the money is in the account = 11

We have $A = PMT * \dfrac{\left(\left(1+\dfrac{r}{n}\right)^{(n*t)}-1\right)}{\left(\dfrac{r}{n}\right)} = 1200 * \dfrac{\left(\left(1+\dfrac{.0647}{12}\right)^{(12*11)}-1\right)}{\left(\dfrac{.0647}{12}\right)} = \$230{,}035.12.$

Putting in $1,200 monthly for 11 years would mean Morandini contributed $1,200 * 11 * 12 = $158,400 so the interest paid would be $230,035.12 − $158,400 = $71,635.12.

Example 2—Suppose you put $150 per month in a retirement account beginning when you are 23 years old. You continue until you retire at age 64. If the interest is 8.4% compounded monthly, how much money will you have when you retire?

A = amount of money in the account = unknown
PMT = amount of money deposited each time the interest is compounded = 150
r = annual interest rate IN DECIMAL FORM = .084
n = number of compoundings of interest per year = 12
t = number of years the money is in the account = 41

$A = PMT * \dfrac{\left(\left(1+\dfrac{r}{n}\right)^{(n*t)}-1\right)}{\left(\dfrac{r}{n}\right)} = 150 * \dfrac{\left(\left(1+\dfrac{.084}{12}\right)^{(12*41)}-1\right)}{\left(\dfrac{.084}{12}\right)} = \$641{,}539.68.$

Example 3—Suppose you put $150 per month in a retirement account beginning when you are 23 years old. You continue until you retire at age 64. If the interest is 8.4% compounded quarterly, how much money will you have when you retire?

At first this seems to have only one difference from the previous example, that being the number of compoundings. But there is actually a second difference. The payment is NOT how much you put in each time you put money in. It is the amount you put in every time the interest is compounded. In the first example, money was put in each month and the interest was compounded each month. This time, however, you may put money in the account in January, February and March but the interest is not compounded until March. So you put in $450 during the time between compoundings.

A = amount of money in the account = unknown
PMT = amount of money deposited each time the interest is compounded = 450
r = annual interest rate IN DECIMAL FORM = .084
n = number of compoundings of interest per year = 4
t = number of years the money is in the account = 41

$$A = PMT * \frac{\left(\left(1 + \frac{r}{n}\right)^{(n*t)} - 1\right)}{\left(\frac{r}{n}\right)} = 450 * \frac{\left(\left(1 + \frac{.084}{4}\right)^{(4*41)} - 1\right)}{\left(\frac{.084}{4}\right)} = \$626{,}034.38.$$

Sometimes, particularly in the case of a special purpose savings account, or one with a relatively short time for investment, the amount desired at the end is the driving factor in how much money is put in. For instance, suppose when Mickey Morandini started to put money in the account cited above, he was assuming a 14-year career and wanted to have $500,000 in his retirement fund. It is a similar problem to the previous kind of problem with one difference. In the previous formula, we know the payment and desire to find the final amount. In this case, we know the final amount we want and need to find the payment that will give us the amount desired.

If a fixed amount of money is regularly deposited in an account with a fixed rate of interest, the amount of money in the account will be given by the following formula.

$$PMT = A * \frac{\left(\frac{r}{n}\right)}{\left(\left(1 + \frac{r}{n}\right)^{(n*t)} - 1\right)}$$

A = amount of money in the account
PMT = amount of money deposited each time the interest is compounded
r = annual interest rate IN DECIMAL FORM
n = number of compoundings of interest per year
t = number of years the money is in the account

Example 4—Morandini wants $500,000 in his retirement fund in 14 years when he expects to retire. Suppose he still has 6.47% interest compounded monthly. How much money must he put in each month?

A = amount of money in the account = 500,000
PMT = amount of money deposited each time the interest is compounded = unknown
r = annual interest rate IN DECIMAL FORM = .0647
n = number of compoundings of interest per year = 12
t = number of years the money is in the account = 14

$$PMT = A * \frac{\left(\frac{r}{n}\right)}{\left(\left(1+\frac{r}{n}\right)^{(n*Y)}-1\right)} = 500000 * \frac{\left(\frac{.0647}{12}\right)}{\left(\left(1+\frac{.0647}{12}\right)^{(12*14)}-1\right)} = \$1836.53.$$

- -

Example 5—Suppose you want to have $100,000 in your child's college fund in 18 years when he is ready to go to college. You find an account that will pay 10.1% interest compounded quarterly. How much money must you put in each month to end up with $100,000?

As before, we changed the number of compoundings. Therefore, the payment amount we end up with in the formula is how much needs to be put in each quarter. We will have to adjust that amount to answer the given question.

A = amount of money in the account = 100,000
PMT = amount of money deposited each time the interest is compounded = unknown
r = annual interest rate IN DECIMAL FORM = .101
n = number of compoundings of interest per year = 4
t = number of years the money is in the account = 18

$$PMT = A * \frac{\left(\frac{r}{n}\right)}{\left(\left(1+\frac{r}{n}\right)^{(n*Y)}-1\right)} = 100000 * \frac{\left(\frac{.101}{4}\right)}{\left(\left(1+\frac{.101}{4}\right)^{(4*18)}-1\right)} = \$502.783.$$

Before we deal with the monthly vs. quarterly issue, note that I did not round off to two decimal places as we typically do when dealing with money.

Normal rounding would say we would write $502.78. But that amount would not yield the amount we want. The amount that would give us the exact $100,000 would be $502.7832057 (or at least as far as the calculator display can tell us). If we pick an amount less than that we will have less than $100,000. So, to end up with at least $100,000, we must round up even if the usual rounding rules would not cause us to do so. So we need $502.79 per quarter. Since there are three months in a quarter, we thus must deposit $502.79/3 = $167.5966667 per month. Rounding up says we will pay $167.60 per month. This will actually have us end up with $100,003.34 but if we had not rounded up we would have finished with $99,997.37.

One last factor to consider for ballplayers or us. Early in our careers, we are likely to make less money than we will be making later in our careers. This makes the problem significantly more complicated so we will not look at actually solving it but we will insert a table here that will show how much Morandini would have had in his account upon retirement if he continued to pay the same percentage of his income into the account as the $1,200 we imagined him depositing at the beginning of his career.

Year	Annual Salary	Monthly Salary	Monthly Payment	End of Year Balance
1	$100,000	$8,333.33	$1,200	$14,914.77
2	$100,000	$8,333.33	$1,200	$30,823.67
3	$180,000	$15,000	$2,160	$59,724.76
4	$300,000	$25,000	$3,600	$108,449.95
5	$750,000	$62,500	$9,000	$227,539.32
6	$1,025,000	$85,416.67	$12,300	$395,582.03
7	$1,900,000	$158,333.33	$22,800	$705,329.65
8	$1,850,000	$154,166.67	$22,200	$1,028,265.66
9	$2,000,000	$166,666.67	$24,000	$1,395,098.64
10	$2,000,000	$166,666.67	$24,000	$1,786,382.34
11	$750,000	$62,500	$9,000	$2,017,311.82

Section 8.3—Loans

Most people would, at some point, like to buy a house. Most people do not, however, have sufficient cash to buy a house without borrowing money. Some home loans are what are called adjustable rate mortgages. In such loans, the interest rate, and thus the payments, change over time depending on various market related factors. When interest rates are high, such loans may be a wise choice for a home buyer since, if the interest rates go down, the monthly payment will go down. When interest rates are low, such a loan is less likely to be a good choice since payments will go up as interest rates increase.

We will consider only "fixed rate mortgages." They are mortgages in which the interest rate does not change over time.

If one borrows money at a fixed rate of interest, the payment will be given by the following formula.

$$PMT = \frac{P*\left(\dfrac{r}{n}\right)}{\left(1 - \left(1 + \dfrac{r}{n}\right)^{(-n*t)}\right)}$$

P = amount of money originally borrowed
PMT = amount of money to be paid each month
r = annual interest rate IN DECIMAL FORM
n = number of compoundings of interest per year
t = number of years over which the loan is to be paid back
For all of the problems we will consider, the interest will be compounded monthly and, therefore, the formula will give the monthly payment.

Example—In 2007, Albert Pujols bought a house for $2 million. Suppose he borrowed the entire amount at 2.76% annual interest, compounded monthly for a 15-year loan. What was his monthly payment?

For this problem, we have the following values for the variables.

P = 2,000,000
PMT = unknown so far
r = .0276
n = 12
t = 15

The monthly payment will be $PMT = \dfrac{2000000*\left(\dfrac{.0276}{12}\right)}{\left(1 - \left(1 + \dfrac{.0276}{12}\right)^{(-12*15)}\right)} = \$13,581.95.$

It should be noted that the actual monthly payment will be more than this amount. Mortgage companies want the house to be covered by insurance and they want the taxes to be paid. In order to be certain these items are paid, they will typically add approximately one-twelfth of the annual tax and insurance costs to each monthly payment. They then make the payments in order to protect their investment. The amount we obtain from the formula only gives the payment going to the mortgage company for paying off the loan.

Example—What is the total of all of the payments you make in the previous example?

Since Pujols was paying $13,581.95 each month for 15 years, we calculate this by multiplying as follows.

$13,581.95 * 12 * 15 = $2,444,751

Obviously having to pay so much in interest is not the best situation. As mentioned above, however, if you do not have a lot of cash available to pay for the house, you do not have a lot of choice. There are two things a borrower can do to lessen the interest. One is using a shorter term loan.

Example—Suppose you are buying a home. The price of the home is $125,000. You make a down payment of $12,500 and borrow the remaining amount. Suppose the loan is for 30 years with an annual interest rate of 5.9%. What will be your monthly payment?

For this problem, we have the following values for the variables.

$P = 125000 - 12500 = 112,500$
PMT = unknown so far
$r = .059$
$n = 12$
$t = 30$

The monthly payment will be $PMT = \dfrac{112500*\left(\dfrac{.059}{12}\right)}{\left(1-\left(1+\dfrac{.059}{12}\right)^{(-12*30)}\right)} = \$667.28$.

That is a total of $240,220.80 in payments. Further, $553.13 of the first payment goes solely to interest so only $114.15 actually pays for the house.

Example—Consider the same house as in the previous example but with a 15 year mortgage with an annual interest rate of 5.75%, what will be your monthly payment?

For this problem, we have the following values for the variables.

$P = 125000 - 12500 = 112,500$
PMT = unknown so far
$r = .0575$
$n = 12$
$t = 15$

The monthly payment will be $PMT = \dfrac{112500*\left(\dfrac{.0575}{12}\right)}{\left(1-\left(1+\dfrac{.0575}{12}\right)^{(-12*15)}\right)} = \$934.21$.

Obviously this is $266.93 more per month than in the previous example. But let us look the difference in costs over the life of the loan. The total of all payments is given by 934.21 * 12 * 15 = $168,157.80. That means you will ultimately pay $72,063 less than you would pay on the 30 year loan in addition to having the house paid off 15 years sooner. So, if you can afford the larger monthly payment, the shorter term loan is a wise investment.

Another way to save money is paying extra principal during the repayment process. Paying as little as $50 extra per month can save a lot of time and pay off the mortgage a lot sooner.

If you borrow $100,000 at 5.75% interest for 30 years, you will have a monthly payment of $583.57 and end up with the total of all your payments being $210,085.20. If you pay an extra $50 per month, the loan will be paid off after 24 years, 8 months and a total of all payments of $187,119.36. That means you will have paid off the house five years, four months sooner and save $22,966.87. If you are able to pay $100 extra each month, then you will finish paying the loan after 21 years, one month, owning the house eight years, 11 months sooner paying a total of $172,633.68 and saving $37,452.55.

You can experiment with extra payments producing savings by going to the Excel spreadsheet at http://fac.hsu.edu/worth/libarts/Excel/4C_Mortg age.xls.

The loan repayment formula is not solely a home mortgage formula. It can be used for any loan.

Example—Derek Jeter is reported to have a 2006 Mercedes S63 AMG. The 2014 S63 AMG lists for $139,500. Suppose you borrow the money to buy that car at 2.1% for five years. How much will you need to pay each month?

For this problem, we have the following values for the variables.

P = 139,500
PMT = unknown so far
r = .021
n = 12
t = 5

The monthly payment will be $PMT = \dfrac{139500 * \left(\dfrac{.021}{12}\right)}{\left(1 - \left(1 + \dfrac{.021}{12}\right)^{(-12*5)}\right)} = \$2451.23.$

Section 8.4—Sports Finance Topics

There are a lot of interesting fringe financial issues involved in various sports. We will look at a couple of examples from various sports.

Baseball's Luxury Tax

Since the days of Babe Ruth, several teams, particularly the Yankees, have been accused of trying to "buy pennants." Over the past few years, a system has been put in place to penalize teams that are paying salaries beyond various set thresholds. The recent thresholds set by Major League Baseball's Collective Bargaining Agreement are as follows.

Year	Threshold
2012	$178 million
2013	$178 million
2014	$189 million
2015	$189 million
2016	$189 million

If a team exceeds $189 million in salary in 2014, then it will be assessed a "tax." The amount of the penalty varies since the system is set up to penalize repeat offenders more severely.

This is how the tax rate were calculated for clubs above the threshold in 2013.

- The tax was 17.5% of the amount over $178 million if the team didn't exceed the tax threshold in 2012.
- The tax was 30% of the amount over $178 million if the team exceeded the 2012 tax threshold in 2012 and paid a 20% penalty that year.
- The tax was 40% of the amount over $178 million if the team exceeded the tax thresholds in both 2011 and 2012.

As the collective bargaining agreement changes, the specific penalties may change but it is likely that the main idea will continue.

Football and Basketball Salary Cap

The National Football League and the National Basketball Association have stricter rules than baseball on salaries. A baseball team may pay whatever amount in salaries they want as long as they are willing to pay the penalty. In the NFL and NBA, the threshold is stricter.

In the NFL, a team is not allowed to pay salaries in excess of the cap which, for 2013, was $123 million. To negotiate contracts in the age of salary caps, teams will sometimes stagger the amounts of contracts. For example, a team may give a player a four-year contract for $40 million. But that may not be $10 million per year. Based on how the team expects its other salary payments to go, they may make it $8 million in the first two years and then $12 million in the last two years when a higher cap will be in place. Also, if a team no longer wants the player he can be released and the team may be able to avoid the larger amounts from later years.

The NFL also has a minimum cap. A team must pay at least 89% of the cap in salaries. For 2013, that was $109.47 million. Signing bonuses, incentive clauses and other factors also play into the NFL salary cap.

The NBA salary cap is similar to that of the NFL but it has several exceptions and is thus called a "soft cap." The main exceptions in the NBA deal with signing free agents. Different rules apply depending on whether the free agent last played with the same team or a different team. Teams are allowed to exceed the cap to retain their own players.

OTHER ISSUES—UNCERTAINTY AND ESTIMATION

There are a number of other issues involving finance that come up in sports. They are not like the savings plans or loan payments problems because no nice formula applies. Yet they are important enough topics for some consideration, particularly because a useful skill comes into play.

In 2016, the Atlanta Braves' lease on Turner Field in Atlanta will expire. So Cobb County in Georgia decided to build a stadium for the Braves. The county believes that bringing the Braves to Atlanta's northern suburbs will be a financial benefit to the area. Whether that is true or not remains to be seen. But the leaders of Cobb County presumably looked at previous stadium shifts and, with estimates of their particular strengths and weaknesses, decided that the move would be to their long-term benefit.

Every four years, some city somewhere in the world, spends huge amounts of money to host the Olympics. Each of those cities must make estimates as to how much the preparation (building any stadium or arena that will be needed, building housing for the athletes, etc.) and costs of running the Olympics (security, temporary hiring of workers, etc.) will cost and how much revenue (tourists, television fees, etc.) will be brought in.

The same sort of thing happens when a city tries to determine if it should try to host an expansion team in a major sport (like Phoenix when the Diamondbacks were born) or try to lure an existing team (like the Supersonics moving to Oklahoma City and becoming the Thunder). What costs will the city incur (building a stadium, parking, etc.)? What revenue will the city realize (taxes, tourist dollars, etc.) from the presence of the team?

Even players sometimes have financial decisions to make that are not easily quantified. Suppose Bryce Harper becomes a free agent and has offers from the Yankees, Blue Jays and Royals. If each team offers the same amount, it is possible that one team's offer is actually significantly better than the others'. Things like tax rates and cost of living come into play. Tax rates vary between the United States and Canada. They vary between states within the United States. It costs a lot more to live in New York City than it does to live in Kansas City. The exact savings or costs of the various residences would vary depending on how much a person makes (tax rates change with income levels), how close to the ballpark he would want to live (housing tends to be more expensive the closer to the city one lives) or other lifestyle choices (apartment or house, acreage or small subdivision, etc.).

Lastly, we often hear about attendance figures at ballgames. It sure sounds better if the Marlins have 30,000 people at the game than if they only have 20,000 people. But, suppose the 30,000 people paid an average ticket price of $30 while the 20,000 people paid an average of $50. The revenue from the 30,000 people would be $900,000 while the 20,000 produce $1 million. Raising ticket prices might produce more revenue even though it reduces attendance. But the important word there is "might."

Example—Estimate the revenue for the Mets in 2014 from tickets, parking and concessions for home games. (I am deliberately not going to try to find out the exact numbers involved in attendance, prices, parking or concession costs. I am going to make estimates on all of them. Some estimates may be high. Some may be low. But in real life estimation problems, the specific numbers may be impossible to know.)

81 home games
Average attendance 35,000
81 * 35000 = 2,835,000 total attendance
Average ticket price $35

Total revenue from tickets—$99,225,000

Average parking costs—$25

Estimated number of vehicles—4,000 per game (I am assuming most fans arrive via subway, train or bus) so 324,000 for the season

Total revenue from parking—$8,100,000

Total attendance 2,835,000

Average spent on food/drink per person $25

Total revenue from concessions—$70,875,000

Total revenue—$178,200,000

Personal Finance

One final topic that comes into play for everyone is personal finance. Every adult has decisions to make regarding finances. Each person who has personal financial responsibility has to consider income and outgo of finances. This is another area that does not fit a nice formula other than (hopefully) INCOME – OUTGO = POSITIVE NUMBER.

In considering one's personal finances there are many different categories and kinds of expenses that must be considered. At http://www.budgetworksheets.org/, the following list of items, with a few additions, is given as a good start for consideration in establishing a personal budget.

Deductions—savings (especially an issue if one's income varies seasonally); legal obligations

Housing—rent or mortgage payments; utilities (keeping in mind that these can vary substantially over the course of a year as heating and/or air conditioning needs vary); homeowner's or renter's insurance; property taxes; fund for home repairs, improvements or maintenance

Debt Payments—credit card payments; student loan payments; any other personal or other kinds of loans

Food—groceries; eating out

Transportation—car payment (loan or lease), insurance, taxes, maintenance/repairs, gas; public transportation, parking, tolls; taxi

Family related expenses—day care/babysitting; leisure activities, recreation, lessons; allowances

Personal and Health—clothing; personal healthcare, haircuts, etc.; gym membership; medical/dental/vision insurance; doctor/dentist visits; prescription and other medications

Education—tuition, fees, books, supplies, etc.

Entertainment—tickets for shows/games/movies; subscriptions; other entertainment

Miscellaneous—charity, gifts, offerings; pets and related costs; entertaining guests; hobbies; pocket money

Many of these expenses can vary throughout the year. If you have children who play baseball, those expenses will be during spring and summer only. Educational expenses typically lessen during the summer. Likewise, income can vary throughout the year. If your income is from teaching, you have a nine or ten month work year but will still have expenses the rest of the year. If you work in construction, your income can be very seasonal so a budgeting process would need to include a heavy dose of savings for times when the income is less robust.

One brief story will illustrate the idea that some people, in this case an athlete, do not view finances the same way normal people do.

In 2005, basketball player Latrell Sprewell was upset at what he termed an "insulting" salary offer of $27 million over three years, saying, "They're not doing anything for me. I'm at risk. I have a lot of risk here. I got my family to feed." Granted, Sprewell had been making $14.6 million per year so a drop to an average of $9 million would be significant. However, it seems many people would welcome the opportunity to try to "feed my family" on $9 million per year.

Chapter 8—Exercises

SECTION 8.1—SIMPLE SAVINGS

1. You put $2,000 in a savings account. The interest rate is 2.3%. No money is added or removed. Fill in the blanks in the chart.

Compounded	*Annually*	*Quarterly*	*Monthly*	*Daily*	*Continuously*
Balance After 1 Year					
Balance After 2 Years					
Balance After 3 Years					
Balance After 5 Years					
Balance After 10 Years					
Balance After 15 Years					
Balance After 20 Years					
Balance After 25 Years					
Balance After 50 Years					

* don't worry about leap year

SECTION 8.2—SAVINGS PLANS

1. Mike Trout started playing regularly at age 21. Suppose he started putting $1,000 per month in his retirement fund and continues to do so until he retires. Suppose he retires at age 40 and the account has an interest rate of 8.725% that is compounded monthly.
   a. How much money will he have when he retires?
   b. What is the total of all of his payments?
   c. How much interest did his money earn?

2. Mike Trout started playing regularly at age 21. Suppose he started putting $1,000 per month in his retirement fund and continues to do so until he retires. Suppose he retires at age 40 and the account has an interest rate of 8.725% that is compounded quarterly.
   a. How much money will he have when he retires?
   b. What is the total of all of his payments?
   c. How much interest did his money earn?

3. Suppose Yasiel Puig started putting money in a savings account. He wants to have $10,000,000 in 12 years. The interest rate of 9.5% is compounded quarterly.
   a. How much money will he have to pay each quarter?
   b. What is the total of all of his payments?

4. Suppose Yasiel Puig started putting money in a savings account each month. He wants to have $10,000,000 in 12 years. The interest rate of 9.5% is compounded quarterly.
   a. How much money will he have to pay each month?
   b. What is the total of all of his payments?

5. You put $200 monthly into a savings account that pays 7.58% interest. Fill in the blanks in the chart.

	Compounded Quarterly	*Compounded Monthly*
Balance After 5 years		
Balance After 10 years		
Balance After 15 years		
Balance After 25 years		
Balance After 30 years		
Balance After 35 years		
Balance After 40 years		
Balance After 45 years		
Balance After 50 years		

Section 8.3—Loans

1. You are buying a house. After the down payment, you need to borrow $125,000. You will take out a mortgage to cover the remaining cost of the house. The interest rate for your 30 year mortgage is 6.455%. Throughout the problem we will ignore escrow payments that might be added to the payment for insurance and taxes.

   a. What will be your monthly payment?

   b. What will be the total of all of your monthly payments?

   c. How much interest will you pay over the life of the loan?

2. Miguel Cabrera is buying a house. After the down payment, he will need to borrow $895,000. He will take out a mortgage to cover the remaining cost of the house. The interest rate for your 10 year mortgage is 3.15%.

   a. What will be his monthly payment?

   b. What will be the total of all of his monthly payments?

   c. How much interest will he pay over the life of the loan?

3. Suppose you take out an auto loan for $8,200 over a period of 4 years at an APR of 7.25%.

   a. What will be your monthly payment?

   b. What will be the total of all of your monthly payments?

   c. How much interest will you pay over the life of the loan?

4. Suppose Justin Verlander takes out an auto loan for $59,400 over a period of 4 years at an APR of 1.3%.

   a. What will be his monthly payment?

   b. What will be the total of all of his monthly payments?

   c. How much interest will he pay over the life of the loan?

5. You are borrowing $120,000 to buy a house. Fill in the blanks in the chart.

	15 Year Loan at 5.25% Interest	30 Year Loan at 5.47% Interest
Monthly Payment		
Total of All Payments		
Interest Paid		

SECTION 8.4—ESTIMATIONS

1. Using reasonable approximations, give an estimate for the number of hot dog eaten at major league ball games each year.

2. Using reasonable approximations, give an estimate for the number of high school baseball players in the United States.

3. Using reasonable approximations, give an estimate for the number of baseballs used in major league ball games each year.

4. (This problem was given in an old copy of *Reader's Digest*.) The Marianas Trench is the deepest place in the ocean. Suppose a very dense weight is dropped in the Marianas Trench. Using reasonable approximations, give an estimate for how long it will take for the weight to hit the bottom of the trench?

5. Using reasonable approximations, give an estimate for how many piano tuners there are in the Chicago metropolitan area?

9—Geometry

"Arithmetic! Algebra! Geometry! Grandiose trinity! Luminous triangle! Whoever has not known you is without sense!"—Comte de Lautreamont

"You can't criticize geometry. It's never wrong."—Paul Rand

Geometry covers a broad array of topics, but it can certainly be defined as including the study of shapes. Those shapes may be two-dimensional. They may be three-dimensional. They can be simple. They can be complicated. In studying the shapes we can talk about areas, lengths, volumes and surface areas. We can take simple shapes to approximate complicated shapes. In this chapter we are going to look at some of these simple ideas about shapes.

Section 9.1—Areas, Perimeters of Plane Figures

Before we begin, we will first look at what we mean by area. For simplicity we will use inches as our units throughout this section.

A square that is one inch by one inch is said to be "one square inch." A square that is one foot by one foot is said to be "one square foot." In general, a square that is one unit by one unit is said to be "one square unit" (Figure 1).

For other shapes, when we say "area" what we are saying is basically "How many squares that are one inch by one inch would fit inside the shape under consideration."

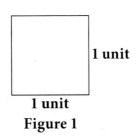

1 unit

1 unit

Figure 1

RECTANGLES

If we have a rectangle that is 2 inches by 3 inches, then we say the area of the rectangle is 6 square inches because that is how many 1 inch × 1 inch squares would fit in it (Figure 2).

This number fits because we will have two rows of three squares each. It is not too hard to see how the "2 inches" by "3 inches" gives us the area of six square inches. Since 2 × 3 = 6, we can see that the area should be 6. Since the 6 things that we counted up are "square inches" we have an area of 6 square inches.

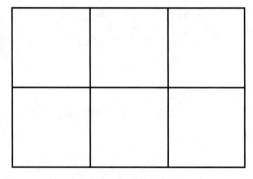

Figure 2

We can also get square inches by thinking multiplicatively.

$$2 \text{ inches} \times 3 \text{ inches} = 2 \times 3 \times \text{inches} \times \text{inches}$$
$$= 6 \text{ (inches} \times \text{inches)}$$
$$= 6 \text{ (inches)}^2$$
$$= 6 \text{ square inches}$$

From all of this it is not hard to figure out the area of a general rectangle. If the rectangle's dimensions are L units by W units, the area would be L × W square units (Figure 3).

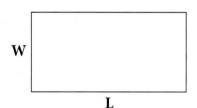

Figure 3

$$A = L \times W$$

Another measurement associated with rectangles is the perimeter. Perimeter can simply be thought of as "how far we have to walk to get around the shape once." Looking again at figure 3, we see that we would walk along two sides that are W units long and two sides that are L units long. Thus, the perimeter for a rectangle would be given by P = 2L + 2W.

The same ideas hold for any shape. For perimeter, if the area is enclosed by straight sides, we just add up the lengths of all the sides. For area, though, it is a little more complicated since it is not always quite as easy to see how many "unit squares" will fit. We may have to cut squares up into pieces to fill everything in.

Parallelograms

We will now look at how we can see why the area of a parallelogram is base × height.

Suppose this parallelogram has base length B and height H (Figure 4). Note that side lengths A, C, and D will just be used for the perimeter.

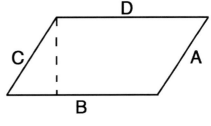

Figure 4

We are going to turn it into a rectangle (Figure 5).

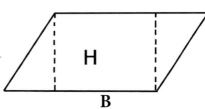

Figure 5

We will take the triangle from the right side and move it to the left. It can be shown (but will not be shown here) that the two triangles are the same size and therefore will form a rectangle when combined (Figure 6).

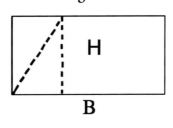

Figure 6

Notice that the height never changed. Neither did the shape (and therefore length) of the bottom edge. So this rectangle has area B × H square inches but also has the same area as the beginning parallelogram.

For this parallelogram the perimeter would be given by P = 2 B + 2 D.

TRAPEZOIDS

We will now look at trapezoids. The approach to figuring out the formula is much the same as with parallelograms in that we'll cut some area off and move it.

Consider a trapezoid with base lengths B_1 and B_2 and height H (Figure 7).

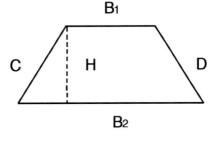

Figure 7

We now move some of the area to another spot in order to make it a rectangle (figures 8 and 9).

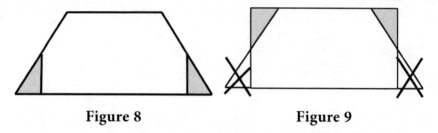

Figure 8   **Figure 9**

Notice the area is the same as it was. Notice the height is the same as it was. The only problem is the length of the resulting rectangle. It is not too hard to convince ourselves that the length is the average, $(B_1 + B_2)/2$, of the original base lengths. Therefore we have the following formula for the area of a trapezoid with base lengths B_1 and B_2 and height H.

$$A = \frac{B_1 + B_2}{2} H$$

The perimeter is simply the sum of the side lengths.

$$P = C + D + B_1 + B_2$$

TRIANGLES

We can also use the area of a parallelogram to find the area of a triangle. Suppose we have a triangle with base B and height H (Figure 10).

We can put two such triangles together to form a parallelogram with base B and height H (Figure 11). The parallelogram would have area B × H square inches. Our original triangle is half of that and therefore the area of the triangle would be A = (1/2) × B × H square inches.

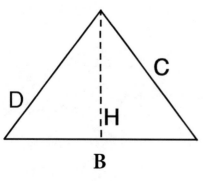

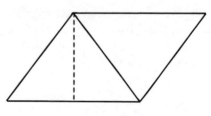

Figure 10   **Figure 11**

Again, perimeter would simply be found by adding the three side lengths together.

$$P = B + C + D$$

There is another formula that we can use to find the area of a triangle if we know the three side lengths but do not know the height. This is another formula we will state without any proof or justification. It is called **Heron's Formula**.

Consider the following triangle.

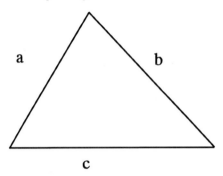

Let $s = (a + b + c)/2$. Notice that is the perimeter of the triangle divided by 2. We call s the **semiperimeter**. Then the area of the triangle is given by

$A = \sqrt{s(s-a)(s-b)(s-c)}$.

One other important thing about triangles is the **Pythagorean Theorem**. If we have a right triangle (a triangle with a right angle, that is, a ninety degree angle), with hypotenuse (the side opposite the right angle) of length c, and the other two sides of length a and b, then it will always be true that $a^2 + b^2 = c^2$.

Circles

Circles are harder to deal with and we will simply find their areas by giving the formula. For a circle of radius R units, the area is given by $A = \pi R^2$ square units and the perimeter, which in the case of the circle has the special name "circumference," is given by $C = 2\pi R$ units.

Important Note—In the formulas for circles and for several others, the number π is used. Keep in mind, π is NOT 3.14 or 22/7. π is a number with an infinitely long decimal representation. Use the π button on your calculator (on the upper right side of TI calculators) to enable you to have as much accuracy as possible. It will use $\pi = 3.141592654$.

Summary of Formulas

Plane Figures		
	Area (square units)	Perimeter (units)
Rectangle	$A = L\,W$	$P = 2L + 2W$
Parallelogram	$A = B\,H$	$P =$ sum of side lengths
Triangle	$A = \dfrac{1}{2}B\,H$ $A = \sqrt{s(s-a)(s-b)(s-c)}$ where $s = (a + b + c)/2$	$P =$ sum of side lengths
Trapezoid	$A = \dfrac{1}{2}\left(B_1 + B_2\right)H$	$P =$ sum of side lengths
Circle	$A = \pi R^2$	(called circumference) $C = 2\,\pi R$

Examples—Find the area and perimeter of each of the following.

1. A rectangle with length 8 cm and width 5 cm
    A = L W = (8 cm) (5 cm) = 40 cm²
    P = 2 L + 2 W = 2 (8 cm) + 2 (5 cm) = 16 cm + 10 cm = 26 cm

2. A circle with radius 8 inches
    A = пR² = п (8 inches)² = 64п square inches = 201.0619 sq. in.
    C = 2 пR = 2 п8 inches) = 16п inches = 50.2654 inches

3. A circle with diameter 6 feet
    Note this says "diameter" not "radius." Thus, R = 3 feet.
    A = пR² = п (3 feet)² = 9п square feet = 28.2743 sq. ft.
    C = 2 п R = 2 п (3 feet) = 6п feet = 18.8495 feet

4. A parallelogram with base length 1 foot and height 9 inches and other side lengths of 14 inches
    Notice here that the units are not the same. So we have base length 12 inches, height 9 inches and other side lengths of 14 inches.
    A = B H = 12 inches 9 inches = 108 sq. in.
    P = sum of side lengths = 12 in. + 12 in. + 14 in. + 14 in. = 52 in.

5. A triangle with base length 21 mm, height 8 mm, and other two sides of length 17 mm and 10 mm
    A = (1/2) B H = (1/2) (21 mm) (8 mm) = 84 mm²
    P = sum of side lengths = 21 mm + 17 mm + 10 mm = 48 mm
    We can also find the area using Heron's Formula.

$$s = \frac{21 + 17 + 10}{2} = \frac{48}{2} = 24$$

$$A = \sqrt{24(24-21)(24-17)(24-10)} = \sqrt{24*3*7*14} = \sqrt{7056} = 84mm^2$$

6. A trapezoid with height 8 inches, base lengths of 12 inches and 33 inches, and other two sides of 10 inches and 17 inches

A = (1/2) (B$_1$ + B$_2$) H = (1/2) (12 in. + 33 in.) 8 in. = 160 in²

P = sum of side lengths = 12 in. + 33 in. + 10 in. + 17 in. = 72 in.

7. In the major leagues, the bases are 90 feet apart. The infield, while typically called a "diamond," is a square.

A = 90 feet * 90 feet = 8100 ft²

P = 90 feet + 90 feet + 90 feet + 90 feet = 360 feet

From our earlier work, we know that the area can be converted to acres.

$$A = A = 8100\ ft^2\ \frac{1\ acre}{43560\ ft^2} = 0.186\ \text{acres}$$

8. If a right triangle has sides of length 5 feet and 8 feet, the area is A = 5 * 8/2 = 20 square feet. By the Pythagorean Theorem, the hypotenuse is $\sqrt{5^2 + 8^2} = \sqrt{89} \approx 9.43$ feet. Thus the perimeter is $5 + 8 + \sqrt{89} = 22.43$.

Section 9.2—*Volumes, Surface Areas of Spatial Solids*

For three dimensional shapes, surface areas are found by finding the areas of the individual parts of the outside of the shape and adding them up. Volumes are found in a way that is analogous to how we found areas. Again, using inches, suppose we have a cube that is 1 inch × 1 inch × 1 inch (Figure 12). We would call that "1 cubic inch" or "1 inch cubed."

We then find volumes by figuring out how many of these "unit cubes" fit in the shape.

"Shoe Boxes"

We will start with finding the volume of a "shoe box." There are more formal names but we will stick with "shoe box." Suppose our shoe box has dimensions L × W × H (Figure 13).

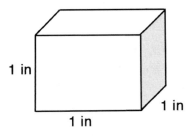

1 in

1 in

1 in

Figure 12

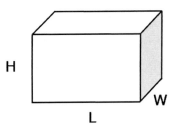

H

L

W

Figure 13

On the bottom of the box we can put L × W unit cubes in the same way we found areas in a rectangle (Figure 14).

The base of the box would have area L × W square units. Since the height is H units, we could put H layers of unit cubes, giving a volume of V = L × W × H units cubed.

Surface area is calculated by realizing there are two faces of the box with area L × W square units, two with area L × H square units, and

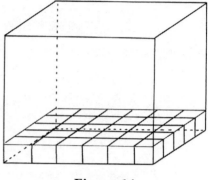

Figure 14

two with H × W square units, giving a surface area of S = 2LH + 2HW + 2 LW units squared.

CYLINDERS

The volume of a cylinder (or tin can) is found in a similar way. Suppose its height is H units and its radius is R units (Figure 15).

Since the bottom is a circle of radius R units, we could fit πR^2 unit cubes on the bottom. As in the case of the box, we could then put H layers of cubes in the cylinder giving a volume of $V = \pi R^2 H$ units cubed.

The surface area is not too hard to figure out. If we were to cut the can straight down the side, cut off the top and bottom and flatten out what is left, we would end up with two circles and a rectangle (Figure 16). The circles would each have area πR^2 square units. The rectangle would be H units high. Its length would be the circumference of the cylinder so its area would be $2\pi RH$ square units. Thus, the surface area would be $S = 2\pi R^2 + 2\pi RH$ square units.

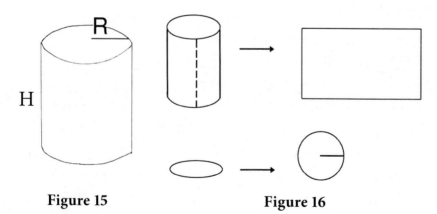

Figure 15   **Figure 16**

CONES

We will just give the formulas here rather than derive them.

For a cone with height, H units, and base radius, R units (Figure 17), the volume is V = π R²H/3.

The slant height, S, is given by $S = \sqrt{R^2 + H^2}$. This is needed to find the total surface area, T given by T = π R² + π R S.

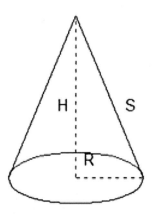

Figure 17

SPHERES

For spheres, as with circles, we will just give the formulas. If the radius is R units, the volume is given by V = (4/3) π R³ units cubed and the surface area is S = 4 πR² square units.

Summary of Formulas

Spatial Solids		
	Volume (units cubed)	Surface Area (square units)
Box	V = L W H	S = 2 L W + 2 L H + 2 H W
Cylinder	$V = \pi R^2 H$	$S = 2 \pi R^2 + 2 \pi R H$
Cone	$V = \frac{1}{3} \pi R^2 H$	$T = \pi R^2 + \pi R S$ where S = $\sqrt{R^2 + H^2}$
Sphere	$V = \frac{4}{3} \pi R^3$	$S = 4 \pi R^2$

Examples—Find the volume and surface area of each of the following.

1. A box with length 8 cm, height 4 cm and width 5 cm
$$V = L\,W\,H = (8\text{ cm})\,(5\text{ cm})\,(4\text{ cm}) = 160\text{ cm}^3$$
$$S = 2\,L\,W + 2\,L\,H + 2\,H\,W$$
$$= 2\,(8\text{ cm})(5\text{ cm}) + 2\,(8\text{ cm})(4\text{ cm}) + 2\,(4\text{ cm})(5\text{ cm})$$
$$= 80\text{ cm}^2 + 64\text{ cm}^2 + 40\text{ cm}^2 = 184\text{ cm}^2$$

2. A cylinder with radius 18 inches and height 2 feet
$$V = \pi R^2\,H = \pi\,(18\text{ in})^2\,(24\text{ in}) = 7776\,\pi\text{ in}^3 \approx 24429.0244\text{ in}^3$$
$$S = 2\,\pi\,R^2 + 2\,\pi\,R\,H = 2\,\pi\,(18\text{ in})^2 + 2\,\pi\,(18\text{ in})(24\text{ in})$$
$$= 1512\,\pi\text{ in}^2 = 4750.0880\text{in.}^2$$

3. A cone with diameter 6 feet and height 30 inches
The radius would be 3 feet or 36 inches.
$$V = (1/3)\,\pi R^2\,H = (1/3)\,\pi\,(36\text{ in})^2\,(30\text{ in}) = 12960\,\pi\text{ in}^3$$
$$\approx 40715.0407\text{ in}^3$$
First we must find S. $S = \sqrt{R^2 + H^2} = \sqrt{36^2 + 30^2} = \sqrt{2196}$ in.
$$T = \pi R^2 + \pi R S = \pi\,(36\text{ in})^2 + \pi\,(36\text{ in})$$
$$T = \pi R^2 + \pi R S = \pi\,(36\text{ in.})^2 + \pi\,(36\text{ in.})\,\sqrt{2196}\text{ in.}$$
$$= 9371.4146\text{ in}^2$$

4. A sphere with radius 9 inches
$$V = (4/3)\,\pi R^3 = (4/3)\,\pi\,(9\text{ in})^3 = 972\,\pi\text{ in}^3 = 3053.6280\text{ in}^3$$
$$S = 4\,\pi R^2 = 4\,\pi\,(9\text{ in})^2 = 324\,\pi\text{ in}^2 = 1017.8760\text{ in}^2$$

5. A baseball has an allowable circumference of 9 to 91/4 inches. Suppose the circumference of a particular ball is 9.1 inches. That would mean that 9.1 = 2πr. Solving for r gives r = 9.1/(2π) = 1.4483 inches. Then the volume of the ball would be $V = \frac{4}{3}\,\pi\,r^3 = \frac{4}{3}\,\pi\,1.4483^3 = 12.7252$ cubic inches.

Section 9.3—Scaling

When traveling in an unfamiliar area, it is helpful to have a map of the region in which you are driving. The map depicts the region, but the map is not the region. When we drive from Arkadelphia, Arkansas, to Little Rock, Arkansas, we don't look at the map and say, "Great, it's only about 5 inches from Arkadelphia to Little Rock!" We may see that the two cities are 5 inches apart on the map but we look at the map and note that it says "1 inch = 13 miles." In Chapter 2 we talked about unit conversions and saw expressions like that but this one is obviously not that sort of conversion. In normal units, 13 miles is 823, 680 inches. So what does this "1 inch = 13 miles" mean? It is the scale of the map. What they really mean, and we understand them to mean is "1 inch on this map represents 13 miles in real life."

In the next section, we are going to look at approximating areas of irregular shapes. One thing that will help us with some of those problems is the idea of scaling. We will now look at a couple of examples of how we can use this idea.

Example—Suppose a map shows a distance that, using a ruler measures 4 inches, but on the map is said to represent 52 miles. You are interested in the distance between two points that on the map are 2.5 inches apart. How far apart are those two points?

This is a simple unit conversion just like in Chapter 2. To make it clear what we are doing, I am going to use the units "real miles" and "map inches."

Note that 4 map inches = 52 real miles. We can use that equation to create

the unit fractions $\dfrac{4\ map\ inches}{52\ real\ miles}$ and $\dfrac{52\ real\ miles}{4\ map\ inches}$.

$$2.5\ map\ inches\ \dfrac{52\ real\ miles}{4\ map\ inches} = 32.5\ real\ miles$$

Example—A map shows two cities as being 126 miles apart. On the map, the distance between them measures 3 inches. Two other cities are 400 miles apart. How many inches apart would they be on this map?

$$400\ real\ miles\ \dfrac{3\ map\ inches}{126\ real\ miles} = 9.5238\ map\ inches$$

Section 9.4—Approximations to Irregular Shapes

Not all areas are nice. Consider the following region. Assume all measurements are given in feet.

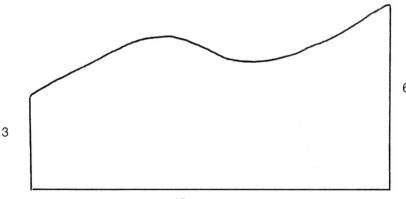

3

6

12

This is not a standard shape for which we have nice formulas for area or perimeter. Calculus is an area of mathematics that develops sophisticated techniques for finding the exact areas of shapes like this one. We are not going to find exact areas, but we will do some approximations. However, we will approach it using the same ideas as are used in calculus. We only know formulas for nice shapes, like rectangles, trapezoids, etc.

We can divide this shape into three regions.

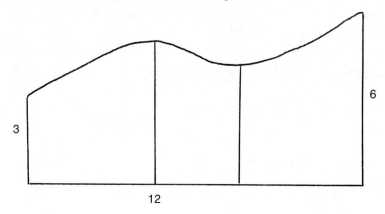

Each of these regions can be approximated by a rectangle and a triangle.

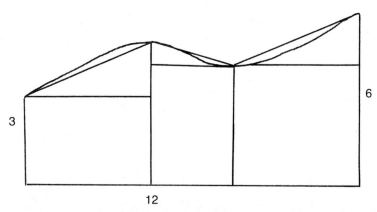

Notice that each rectangle is completely contained in the original region but there are some problems with the triangles. The first one omits a bit of the area of the region. The last one includes area that is not in the original region. The middle triangle includes some area it shouldn't and excludes some area it shouldn't. But the extra areas are about the same as the omitted areas. Therefore we will get a decent approximation to the area with these shapes. Now we need to approximate the needed lengths.

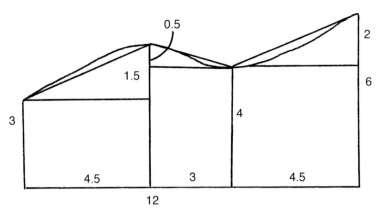

Let's consider the rectangles first, going from left to right.

A1 = 3 * 4.5 = 13.5 ft²
A2 = 3 * 4 = 12 ft²
A3 = 4 * 4.5 = 18 ft²

Now for the triangles, going from left to right.

A4 = .5 * 4.5 * 1.5 = 3.375 ft²
A5 = .5 * 3 * .5 = 0.75 ft²
A6 = .5 * 4.5 * 2 = 4.5 ft²

Adding the six areas together, we get the following approximation to the area.

$$A = 13.5 + 12 + 18 + 3.375 + .75 + 4.5 = 52.125 \text{ ft}^2$$

We can do something similar for the perimeter. The left side, bottom and right side are not problems for us since we know they are 3 feet, 12 feet and 6 feet, respectively. So the perimeter will be 21 feet plus whatever the length of the curving portion is.

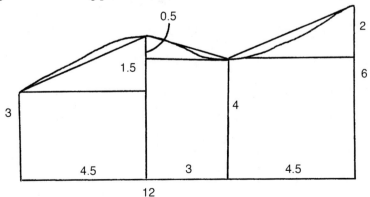

Looking at the three triangles, we can see that the three hypotenuses are a little bit less than the length of the curved edge of the region. We can use the Pythagorean theorem to find the lengths of the hypotenuses, going from left to right.

$$L1 = \sqrt{4.5^2 + 1.5^2} = 4.74\,\text{feet}$$

$$L2 = \sqrt{3^2 + .5^2} = 3.04\,\text{feet}$$

$$L3 = \sqrt{4.5^2 + 2^2} = 4.92\,\text{feet}$$

These three lengths add up to 12.7 feet. We can adjust for the fact that the curved edge is a little longer by calling it 13 feet. So we have an approximation for the perimeter of the entire region by taking 21 + 13 = 34 feet.

A baseball bat does not have a nice shape for calculating volume or surface area. But we can do the same kind of thing as above and approximate the volume and surface area. Suppose a bat has a length of 35 inches and a maximum diameter of 2¾ inches. Also, suppose the knob is 1.5 inches wide and 1 inch long. We can view the bat as a long, thin cone with a small cylinder on the end.

The cylinder is the knob. It has a diameter of 1.5 inches, so a radius of .75 inches, and a height of 1 inch. Then its volume is $V1 = \pi r^2 h = \pi\, 0.75^2 * 1 = 1.7671\ \text{in}^3$. Its surface area would be $A1 = 2\pi r^2 + 2\pi rh = 2\,\pi\,0.75^2 + 2\,\pi\,0.75 * 1 = 8.2467\ \text{in}^2$.

The cone is the barrel of the bat. It would have a diameter of 2¾ = 11/4 inches, so a radius of 11/8 inches, and a height of 34 inches. Thus, the volume is $V2 = (1/3) * \pi r^2 h = (1/3) * \pi\, (11/8)^2\, 34 = 67.3152\ \text{in}^3$. The surface area is $A2 = T = \pi r^2 + \pi r \sqrt{r^2 + h^2} = \pi\,(11/8)^2 + \pi\,(11/8)\,\sqrt{(11/8)^2 + 34^2} = 152.9291\ \text{in.}^2$

Then our approximation for the volume of the bat is $V = V1 + V2 = 1.7671 + 67.3152 = 69.0823\ \text{in}^3$. Our approximation for the surface area is $A = A1 + A2 = 8.2467 + 152.9291 = 161.1758\ \text{in}^2$.

FIELD APPROXIMATION #1

Now let's look at a baseball field. The following picture is of the old Philadelphia ballpark, Baker Bowl. It was the home field of the Philadelphia Phillies from 1895 to 1938.

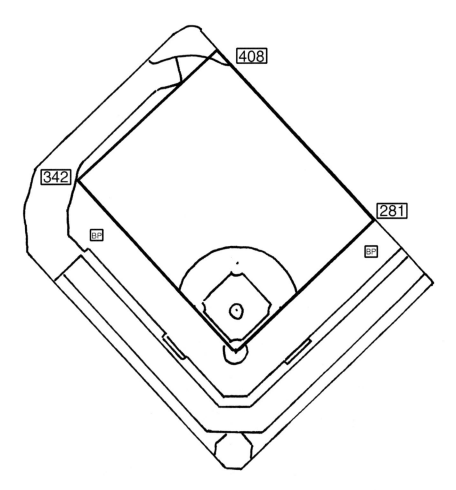

Picture courtesy of Andrew G. Clem, © Andrew G. Clem, 2006. Used with permission.

Suppose we want to have an approximation to the area of fair territory. This field's shape makes for a fairly simple approximation. A first step toward the approximation would be a rectangle using the foul lines as two sides.

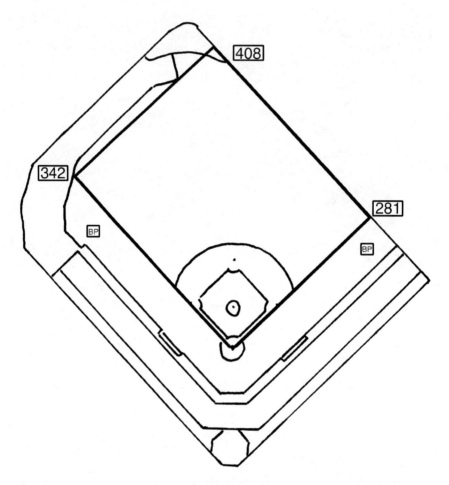

This rectangle is 281 feet by 342 feet for an area of 96,102 square feet. It includes just a bit of some area that should not be included. Now we will add another rectangle.

There are three parts of the field not included in the second rectangle. The non-playing area included in the first rectangle is about the same as the excluded portion in the left field corner plus the smaller of the two excluded portions in center. The larger excluded portion in center is about the same as the non-playing area included in the second rectangle. So these two rectangles do a decent job of approximating the area. Using some measuring and scaling based on known area, the smaller rectangle appears to be about 227 feet by 18 feet, giving an area of 4086 square feet.

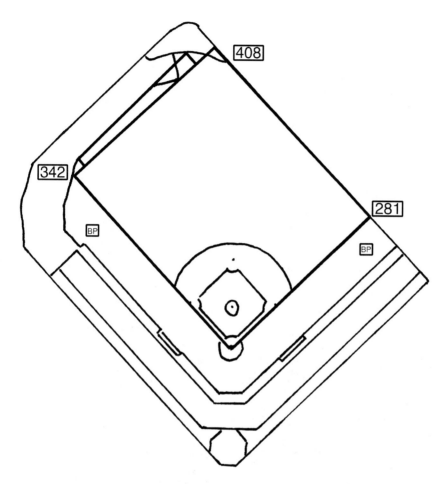

The two rectangles together give 100,188 square feet. What is this in acres?

$$100{,}188\ ft^2\ \frac{1\ acre}{43{,}560\ ft^2} = 2.3\ acres$$

FIELD APPROXIMATION #2

The following picture is of Forbes Field, home of the Pittsburgh Pirates from 1909 to 1970 and the Homestead Grays from 1939 to 1948. Forbes Field was particularly known for the depth to the area just to the left of dead center field.

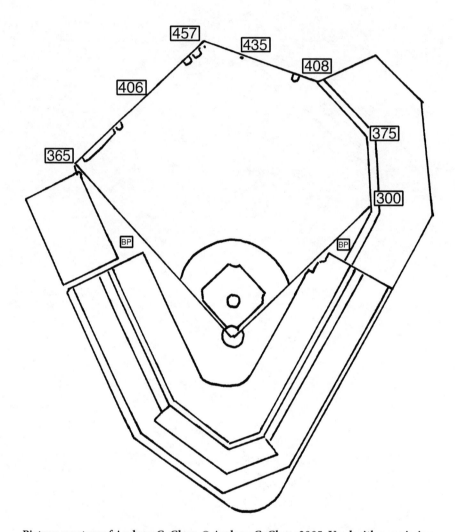

Picture courtesy of Andrew G. Clem, © Andrew G. Clem, 2005. Used with permission.

The easiest way to approximate this playing area is with four triangles.

Going from left to right, we will call the triangles #1, #2, #3 and #4. Triangle #1 has two sides with length 365 feet and 457 feet. Triangle #2 has two sides with length 457 feet and 408 feet. Triangle #3 has two sides with length 408 feet and 375 feet. Triangle #4 has two sides with length 375 feet and 300 feet. By measuring and scaling, we get approximations for the third side for triangle #1 to be 280 feet, for triangle #2 to be 190 feet, for triangle #3 to be 115 feet and for triangle #4 to be 105 feet.

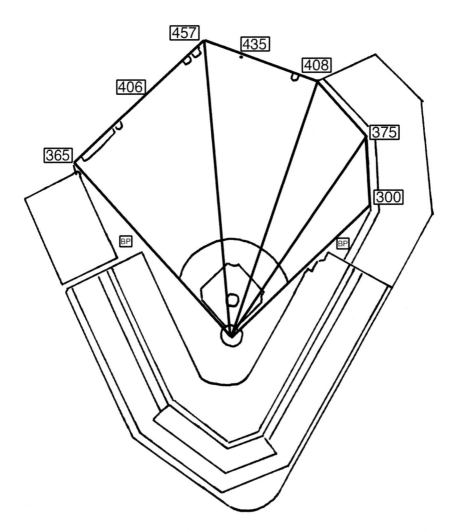

We will then use Heron's formula on each triangle to find the area of the four triangles.

Triangle #	Side 1	Side 2	Side 3	Area
1	365	457	280	51095.29 square feet
2	457	408	190	38728.14 square feet
3	408	375	115	21330.66 square feet
4	375	300	105	12249.59 square feet

Adding these areas together gives 123,403.67 square feet or 2.72 acres or about 18 percent more area than Baker Bowl.

FIELD APPROXIMATION #3

Our last field approximation will be for Wrigley Field, shown in the picture below.

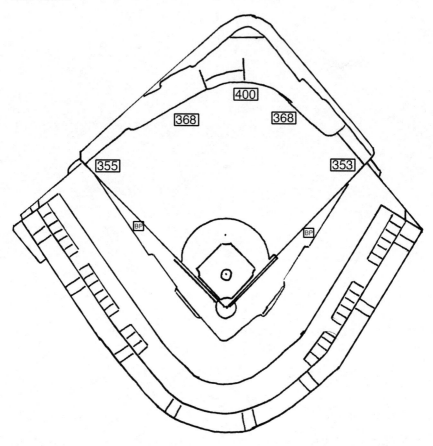

Picture courtesy of Andrew G. Clem, © Andrew G. Clem, 2008. Used with permission.

Wrigley Field has a much less uniform shape. In this case, we will use some triangles and a portion of a circle.

The letters will represent the corners of the various triangles. We have some of these lengths and will need to find the rest.
HA = 355 feet
HC = 368 feet
HD = 368 feet
HG = 353 feet

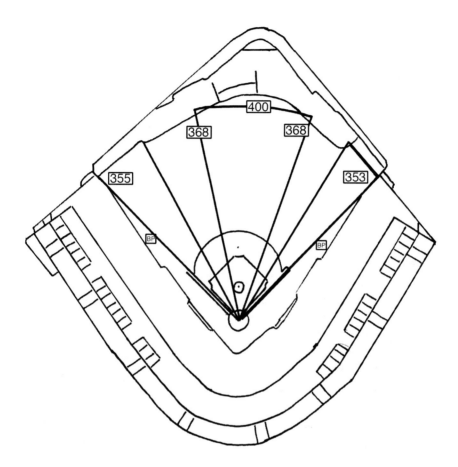

I set up the circular portion at the center field fence to be about 384 feet (the average of 368 and 400). That includes non-playing area and excludes some playing area.

By measuring and scaling, we get an estimate of 100 feet for AB. Treating ABH as a right triangle, we use the Pythagorean Theorem and get BH to be approximately 368.8 feet.

By measuring and scaling, we get an estimate for FG of 78 feet. Treating FGH as a right triangle, we use the Pythagorean Theorem and get HF to be approximately 361.5 feet. Measuring and scaling give us BC = 114 feet and DE = 80 feet. We will estimate HE to be the same as HG, or 353 feet.

Since we assumed ABH and FGH were right triangles, we have their base and height and thus can figure out the area by using A = .5 (base)(height). For BCH and DEH, we can use Heron's Formula.

Triangle	Area
ABH	17,750 square feet
BCH	20,745.42 square feet
DEH	14,076.79 square feet
EFH	13,767 square feet

Lastly we need to find the area of the circular portion. For that, we need the formula $A = \theta r^2/360$, where θ is the angle of the circular portion in degrees and r is the radius. Approximating the angle with a protractor, we get 32°. So our area for the circular portion is $A = 32 * 384^2/360 = 41{,}117.48$ square feet. Adding all the areas together gives us 107,516.69 square feet or 2.47 acres.

Chapter 9—Exercises

SECTION 9.1—AREAS, PERIMETERS OF PLANE FIGURES

HERON

In #1–8, find the area and perimeter of the given shape. The units are shown by the shape.

1. yards

2. miles

3. millimeters

4. inches

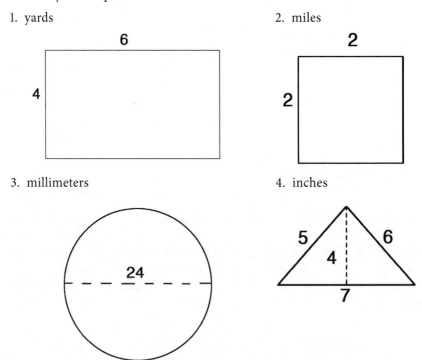

5. centimeters

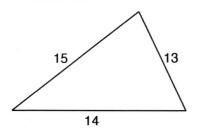

6. meters

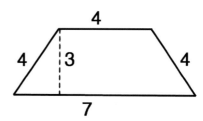

7. feet

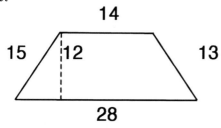

8. feet

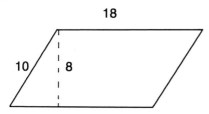

9. The window below is shaped like a rectangle with a semi-circle on top. What are the area and perimeter of the window?

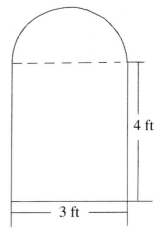

10. The shape below is a rectangle with a semi-circle on each end. Find the area and perimeter.

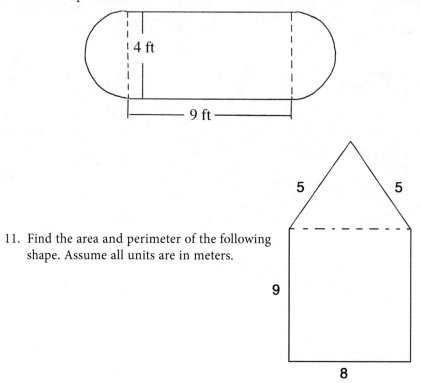

4 ft

9 ft

11. Find the area and perimeter of the following shape. Assume all units are in meters.

5   5

9

8

12. Home plate has dimensions as given by the rule book statement below. Find the area and perimeter of home plate.

Home base shall be marked by a five-sided slab of whitened rubber. It shall be a 17-inch square with two of the corners removed so that one edge is 17 inches long, two adjacent sides are 8½ inches and the remaining two sides are 12 inches and set at an angle to make a point. It shall be set in the ground with the point at the intersection of the lines extend-

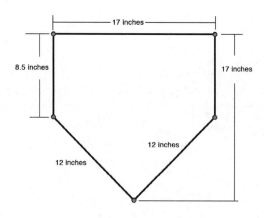

17 inches

8.5 inches

17 inches

12 inches

12 inches

ing from home base to first base and to third base; with the 17-inch edge facing the pitcher's plate, and the two 12-inch edges coinciding with the first and third base lines. The top edges of home base shall be beveled and the base shall be fixed in the ground level with the ground surface.

Section 9.2—Volumes, Surface Areas of Spatial Solids

1. A cylindrical storage drum has a height of 2 feet and a radius of one yard. Find the volume and surface area.
2. A collegiate women's basketball has a diameter of 11 inches. Find the volume and surface area.
3. A conical storage drum has a height of 2 feet and a diameter of one yard. Find the volume and surface area.
4. A men's basketball has a diameter of 12 inches. Find the volume and surface area.
5. Find the volume and surface area of the box shown below. Assume all measurements are in feet.

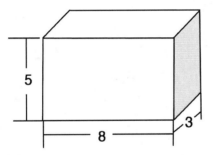

6. Find the volume and surface area of the solid shown below. It is a cylinder with a cone on top and a hemisphere on the bottom. The cylinder has radius 4 feet and height 10 feet. The cone has height 8 feet.

7. A spherical balloon is being blown up. If its radius increases by a factor of two (that is, it doubles), what happens to the volume? the surface area?

SECTION 9.3—SCALING

1. On a map, the scale is 1 inch = 16 miles.
   a. If the distance between two cities on the map is 4¼ inches, how many miles apart are the cities?
   b. If two cities are 100 miles apart, how far apart would they be on the map.
   c. Suppose two cities on the map are 5 inches apart. If you can average 40 miles per hour on the road connecting the two cities, how long will it take you to drive from one city to the other?

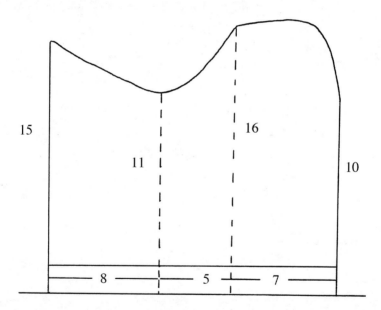

2. Estimate the area and perimeter of the shape below. All measurements are in inches.

   Estimate the fair territory playing area of the following two ballparks.

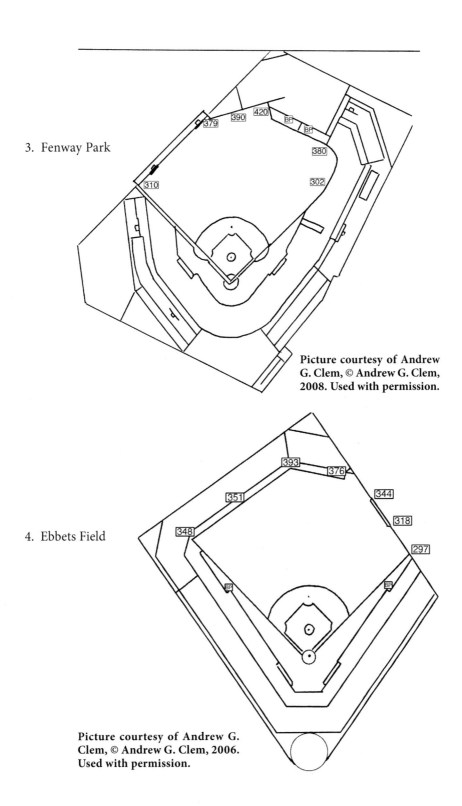

3. Fenway Park

Picture courtesy of Andrew
G. Clem, © Andrew G. Clem,
2008. Used with permission.

4. Ebbets Field

Picture courtesy of Andrew G.
Clem, © Andrew G. Clem, 2006.
Used with permission.

10—Modeling

"A good physicist ignores the things that make a problem hard."—Fred Worth

"An engineer thinks that his equations are an approximation to reality. A physicist thinks reality is an approximation to his equations. A mathematician doesn't care."—unknown

Mathematics is a means of describing the world. In Chapter 9 we discussed shapes and several mathematical ways to discuss and describe shapes. In Chapter 8 we discussed finances and various mathematical ways to calculate assets or costs of borrowing. These are all examples of what we call "mathematical modeling."

By modeling, we do not mean building model airplanes or wearing designer clothes for an audience. What we mean is development of a mathematical formula to describe some physical phenomenon. Basically any mathematical formula you know is a mathematical model for something.

area of a rectangle	area = length × width
travel	distance = rate × time
total cost	total_cost = price × unit_cost

Section 10.1—Linear, Quadratic and Exponential

In high school algebra you learned about linear functions. A linear function is anything that can be written in the form $y = mx + b$, where m and b are fixed numbers.

Example 1—Suppose you are driving 45 miles per hour. Then the distance you have traveled is $d = 45t$, where d = distance and t = time.

Example 2—Suppose a rectangle has a length of 9 feet. Then its perimeter is given by p = 2w + 18, where p = perimeter and w = width.

Example 3—If a product costs $5 per item, the cost, C, of buying n of the item would be C = 5n.

Example 4—If Randy Johnson threw a fastball 100 miles per hour, how long would it take for the ball to reach home plate?

From Chapter 2, we know this would be 146.6667 feet per second. From the first example above, we know we would have d = 146.6667t. Assuming Johnson's release point is 54 feet from home plate, we would have 54 = 146.6667t. Dividing both sides by 146.6667, gives us t = 0.368 seconds.

Each of these is an example of a linear model. Such models abound in baseball. Sometimes we have some "round off error" that can come into play.

Example 5—Suppose a player batted .321 for the season during which he had 452 at-bats. Since average = hits/at bats, it is also true that hits = average × at bats. So, in this case, we would have hits = .321 × 452 = 145.092. The only problem with this is hits cannot be a fraction. So, if the player has 452 at-bats, we would guess that hits was actually 145. If that is the case, the batting average was actually .32079646 but only .321 is generally reported.

Example 6—Suppose a pitcher has a 2.98 ERA. Since ERA = 9*ER/IP, we would have ER = ERA*IP/9 or IP = 9*ER/ERA. In this case, that would be IP = 9*ER/2.98. If this pitcher has allowed 45 earned runs, we would have IP = 9*45/2.98 = 135.9060403. He cannot pitch 135.9060403 innings. It would have to be either 135.667 or 136. Checking, we see that 135.667 IP would give an ERA of 2.99 and 136 IP would give the correct 2.98.

Another simple model you saw in high school algebra was a quadratic model. That is any model that can be written $y = ax^2 + bx + c$, where a, b and c are fixed numbers.

Example 7—The area of a circle with radius, r, is a quadratic model with $A = \pi r^2$.

Example 8—The area of a square with side length, x, is $A = x^2$.

An exponential model is any that can be written in the form y = c a^x, where a and c are fixed numbers.

Example 9—If you put $500 in the bank at 4% interest compounded quarterly, your balance will be P = A * 1.01$^{(y*4)}$, where y is the number of years the money is in the bank.

Example 10—If a town's population was 100 in 1900, and doubles every 11 years, then the population will be y = 100 * 2$^{x/11}$, where x is the number of years since 1900.

There are four formulas that give us the capability of working with exponential models. There are two kinds of exponential models, exponential growth (when the quantity is growing) and exponential decay (when the quantity is decreasing). We have two formulas for each case. Which formula to use will depend on what description we have of the change of the quantity. One feature of exponential growth is that the quantity will always go up the same percentage every unit of time. For example, if the quantity goes up 10% this year, it will go up 10% next year, and the next year, etc. Another way of looking at it is that the quantity will always double over the same unit of time. That is, if the quantity doubles in five years, it will double again during the next five years and the next five years, etc. This is in contrast with a linear model in which the quantity will change the same amount every unit of time. For example, if the quantity goes up five in the first year, it will go up five every subsequent year. If it goes down four in the first year, it will go down four every subsequent year.

Example 11—Suppose the population of a town was 4000 in 1903. In 1904, it was 4240. If the population continues to grow according to the same exponential model, what was the population in 1905?

We need to figure out the percentage growth. The part will be the amount of growth.

$$\frac{part}{whole} = \frac{PART}{WHOLE}$$

$$\frac{x}{100} = \frac{240}{4000}$$

$$x = 6$$

So the growth rate is 6%. Computing a 6% growth for the next year gives us the following.

$$\frac{part}{whole} = \frac{PART}{WHOLE}$$

$$\frac{6}{100} = \frac{x}{4240}$$

$$x = 254.4 \text{ people}$$

Since the unit is "people," the fractional portion makes no sense. Therefore, we will say the growth was 254, giving a 1905 population of 4494 people.

Exercise 12—Suppose the population of some town was 150 in 1823 and 300 in 1842. If the population continues to grow according to the same exponential model, what will the population be in 1861?

Notice the population doubled in 19 years. If it follows an exponential model, then it will double every 19 years. Since 1861 is 19 years after 1842, the population would be 600 in 1861.

These examples are not hard but the method used is difficult to use if we are working with longer periods of time. For such cases, the following formulas will be useful.

Exponential Growth

When you know the *Doubling Time*

$$new = old \times 2^{\left(t/T_d\right)}$$

When you know the *Percentage Change*

$$new = old \times (1 + r)^t$$

Example 13—Consider the town from Example 11. What would the population be in 2009?

In this case we know the percentage rate of population growth. Therefore we will use the second formula from above. "Old" will refer to the population in 1903, r is the percentage change in decimal form. And t is time using the same unit over which the percentage change occurred, in this case, years.

$$new = 4000 \times (1 + .04)^{106} = 255619.4859$$

Again, since the answer is people, we will round off to a population of 255,619 people in 2009.

Example 14—Consider the town from Example 12. What would the population be in 2009?

In this case we know how long it takes the population to double so we will use the first formula above. "Old" refers to the population in 1823, T_d refers to the time it took the quantity to double, and t refers to the time elapsed in whatever unit we are given for the doubling time.

$new = 150 \times 2^{(186/19)} = 132744.4828$

Once again, since the unit is "people" we round off, reporting the answer as 132,744 people in 2009.

Exponential Growth
When you know the *Doubling Time*
$$new = old \times 2^{\left(t/T_d\right)}$$
When you know the *Percentage Change*
$$new = old \times (1 + r)^t$$

The same kind of thing happens if the quantity decreases. Here are the formulas for that case.

Exponential Decay
When you know the *Half Life*
$$new = old \times \left(\frac{1}{2}\right)^{\left(t/T_h\right)}$$
When you know the *Percentage Change*
$$new = old \times (1 - r)^t$$

Example 15—A radioactive substance decays exponentially. Suppose it has a half-life of 18 hours. If you start with 16 grams, how much will you have after two days?

The first formula above. "Old" refers to the starting amount, T_h refers to the **half-life**, that is, the time it takes the quantity to be cut in half, and t refers to the time elapsed in whatever unit we are given for the half life. Note that we have to be careful about units here.

$$new = 16 \times (1/2)^{(48/18)} = 2.5198421 \text{ grams}$$

Note that fractions are fine when working with weight.

Example 16—Suppose the population of a city dropped 3% from 1984 to 1985. If the 1984 population was 2100, what would the population be in 2009 if it continued to decay exponentially?

In this case we know the percentage rate of population decay. Therefore we will use the second formula from above. "Old" will refer to the population in 1984, r is the percentage change in decimal form. And t is time using the same unit over which the percentage change occurred, in this case, years.

$$new = 2100 \times (1 - .03)^{25} = 980.646881$$

Again rounding, we have a population of 981 people.

Review

Most of what we are doing in this chapter falls under the category of algebra. In algebra, we often use something called "function notation." That is helpful when one quantity is dependent on the value of another quantity. For example, in Example 8 above, we said $A = x^2$. To write this in function notation, we would write $A(x) = x^2$. The only difference is the "(x)" on the left side. It does not affect the calculations at all. It simply emphasizes the dependence of Area on x.

If we write $f(x) = 3x^2 + 4x + 1$, that means we have the function named f, that is dependent on the variable x. The x on the left simply tells the independent variable, x, on which the dependent variable, f, depends. Then, in calculations, whatever goes in place of x on the left, goes in place of x on the right and we then do any simplification possible. Here are some examples.

$$f(5) = 3^*(5)^2 + 4^*(5) + 1 = 75 + 20 + 1 = 96$$
$$f(-5) = 3^*(-5)x^2 + 4^*(-5) + 1 = 75 - 20 + 1 = 56$$
$$f(a) = 3a^2 + 4a + 1$$
$$f(x + 1) = 3(x + 1)^2 + 4(x + 1) + 1 = 3x^2 + 6x + 3 + 4x + 4 + 1 = 3x^2 + 10x + 8$$

Caution—For the upcoming material, it will be important that you have your graphing calculator handy.

Section 10.2—Projectile Motion—One Dimension

Physics includes many topics. The main one we will consider is that portion of physics dealing with the mathematics of motion. The mathematics involved in physics is often quite complicated. Because of that, it is not uncommon for physicists to make certain assumptions or ignore certain factors in order to make the problems easier to handle. In many of those cases, the things being ignored do not really make much difference as long as the experiment does not go on very long. The case that we will consider here and in Section 10.4 is projectile motion, that is, the physics of an object propelled through the air. This can be complicated depending on the particular setting and our assumptions. For our purposes, we will concern ourselves only with cases for which the only force acting on the object, once it has begun its flight, is gravity. Air resistance is one of the things that complicates the problem and therefore we will ignore it.

The case we will consider here is the one dimensional case. That is, the object has only vertical motion, such as an object dropped from a height or an object thrown straight up or down. When that is the case, the formula describing the height of the object at time, t, is $s(t) = -16t^2 + v_0 t + s_0$, where s is the height at time, t, v_0 is the initial velocity (positive if directed up, negative if directed down) and s_0 is the initial height of the object. The units, for this version of the formula, are feet and seconds. Another formula related to the problem tells us the velocity of the object at time, t. This formula is $v(t) = -32t + v_0$.

Example—Suppose a ball is thrown straight up in the air with a velocity of 80 feet per second. Assume the point of release of the ball is 6 feet above the ground.

In this case, our formula is $s(t) = -16t^2 + 80t + 6$. Realize the 80 is positive because the ball is thrown UP. If it were being thrown down, the 80 would be negative. Press the <Y=> button on your calculator and, in Y1, enter $-16x^2 + 80x + 6$. Press the <WINDOW> button and set the parameters as follows:

$$Xmin = 0$$
$$Xmax = 6$$
$$Xscl = 1$$
$$Ymin = 0$$
$$Ymax = 130$$
$$Yscl = 10$$

Press <GRAPH>. You will see a parabola, opening down. Keep in mind, this is not showing horizontal movement of the ball. It shows the height of the ball as time changes. The horizontal movement is time change, not position change. Now we want to answer some questions about the ball.

How high does the ball go? When does it get that high?

To answer these questions, press <2nd><CALC> and choose "maximum." The calculator is asking for a "Left Bound." This means we use the left arrow to move the cursor to the left of the peak. Then press <ENTER>. Now you are being asked for a "Right Bound." Use the right arrow button to move the cursor to the right of the peak and press <ENTER>. You are now asked for a "Guess." Just press <ENTER>. At the bottom you should see x = 2.5 and Y = 106. Then the ball's maximum height is 106 feet and that occurs at 2.5 seconds.

When does the ball land?

If you remember the quadratic formula from algebra, you can set $-16t^2 + 80t + 6 = 0$ and solve. You will get two answers. Because of the physical context of the problem, the negative answer makes no sense so only the positive answer is used. Whether or not you remember the quadratic formula, we can also do this using the calculator. You see a point where the graph touches the x-axis. That is the point we want to find. Assuming you are using a TI-82, 83, or 84, press <2nd><CALC> and choose "zero." You are asked for a "Left Bound." Using the left or right arrow buttons to move the cursor close to but to the left of the point where the graph touches the x-axis, the press <ENTER>. You are now asked for a "Right Bound." Use the right arrow button to move the cursor to the right of that point. Because of how we have the WINDOW set up, the cursor go off the bottom of the screen (make sure the Y values showing at the bottom become negative). Press <ENTER>. You are asked for a "Guess." Just press <ENTER>. Now you see that the ball hits the ground at a time of 5.07 seconds. (The Y value may give something like 1E − 11. That is calculator notation for the scientific notation expression 1×10^{-11}. In regular notation, that is 0.00000000001. That is not 0 but it is simply a round off error issue.)

How high is the ball after 3 seconds?

Press <2nd><CALC> and choose "Value." You will see "X=." Enter 3 and press <ENTER>. The ball is 102 feet high.

How fast is the ball moving after 3 seconds? How fast is it moving at the instant it hits the ground?

Recall the general formula for velocity for these problems is $v(t) =$ $-32t + v_0$. For our particular problem, it would be is $v(t) = -32t + 80$. To find the velocity at 3 seconds, simply substitute 3 in place of t. We get $v(t)$ $= -32*3 + 80 = -96 + 80 = -16$ feet per second. The negative tells us the ball is coming back down after passing its peak. To find the speed at which the ball is moving when it hits the ground, recall from above that the ball hit the ground after 5.07 seconds. So insert 5.07 in place of t in the velocity formula to obtain $v(t) = -32*5.07 + 80 = -82.24$ feet per second.

Section 10.3—Basic Trigonometry

It is possible to have a complete semester-long or yearlong course in trigonometry. In fact, you may have had one. We are not going to spend very much time on trigonometry. We will look only at a couple of basic ideas and let our calculator do the majority of the work.

Trigonometry is the algebra of right-triangle geometry. For a right triangle with certain values for the other two angles, there are numbers that will correspond to the ratios of different side lengths of the triangle. Consider the following right triangle and the angle, θ.

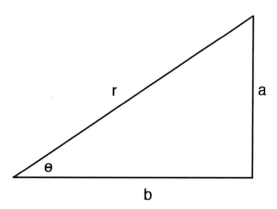

The three ratios of interest to us are sine, cosine and tangent of θ. They will be written sin θ, cos θ and tan θ, respectively. A simple acronym that will help us remember which ratio goes with which function is SOHCAH-TOA. That stands for

Sine is Opposite over Hypotenuse, Cosine is Adjacent over Hypotenuse, Tangent is Opposite over Adjacent.

For the triangle above, then, we would have sin θ = a/r, cos θ = b/r and tan θ = a/b.

Let us do it again, this time with some numbers.

Example

For this triangle, sin θ = 12/20 = 3/5, cos θ = 16/20 = 4/5 and tan θ = 12/16 = 3/4.

Notice again that we are using function notation here. The function names are sin, cos, tan and they are dependent on the variable θ.

If we know the angle, θ, our calculator can tell us the values for sin θ, cos θ and tan θ even if we do not know any of the lengths of the triangle.

Example—Find sine, cosine and tangent for the angle θ = 52°.

First we must make sure we have our calculators in the right mode. Press <MODE>. If the word "DEGREE" is highlighted, you are set. If not, move the cursor until it is on the word "DEGREE." Then press <ENTER>. Now go back to the home screen and evaluate sine, cosine and tangent for the angle θ = 52°.

sin(52)	.7880107536
cos(52)	.6156614753
tan(52)	1.279941632

Section 10.4—Projectile Motion—Two Dimensions

We are now going to take the projectile motion problem we considered in Section 10.2 and extend it to two dimensions. This will still involve a simplification of the real situation. We are still going to ignore air resistance. We are going to ignore wind. We will ignore the fact that the ball sometimes curves toward or away from a fielder. We will just assume all balls go perfectly straight in whatever direction they started.

This model is a little different than others we have considered. It has two parts, one for the horizontal part of the motion of the object and one for the vertical. We will call the horizontal part x and the vertical part y.

$$x(t) = v_0 (\cos \theta) t$$
$$y(t) = -16t^2 + v_0 (\sin \theta) t + y_0$$

where

  x is the horizontal position of the object in feet
  y is the vertical position of the object in feet
  t is time in seconds
  v_0 is the initial velocity of the object
  θ is the initial angle of elevation of the object
  y_0 is the initial height of the object

In order to work with this model, we need to put our calculator in Parametric mode. Press <MODE>. Move the cursor onto "PAR" and press <ENTER>.

Example—Suppose a ball is hit from a height of 3 feet with a velocity of 80 miles per hour at an angle of elevation of 53°.

In order to work with this problem we must first convert 80 miles per hour into feet per second.

$$\frac{80 \; miles}{hour} \; \frac{1 \; hour}{60 \; minutes} \; \frac{1 \; minute}{60 \; seconds} \; \frac{5280 \; feet}{1 \; mile} = \frac{117.3333 \; feet}{second}$$

Press <Y=>. Notice it looks different than it did before.

In X_{1T} enter 117.3333 (cos(53)) t and in Y_{1T} enter $-16t^2$ + 117.3333 (sin(53)) t + 3.

Press <WINDOW> and set up the following parameters:

Tmin = 0
Tmax = 6
Tstep=.03
Xmin = 0

$$Xmax = 450$$
$$Xscl = 20$$
$$Ymin = 0$$
$$Ymax = 150$$
$$Yscl = 10$$

Then press <GRAPH>. This time, what you see is the approximate path of the ball. We lose a little bit of realism in this model. An actual baseball will not carry as far as this model predicts. Ignoring the wind resistance creates some inaccuracy.

To find out approximately how far the ball goes, press <TRACE>. Use the right arrow button to move the cursor along the curve. Keep going until the Y value gets close to 0. You'll see that this model predicts the ball will fly for about 5.88 seconds (the T value) and travel about 415 feet (the x value).

Suppose the fence is 405 feet from home plate and is 10 feet high. Would this be a homerun? Move the cursor to get it as close to x = 405 as you can. At x = 404.6, Y = 14.6. So the ball is 14.6 feet high just before the fence. So this is a homerun.

Suppose the fence is 410 feet from home plate. Is it still a homerun? When x = 408.8, Y = 9.17. So it would not be a homer.

Example—Suppose a batter hits the ball at 120 feet per second at an angle of 29° with an initial height of 2 feet. Doing what we did in the previous example, we find that the ball will land after 3.66 seconds at a point about 385 feet from home plate.

Suppose the centerfielder can run 20 miles per hour and started off 110 feet from the spot where the ball lands. Would he get to the ball in time to catch it?

First we find the outfielder's speed in feet per second.

$$\frac{20\ miles}{hour}\quad \frac{1\ hour}{60\ minutes}\quad \frac{1\ minute}{60\ seconds}\quad \frac{5280\ feet}{1\ mile} = \frac{29.3333\ feet}{second}$$

He has 3.66 seconds so he can run 3.66 * 29.3333 = 107.36 feet. If he takes a good path to the ball and dives, he might catch the ball.

One additional factor that we mentioned above is that we are ignoring certain complicating factors. The ball will not travel as far as our model suggests. Air resistance affects the flight of the ball so it will not travel as far as the numbers we get. As we mentioned in Chapter 6, the ball travels farther in Denver than it does at lower altitudes. This is because air resistance is less at higher altitudes. If there is wind, the ball can travel farther or less far depending on whether it is going with the wind or against the wind.

Section 10.5—Bounce and Force

Anyone who has ever played baseball knows that hitting the ball on the middle barrel of the bat produces a better hit than one on the handle or the end of the bat. The complete description as to why is beyond the scope of this text. We will consider a simple explanation.

When the ball hits the bat, there is some vibration. Vibration dampens, or minimizes, the force the bat can exert on the ball. The greater the bat's mass near the point of impact, the less the vibration will be. So, if the ball hits on the handle, a small amount of the mass of the bat is there so there is more vibration. Therefore a smaller amount of the force of the bat will be transferred to the ball, causing the ball to not travel as far. Likewise, if the ball hits on the end of the bat, there will be a large amount of vibration, as anyone who has ever hit a ball on the end of the bat on a cold day will attest. If the ball hits in the middle of the barrel, the vibration is minimal, thus transferring the greatest amount of the bat's force to the ball.

The hardness of the wood in the bat also affects the distance the ball travels. If a bat is soft, it will absorb much of the force from the ball, lessening the amount of force transferred back to the ball. If the bat is hard, like an ash or maple bat, this does not happen as much. Additionally, the bat, during a swing, will bend, though the amount of the bend is so small you cannot see it without the help of some very good photographic equipment.

The ball also factors into this discussion. There is something in physics, called the **coefficient of restitution**. Basically that deals with how much of the force of an object is retained by that object during a collision with an immovable object. If the coefficient of restitution is small, the object will not bounce very far. If it is high, the object will bounce farther. That is part of why a softball will not travel as far as a baseball. Or why an old baseball will not travel as far as a new baseball.

Section 10.6—Linear Regression

Recall the following chart from chapters 5 and 6. This scatter plot gives the walks vs. strikeouts comparison of the top 77 strikeout pitchers from 1965. We are going to use technology to do **linear regression** on these data.

Linear regression means finding the line that best approximates a given set of data. Using the linear regression command from Microsoft Excel with these data values gives $y = 0.210451724x + 35.18181866$ as the **line-of-best-fit** for these data. This means that if a pitcher has x strikeouts, we could expect him to have y walks. As we saw in chapter 6, the correlation is not

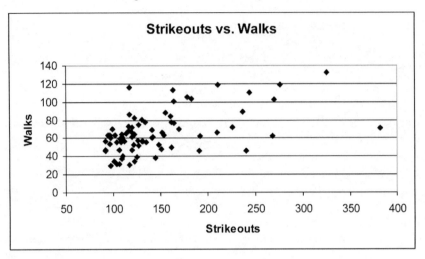

very strong, since the correlation coefficient was only 0.522798368. But we can still use this function to estimate other pitchers' walks, given a number of strikeouts.

Here is the chart again with that line (slope = 0.210451724, y-intercept (0, 35.18181866) included).

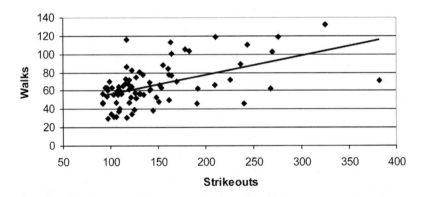

So if a pitcher had 200 strikeouts, this line would suggest he would have 77 walks (well, it actually tells us 77.27216345 but fractional walks don't happen). None of the pitchers had exactly 200 strikeouts. The closest were Don Drysdale with 210 (66 walks) and Denny McLain with 192 (62 walks). Chris Short struck out 237 batters. Our line-of-best-fit suggests he would have 85 walks. His actual total was 89 so he is one for whom the line does a good job.

Example—The following chart shows the strikeout to HR comparison for all players with at least 550 at-bats in 1976.

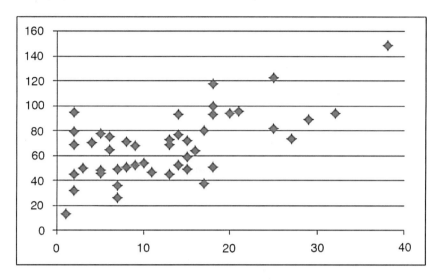

Using technology we get a correlation of 0.63501711, so there is a decent correlation between the two quantities (remember, correlation does not necessarily mean causation). The next chart shows the data with the line-of-best-fit, $y = 0.209865186x - 1.645759413$.

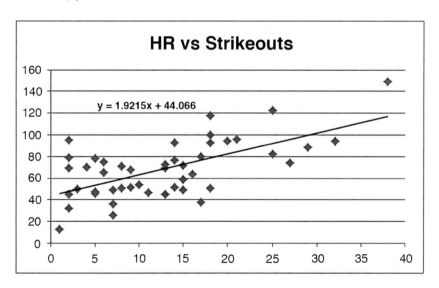

The player with the most home runs was Mike Schmidt. Schmidt struck out 149 times. Our line suggests he should have had only 30 home runs (rounding 29.62415). The diamond nearest the 100 on the vertical axis is Bill North who struck out 95 times. According to the estimate of the line, he should have had 18 home runs, not the two he actually had. The following chart gives all the players with their actual numbers and the "predicted HRs." You will see that some are fairly close.

Name	SO	HR	predicted HR	Name	SO	HR	predicted HR
Mike Schmidt	149	38	30	John Mayberry	73	13	14
Graig Nettles	94	32	18	Willie Montanez	47	11	8
George Foster	89	29	17	Pete Rose	54	10	10
Sal Bando	74	27	14	Rod Carew	52	9	9
George Hendrick	82	25	16	Dave Concepcion	68	9	13
Jim Rice	123	25	24	Mickey Rivers	51	8	9
Richie Zisk	96	21	19	Phil Garner	71	8	13
Gary Matthews	94	20	18	George Brett	36	7	6
Amos Otis	100	18	19	Buddy Bell	49	7	9
Cesar Cedeno	51	18	9	Bill Buckner	26	7	4
Jeff Burroughs	93	18	18	Ken Griffey, Sr.	65	6	12
George Scott	118	18	23	Rick Manning	75	6	14
Thurman Munson	38	17	6	Ken Reitz	48	5	8
Chris Chambliss	80	17	15	Bill Russell	46	5	8
Bob Watson	64	16	12	Von Joshua	78	5	15
Don Baylor	72	15	13	Manny Trillo	70	4	13
Rusty Staub	49	15	9	Al Cowens	50	3	9
Toby Harrah	59	15	11	Rennie Stennett	32	2	5
Roy White	52	14	9	Enos Cabell	79	2	15
Jorge Orta	77	14	15	Bucky Dent	45	2	8
Larry Hisle	93	14	18	Robin Yount	69	2	13
Steve Garvey	69	13	13	Bill North	95	2	18
Rico Carty	45	13	8	Dave Cash	13	1	1

If data sets have different shapes, we might use different kinds of regression. If the data start off going up slowly then start getting bigger faster, we might use exponential regression. If the data start high, go down, then go back up, we might use quadratic regression. For the purposes of this book, however, we will just do linear regression.

Chapter 10—Exercises

Section 10.1—Linear, Quadratic and Exponential

1. Write a linear model expressing the relationship between pounds and ounces.

    Use that model to find the number of ounces in
    a. four pounds.
    b. 6.5 pounds.
    c. one ton (2000 pounds).

Use that model to find the number of pounds corresponding to
a. 144 ounces.
b. 2000 ounces.

2. Write a linear model describing the relationship between distance and time if a car is traveling at 45 miles per hour.

Use that model to find the number of miles traveled in
a. 3 hours.
b. 45 minutes.

Use that model to find the amount of time it takes to travel
a. 90 miles.
b. 250 miles.

3. According to microbiologist, Dr. Chuck Gerba, one of three chickens is contaminated with salmonella. The vast majority of contaminated chickens have fewer than 300 salmonella, all killed in the cooking. Even if they survived, it usually takes several thousand to cause illness. However, if the salmonella gets transferred during food preparation to the potato salad, the warm, moist environment allows them to double in population every 20 minutes. Suppose 100 salmonella got into the potato salad. How many would there be 6 hours later? (*Reader's Digest*, February 1995).

4. In 1870, Searcy, Arkansas, had a population of 874. By 1880 the population had dropped to 840 (that's a drop of 3.8902% over the 10 year period). If that rate had remained the same, what would the population of Searcy be in 2005?

5. In 1985, the highest paid major league baseball player made $2,130,300. In 1986, the highest paid player earned $2,800,000. That was an increase of 31.4369%. If salaries continued to grow exponentially at that rate, what would the highest paid player have earned in 2005? (The highest paid player in 2005 made $26,000,000.)

6. Over a period of time, Brazil experienced hyperinflation. Suppose the rate of inflation was 75.5% per month. If something cost the equivalent of $1.45, what would its price be after one year of this hyperinflation rate?

7. Americium-241 has a half-life of 16.02 hours. If you have 15 grams of Americium-241, how much will you have left in 8 days?

8. According to the United States Energy Information Administration's *Monthly Energy Review*, the average price of a gallon of gasoline in 1949 was $0.27. In 1999, it was $1.17. Adjusting for an average annual inflation rate of 3.9685% (data due to NASA), was gasoline more or less expensive in 1999 than it was in 1949? Be sure to show all work.

9. Barium-140 has a half life of 12.74 days. If you have nine grams of Barium-140, how much will you have left in 12 hours?

10. Write a model for the time it takes for a pitch of varying speeds to reach home plate. Assume the pitcher's hand is 55 feet from home plate at the point of release.

    a. How long will it take an Aroldis Chapman 105 miles per hour fastball to reach home?

    b. How long would Tim Wakefield's 66 miles per hour knuckle ball take to reach home?

SECTION 10.2—PROJECTILE MOTION—ONE DIMENSION

1. A ball is thrown from the top of a 75 foot tall building. It is thrown up with a velocity of 45 feet per second. Find the following.

    a. the time it takes for the ball to hit the ground

    b. the velocity when it hits the ground

    c. the peak height the ball reaches

    d. how long it takes to reach the peak

2. A ball is thrown from the top of a 75-foot tall building. It is thrown down with a velocity of 45 feet per second. Find the following.

    a. the time it takes for the ball to hit the ground

    b. the velocity when it hits the ground

3. A ball is dropped from the top of the Empire State Building (1350 feet). Find the following.

    a. the time it takes for the ball to hit the ground

    b. the velocity when it hits the ground

4. On August 21, 1908, Washington Senators catcher Gabby Street caught a baseball dropped from the top of the Washington Monument. That is a distance of 555 feet.

    a. Find the time it took for the ball to reach Street's glove (assume he caught it at a height of 6 feet from the ground).

    b. Find the velocity when it hit his glove.

SECTION 10.3— BASIC TRIGONOMETRY

For each of the following triangles, fill in the blanks.

	Triangle	$\sin \theta$	$\cos \theta$	$\tan \theta$
1.)	45, 27, 36, θ			
2.)	12, 13, 5, θ			
3.)	12.36, 15, 8.5, θ			

Fill in the blanks.

	Angle	$\sin \theta$	$\cos \theta$	$\tan \theta$
4.)	32°			
5.)	45°			
6.)	63°			
7.)	74.5°			

SECTION 10.4—PROJECTILE MOTION—TWO DIMENSIONS

1. Suppose a ball is hit from a height of four feet with a velocity of 83 miles per hour at an angle of elevation of 43°. Find the following.
   a. how far it travels
   b. how long it takes to land
   c. whether it is a home run over an 8 foot tall fence at 400 feet

2. Suppose a ball is hit from a height of two feet with a velocity of 88 miles per hour at an angle of elevation of 25°. Find the following.

    a. how far it travels

    b. how long it takes to land

    c. whether it is a home run over an 8 foot tall fence at 400 feet

SECTION 10.6—LINEAR REGRESSION

1. The following chart gives the doubles and triples for all players with at least 525 at-bats in 1960.

	2B	3B		2B	3B
Vada Pinson, Reds	37	12	Marv Breeding, Orioles	25	2
Tito Francona, Indians	36	2	Tony Taylor, Cubs/Phillies	25	7
Orlando Cepeda, Giants	36	3	Don Hoak, Pirates	24	9
Bill Skowron, Yankees	34	3	Nellie Fox, White Sox	24	10
Bob Skinner, Pirates	33	6	Ron Hansen, Orioles	22	5
Ernie Banks, Cubs	32	7	Roberto Clemente, Pirates	22	6
Minnie Minoso, White Sox	32	4	Bill Mazeroski, Pirates	21	5
Al Smith, White Sox	31	3	Bill Tuttle, A's	21	3
Frank Malzone, Red Sox	30	2	Hank Aaron, Braves	20	11
Willie Mays, Giants	29	12	Luis Aparicio, White Sox	20	7
Al Kaline, Tigers	29	4	Frank Bolling, Tigers	20	4
Pete Runnels, Red Sox	29	2	Jim Gilliam, Dodgers	20	2
Brooks Robinson, Orioles	27	9	Jerry Lumpe, A's	19	3
Bill White, Cardinals	27	10	Eddie Mathews, Braves	19	7
Bill Bruton, Braves	27	13	Rocky Colavito, Tigers	18	1
Vic Power, Indians	26	3	Mickey Mantle, Yankees	17	6
Ken Boyer, Cardinals	26	10	Richie Ashburn, Cubs	16	5
Billy Gardner, Senators	26	5	Del Crandall, Braves	14	1
Dick Groat, Pirates	26	4	Jim Lemon, Senators	10	1
Tony Kubek, Yankees	25	3			

    a. Use the linear regression command on your calculator to determine the correlation coefficient between doubles and triples for these hitters.

    b. Is there a strong correlation?

2. The following chart gives the ERA and winning percentage for National League pitchers from 1985 who had at least 162 IP.

	ERA	WPCT		ERA	WPCT
Dwight Gooden, Mets	1.53	.857	Kevin Gross, Phillies	3.41	.536
John Tudor, Cardinals	1.93	.724	Ed Lynch, Mets	3.44	.556
Orel Hershiser, Dodgers	2.03	.864	LaMarr Hoyt, Padres	3.47	.667
Rick Reuschel, Pirates	2.27	.636	Rick Mahler, Braves	3.48	.531
Bob Welch, Dodgers	2.31	.778	Bill Gullickson, Expos	3.52	.538
Fernando Valenzuela, Dodgers	2.45	.630	Tom Browning, Reds	3.55	.690
Sid Fernandez, Mets	2.80	.500	Bob Knepper, Astros	3.55	.536
Danny Cox, Cardinals	2.88	.667	Dave LaPoint, Giants	3.57	.292
Ron Darling, Mets	2.90	.727	Mario Soto, Reds	3.58	.444

	ERA	WPCT		ERA	WPCT
Bryn Smith, Expos	2.91	.783	Joe Niekro, Astros	3.72	.429
Jerry Reuss, Dodgers	2.92	.583	Atlee Hammaker, Giants	3.74	.294
Dave Dravecky, Padres	2.93	.542	Charles Hudson, Phillies	3.78	.381
Dennis Eckersley, Cubs	3.08	.611	Nolan Ryan, Astros	3.80	.455
Eric Show, Padres	3.09	.522	John Denny, Phillies	3.82	.440
Andy Hawkins, Padres	3.15	.692	Steve Bedrosian, Braves	3.83	.318
Mike Scott, Astros	3.29	.692	Jay Tibbs, Reds	3.92	.385
Shane Rawley, Phillies	3.31	.619	Rick Rhoden, Pirates	4.47	.400
Mike Krukow, Giants	3.38	.421	Jose DeLeon, Pirates	4.70	.095
Joaquin Andujar, Cardinals	3.40	.636			

a. Use the linear regression command on your calculator to determine the correlation coefficient between ERA and WPCT for these pitchers.

b. Is there a strong correlation?

11—Voting Theory

At first, one might not think voting has much to do with baseball. There are, however, a number of situations where various types of voting are found in baseball. Each year there are various awards or honors given. The league leader in batting average or strikeouts is strictly a numerical issue. Who has the highest batting average among qualifiers? Who has the most strikeouts among pitchers. But there are other kinds of awards or honors, such as the Most Valuable Player, Cy Young award and Golden Glove award, that are subjectively determined based on voting systems.

Section 11.1—Majority, Plurality, Supermajority

The two most familiar forms of voting are majority voting and plurality voting. If there are only two options in the election, plurality and majority are the same thing. If there are more than two options, they differ in important ways.

Majority vote—In order to win an election decided by majority vote, an option must get *more than half* of the votes.

People often misstate what a majority vote requires.
"at least half of the votes"—In an election with two candidates, each candidate could get exactly 50% of the votes. So BOTH candidates could get "at least half of the votes." But in this case, neither would win. The correct statement is "*more than half* of the votes."
"at least 51% of the votes"—It is not necessary to get 51% to win a major-

ity vote. Getting 50.1% is sufficient. So is getting 50.01%. So is getting 50.000000001%. The correct statement is *"more than half* of the votes."

"half of the votes plus one"—If only seven votes are cast, "half of the votes" would be 3.5 votes. "Half of the votes plus one" would be 4.5 votes. But only four votes would be necessary to win a majority vote. The correct statement is *"more than half* of the votes."

"win by at least half of the vote"—"Half of the vote" is 50% of the vote. "Win by at least half of the vote" would mean one option would have a percentage at least 50 greater than the next most popular option. That is far more than is necessary in a majority vote. The correct statement is *"more than half* of the votes."

"win a majority of the votes"—While this is certainly true, it is poor form to define a term by using the term.

The correct statement is *"more than half* of the votes."

In many jurisdictions, political elections are majority elections. If there are only two candidates, then either the two candidates tie or one has a majority. Different jurisdictions have different rules for how to handle a tie. In some cases, a new election is held. In some cases, the winner is chosen by some game of chance. The candidates may each pull a card from a deck of cards with the candidate getting the higher card winning. The election could be decided by a coin flip.

When there are more than two candidates, it is possible to have neither a tie nor have someone win a majority of the votes. In such cases, the typical procedure is to have the two candidates with the highest vote totals participate in a second election, called a runoff. In most cases, this is done by holding a second election some number of weeks after the first election.

Since holding elections takes a lot of time and can cost a lot of money, some jurisdictions have begun using "instantaneous runoffs." This can be done a variety of ways. One way can be illustrated by supposing we have three candidates for a position, Alan Adams, Beatrice Baxter and Clarence Compton.

The ballot might be set up in two parts. The first part could be a typical ballot.

Alan Adams   _____
Beatrice Baxter   _____
Clarence Compton   _____

Each voter selects a candidate on both parts of the ballot. These votes are tallied. If a candidate receives a majority of the votes on the first part of the ballot, the election is over and the second part of the ballot is ignored. The second part of the ballot could look like this.

| Alan Adams | _____ |
| Beatrice Baxter | _____ |

| Alan Adams | _____ |
| Clarence Compton | _____ |

| Beatrice Baxter | _____ |
| Clarence Compton | _____ |

In each pair of candidates, the voter would choose one from each pair. If no candidate received a majority of the votes on part one of the ballot, election officials would turn to part two of the ballot and look at the pair above consisting of the two candidates with the two highest vote totals. The votes cast on that pairing would be counted. Whoever receives a majority in this count would win.

Ballot questions are typically decided by majority vote. These will not generally require a runoff since there are generally only two choices.

The presidential election is decided by a majority vote but there is a twist here. It is not the majority of the votes of the people that count. Each state and territory has a certain number of electoral votes. In most cases, whichever candidate gets the most votes in a given state gets that state's electoral votes. Then, the candidate who gets the majority of the electoral votes wins the election. (Some states have a mechanism by which more than one candidate can receive electoral votes from that state.)

Plurality vote—In order to win an election decided by plurality vote, an option must *get the most votes.*

In any election decided by plurality voting, if there is not a tie, then someone wins. In baseball, the voting for the all-star team is decided by plurality voting. Some political elections are decided by plurality voting.

Supermajority vote—If an election requires a super-majority, then some percentage greater than 50% must be met or exceeded for an option to pass.

The Baseball Hall of Fame is intended to honor only the greatest players in baseball history. In order to try to assure that happens, a number of procedures are followed. Players who do not get at least 5% of the votes cast do not get on the ballot again. Players may only be on the ballot for 15 years. Voters are permitted to vote for at most ten candidates. A player, in order to be elected, must be named on at least 75% of the ballots that are cast. That last requirement is an example of the requirement of the super-majority of the vote. There is no requirement that anyone be elected. In fact, there have been years where no one was elected.

Jury trials generally require a super-majority. In many cases, a criminal trial jury must vote unanimously to convict a defendant.

Overriding a presidential veto requires a 2/3 vote in both the Senate and the House of Representatives.

Ending a filibuster in the U.S. Senate requires a 60% vote.

Section 11.2—Other

A track meet is not an election but its method of scoring helps illustrate another method of doing elections. Various track meets are scored in different ways. One method of scoring a track meet awards points to the top five finishers in each event. The first-place finisher earns five points for his or her team. The second-place finisher earns four points. Third place earns three points, fourth place earns two and fifth place earns one. Anyone finishing in sixth place or worse earns no points. Then, each team's points from all of the events are added up. Whatever team gets the most points wins.

Track meet scoring is basically the idea behind a Borda Count vote. In the voting for National and American League Most Valuable Player (MVP), a majority vote would almost never produce a winner. A plurality vote might not be very satisfying since, of the hundreds of players in each league, dozens might receive votes. The one with the most votes might only receive 10–20%. The MVP voting is currently handled by having each voter vote for 10 players. The voter ranks the players chosen. Whatever player is ranked first receives 14 points. The player ranked second gets nine points. Third place gets eight, fourth place gets seven, and on down to 10th place which earns one point. Each player's points are added up and the player with the most points is the MVP. In 1979, the National League ended up with a tie in the MVP voting between Keith Hernandez of the Cardinals and Willie Stargell of the Pirates. Every other year, however, has produced a single winner. Below is the National League MVP voting from 2008, as reported by MLB.com.

2008 NL MVP Award Voting

Player, Club	1st	2nd	3rd	4th	5th	6th	7th	8th	9th	10th	Points
Albert Pujols, STL	18	10	2	1			1				**369**
Ryan Howard, PHI	12	8	6		1	1	2			1	**308**
Ryan Braun, MIL		2	3	5	5	2	2	3	2	1	**139**
Manny Ramirez, LAD		2	4	7	2	3	2		1	2	**138**
Lance Berkman, HOU		2	4	4	1	3	3	4	1	1	**126**
CC Sabathia, MIL		4	5	1	2	2	3		1	2	**121**
David Wright, NYM		2	1	4	3	3	2	5	2	1	**115**

Player, Club	1st	2nd	3rd	4th	5th	6th	7th	8th	9th	10th	Points
Brad Lidge, PHI	2		2		4	3	2	3	1	2	104
Carlos Delgado, NYM		5		1	2		5	2	3		96
Aramis Ramirez, CHC				2	4	1	1	4	3	1	66
Hanley Ramirez, FLA				2	2	2	1	2	2	5	55
Chipper Jones, ATL				1	2		4	1	2	2	44
Geovany Soto, CHC				3	1		3		1		41
Johan Santana, NYM			1	1	1		1		2	1	30
Chase Utley, PHI				1	1	1	1		3	2	30
Ryan Ludwick, STL							1	2	3	1	17
Brandon Webb, ARI					2				1		14
Adrian Gonzalez, SD							1	1	1	4	13
Matt Holliday, COL						1	1	1		1	13
Prince Fielder, MIL						1		1	1	1	11
Derrek Lee, CHC					1		1				10
Carlos Beltran, NYM					1			1		1	10
Tim Lincecum, SF						1			1	2	9
Jose Reyes, NYM								1			3
Jose Valverde, HOU								1			3
Stephen Drew, ARI									1		2
Nate McLouth, PIT										1	1

The Cy Young award voting is also a Borda Count. Voters vote for three pitchers. The man ranked first gets five points, second place gets three points and third place one.

In college sports, the NCAA rankings are an example of an election held by a Borda Count. Depending on the sport and division, different numbers of teams are ranked. In football, 25 teams are ranked. First place gets 25 points, second gets 24, down to 25th place which gets one point. Then, again, each team's points are totaled with the leading point total producing the top ranked team.

Like track meet scoring, cross-country scoring is not a vote but it provides another way to handle scoring. In cross-country, a team has at least five runners compete in the race. At the end of the race, each team's top five finishers score points. But in this case, the number of points corresponds to the runner's finish in the race. The first place runner gets one point, the second place gets two, etc. Then, each team's top five runners points are added up with the winner being the team with the LOWEST point total.

Our last example is the Bowl Championship Series (BCS) rankings. It is not strictly a voting method but uses various votes. As of December 2008, the BCS ranking is based on two polls, the Harris Poll and the USA Today poll, and six computerized ranking systems. The Harris Poll is a Borda count and has a total possible of 2850 points. Each team gets a score based on the percentage of those possible points that it received in the Harris poll. So, if a team has 990 total points in the Harris Poll, they receive a score of 990/2850 = .3474. The same is done with the USA Today poll which has a maximum of 1575 possible points. Teams listed in the computer rankings are given 25 points if ranked first, 24 if second, down to one if ranked 25th. The best and worst computer ranking for each team is dropped and the remaining four are added together and divided by 100 to obtain a "computer ranking percentage." The BCS average is then the average of the Harris percentage, *USA Today* percentage and computer ranking percentage. Here are the BCS rankings from December 7, 2008, as reported by ESPN.com.

	BCS		Harris Poll			USA Today			Computer Rankings							
Team	BCS AVG	PRVS	RK	PTS	%	RK	PTS	%	COMP AVG	A&H	RB	CM	KM	JS	PW	%
1 Oklahoma	.9757	2	2	2699	.9554	1	1482	.9718	1	25	25	25	25	25	25	1.000
2 Florida	.9479	4	1	2776	.9827	2	1481	.9711	3	22	24	23	21	22	22	.890
3 Texas	.9298	3	3	2616	.9260	3	1408	.9233	2	23	22	24	23	24	24	.940
4 Alabama	.8443	1	4	2442	.8644	T4	1309	.8584	6	20	21	21	20	20	19	.810
5 USC	.8208	5	5	2413	.8542	T4	1309	.8584	7	17	23	19	19	19	18	.750
6 Utah	.7846	6	7	2119	.7501	7	1134	.7436	5	24	19	22	22	21	21	.860
7 Texas Tech	.7840	7	8	2090	.7398	8	1132	.7423	4	21	20	20	24	23	23	.870
8 Penn State	.7387	8	6	2186	.7738	6	1193	.7823	9	18	16	17	16	16	17	.660
9 Boise State	.6980	9	9	1938	.6860	9	1034	.6780	8	19	18	18	18	18	20	.730
10 Ohio State	.6354	10	10	1858	.6577	10	1004	.6584	11	16	17	16	12	11	15	.590
11 TCU	.5848	11	11	1580	.5593	11	877	.5751	10	15	14	12	17	17	16	.620
12 Cincinnati	.5384	13	12	1528	.5409	12	830	.5443	12	14	10	15	13	12	14	.530
13 Oklahoma St	.4866	14	13	1402	.4963	14	722	.4734	13	9	13	8	14	15	13	.490
14 Georgia Tch	.4516	15	14	1221	.4322	15	690	.4525	14	10	12	10	15	14	11	.470
15 Georgia	.3775	16	17	1018	.3604	17	537	.3521	15	13	11	13	8	9	9	.420
16 BYU	.3580	18	16	1071	.3791	16	541	.3548	16	8	15	6	7	7	12	.340
17 Oregon	.3395	19	15	1211	.4287	13	747	.4898	T-23	0	9	4	0	0	6	.100
18 Michigan St	.2866	21	18	831	.2942	18	466	.3056	19	11	6	11	2	1	7	.260
19 Virginia Tech	.2440	25	22	511	.1809	19	337	.2210	17	6	1	7	10	13	10	.330
20 Pitt	.2377	23	19	638	.2258	21	316	.2072	18	12	3	14	3	5	8	.280
21 Missouri	.1627	20	24	382	.1352	23	218	.1430	T-20	7	7	3	5	4	5	.210
22 Ball State	.1464	12	20	609	.2156	22	219	.1436	25	1	4	9	0	0	3	.080
23 Northwestern	.1377	22	21	548	.1940	20	334	.2190	NR	0	0	0	0	0	0	.000
24 Boston Coll	.1046	17	26	172	.0609	26	96	.0630	22	4	0	5	9	8	2	.190
25 Mississippi	.0837	NR	23	413	.1462	24	160	.1049	NR	0	5	0	0	0	0	.000

Chapter 11—Exercises

SECTION 11.1—MAJORITY, PLURALITY, SUPERMAJORITY

1. Explain the difference between elections that are determined by majority and plurality voting.

2. Define a super-majority vote.

3. Give examples of four elections that require a super-majority vote. Be sure to give the percentage or fraction required in each vote.

4. In a vote for the Hall of Fame, if 454 votes are cast, how many votes are necessary for election.

5. The chart below gives results of a number of elections. In the column marked "Majority," put the option, if any, that wins if the vote requires a majority. In the column marked "Plurality," put the option, if any, that wins if the vote requires a plurality. In the column marked "60% Super-

Majority," put the option, if any, that wins if the vote requires a 60% super-majority. In each case, if no option has the requisite number of votes, write "none."

	Votes		Majority	Plurality	60% Super-Majority
a.)	**option** A B C D	**votes** 45 34 23 22			
b.)	**option** A B C D	**votes** 74 145 35 32			
c.)	**option** A B C D	**votes** 145 174 643 90			
d.)	**option** A B C D	**votes** 145 174 613 90			
e.)	**option** A B	**votes** 145 174			
f.)	**option** A B C	**votes** 145 174 319			

Section 11.2—Other

1. Explain how a Borda Count works.

2. Suppose the following are the votes received for the Most Valuable Player. Calculate the total points for each player (use the point distribution given in the text). Rank all the players and see who wins.

National League Most Valuable Player Award Voting

Player, Club	1st	2nd	3rd	4th	5th	6th	7th	8th	9th	10th	Points
Albert Pujols, STL	6	10	3	7	4	2					
Lance Berkman, HOU		2	2	1	5		5	2	5	9	1
David Wright, NYM	10	15	6	1							
Carlos Delgado, NYM			3	5	4		5	11	4		
Aramis Ramirez, CHC		2	7	8		4	3	7			1
Geovany Soto, CHC			1	2	1		5	7	10	6	
Johan Santana, NYM		2	1	1		2	2	3	6	15	
Chase Utley, PHI	1		4	2	4	1	5	2	5	8	
Matt Holliday, COL			4	4	4	12	4	4			
Prince Fielder, MIL	15	5	6	3					2	1	
Derrek Lee, CHC	6	10	3	7	4	2					
Carlos Beltran, NYM		2	2	1	5		5	2	5	9	1
Jose Reyes, NYM	10	15	6	1							

3. Suppose the following are the votes received for the 1952 National League Cy Young award voting. Calculate the total points for each player (use the point distribution given in the text). Rank all the players and see who wins.

1st	2nd	3rd	Points
Hoyt Wilhelm	4	7	
Warren Hacker	2	1	4
Robin Roberts	6	6	1
Billy Loes		1	1
Carl Erskine	2		2
Bob Rush			1
Karl Drews			1
Ken Raffensberger	1		2
Curt Simmons	1	1	3
Sal Maglie			1

12—Recording Statistics

"Always keep a record of data. It indicates you've been working."—Unknown

"You can have data without information, but you cannot have information without data."—Daniel Keys Moran

The statistics we have been discussing throughout the book would never have existed for us to examine unless people had recorded them for posterity. There are two aspects to that recording of data. The first is keeping the individual game records, also called "scoring the game," and accumulating seasonal, career, individual, team, league and historical data. The latter part of that, as we have discussed earlier, is much easier now that we have computers so easily accessible.

Section 12.1—Scoring a Game

There are as many different systems for scoring games as there are people doing the scoring. Some people keep minimal information, such as hits, walks and outs. Others careful record hits, including their location and the count on which they occurred, what kinds of outs were made and the fielders involved, whether a spectacular play occurred, etc. We will aim for a middle ground.

WHO IS WHO?

We will keep track of who did what defensively. In order to do that, we will want a shorthand way to refer to the different defensive positions. This is one aspect of scoring that is fairly standard.

1 pitcher
2 catcher

3	1st baseman
4	2nd baseman
5	3rd baseman
6	shortstop
7	left fielder
8	center fielder
9	right fielder

So, if a batter grounds out from shortstop to first, we might denote it by "6-3." Some people give a little more detail indicating a ground ball out by "G 6-3." A second base to shortstop to first base double play might be denoted "4-6-3." However, it is possible that a second baseman might get a ground ball, flip it to the shortstop who throws it to first just to get the batter out. So, for the double play we might write "DP 4-6-3" or "GDP 4-6-3."

Other notations could be as follows:

F	fly out
L	line out
P	pop out
K	strikeout
G	ground out
SB	stolen base
SAC	sacrifice bunt
SF	sacrifice fly

For a strikeout, some people will use "KO" and some "SO." Some people differentiate between a swinging strikeout and a batter who is called out looking. Usually the way that is done is:

K	swinging strikeout
Ʞ	strikeout looking

The defensive notations are more standard than the offensive notations. For a walk, the notation is usually "BB" or "W." For hits, various notations, both alphanumeric and geometric, are used. Here are a few that are used by various people.

single	1B	—	╱	—
double	2B	=	⟩	⌐
triple	3B	≡	⬦	⌐
home run	HR	≣	◇	□

Obviously, you can use any symbols you want to use. It is nice if the symbols you choose can be easily interpreted by other people but the specifics are a matter of personal preference.

The scorecard form can vary substantially. Some are very simple.

Name	Pos	1	2	3	4	5	6	7	8	9	10

Team	1	2	3	4	5	6	7	8	9	10	R	H	E

　　The above gives a place for the batters name and position and a column for each inning's results. It also gives a spot for tallying the runs scored each inning and places for summarizing the runs, hits and errors for each team.

　　There are more complicated forms. An example can be seen at http://www.printyourbrackets.com/printable-baseball-score-sheet.html. Some forms give three lines for each spot in the batting order to allow for substitutions. An inning column would allow the scorer to note the inning in which the substitute entered. A small baseball diamond in each square allows the scorer to note how far a batter advances, both on his at-bat and on subsequent players' at-bats. Small notations next to the diamond can allow the scorer to tell whether the batter reached on a single, double, triple, etc. Finally, small squares in the bottom right can allow notations of balls (the bottom three squares) and strikes (the top two squares). If a batter hit a single on a 3 balls, 1 strike count, the scorer would circle "1B" and then "X" one of the "strike" squares and all three "ball" squares.

Forms typically give a set of summary rows for each inning, allowing notations for runs, hits and errors for each inning.

Much of the remainder of the process for scoring will depend on whether you plan to tally statistics when you are done. For example, many scorecards have a "game summary" section for each player.

Some people will make a horizontal line in the scorecard at the point where a pitcher is removed from the game. This allows for easier recording of statistics at the end of the game.

Most versions provide columns for at-bats, runs, hits, runs batted in, walks, strikeouts, doubles, triples and home runs. In order to keep track of runs and runs batted in, some people will make a notation in the inning columns when a player scores a run. This can be done by putting an "R" in a corner of the box or in the diamond. Similarly "RBI" can be put in the box or diamond if a player knocks in a run.

Here is a sample.

Suppose the game has the following play by play in the first two innings. I will use the 1969 Mets for an example.

1ST INNING

Tommie Agee (cf) singles.
Bud Harrelson (ss) strikes out while Agee steals second.
Cleon Jones (lf) doubles, scoring Agee.
Donn Clendenon (1b) homers, scoring Jones.
Art Shamsky (rf) walks.
Ken Boswell (2b) grounds into a double play, short to second to first.

Name	Pos	1	2
Agee	8	/ sb, r	
Harrelson	6	KO	
Jones	7	⟩ rbi, r	
Clendenon	3	◇ 2rbi, r	
Shamsky	9	BB	
Boswell	4	DP, 6-4-3	

Name	Pos	1	2
Garrett	5		
Grote	2		
Seaver	1		

2ND INNING

Wayne Garrett (3b) singles.

Jerry Grote (c) singles.

Tom Seaver (p) sacrifice bunts, catcher to first, moving Garrett to third, Grote to second.

Agee triples, scoring Garrett and Grote.

Harrelson is hit by the pitch.

Jones doubles, scoring Agee and Harrelson. The pitcher is replaced.

Clendenon flies out to left.

Shamsky lines out to second.

Name	Pos	1	2
Agee	8	SB, r	2 rbi, r
Harrelson	6	KO	HBP r
Jones	7	rbi, r	2 rbi
Clendenon	3		F 7 / 2rbi, r
Shamsky	9	BB	L 4
Boswell	4	DP 6-4-3	
Garrett	5		r
Grote	2		r
Seaver	1		SAC 2-3

Section 12.2—Using Excel to Record and Calculate Statistics

Game and season statistics are easily tallied and analyzed using Microsoft Excel or other spreadsheet program.

Let's look at a brief introduction into Excel. Different versions of Excel will have slight differences but the majority of it will follow this pattern.

INTRODUCTION TO EXCEL

Excel is a spreadsheet, which is a fancy way of saying it is a means of using, storing and displaying data. In this introduction, we will look at some very basic terminology and some of the uses of Excel.

Terminology

Excel worksheets are divided into 16384 **columns** and 1,048,576 **rows**, forming 17,179,869,184 **cells**. Obviously it is rare that we will use a significant portion of the cells. The cells are where the data is entered and where calculations are made. Rows are "named" using numbers. Columns are "named" using letters.

Columns   **Rows**

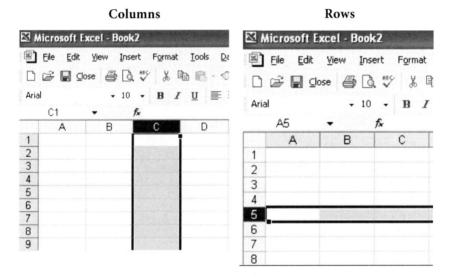

Cells

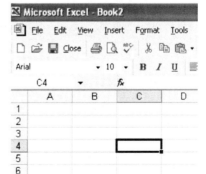

We will identify cells by their column letter and row number. The cell shown in the figure to the right is identified as C4, as you can see in the small window on the **command line**.

Open up Excel and work through the following simple examples.

Example 1—Entering Data

To enter data into a cell, simply click on the cell you want to use and type the data. Data can be numeric or alphabetic. Let us start by putting the numbers 4, 5 and 6 into cells A1, A2 and A3 respectively. After typing the number, you can either use the arrow keys or <ENTER> to move on to the cell below.

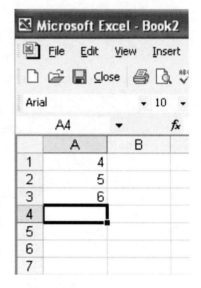

Example 2—Adding Data Values

Suppose we want to add the numbers in Example 1 and put the sum in cell B1. There are three ways we can do this. Simply typing 4 + 5 + 6 will not work. To tell Excel that you want to do a calculation, you first type "=". Then type the calculation. See below.

Enter the calculation ...   ... and hit <ENTER>.

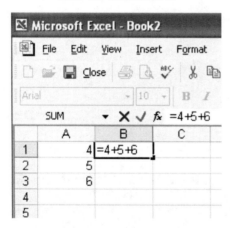 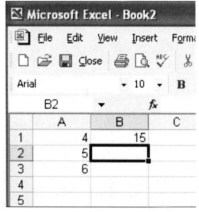

Sometimes the numbers are messy enough that we do not want to type them in, especially if we already have them typed in other cells. In that case, we can use the cell labels in the calculation.

Enter the calculation ...   ... and hit <ENTER>.

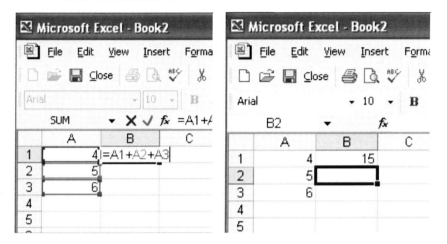

Another way to do it is using the built in Excel command called "SUM." The syntax shown in the figure below on the left means we want Excel to take the sum of all cells from A1 down through A3.

Enter the calculation ...   ... and hit <ENTER>.

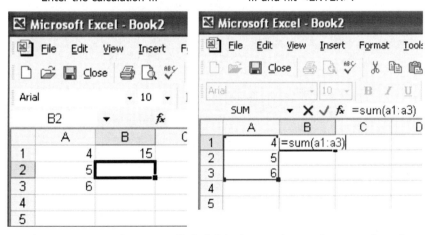

The sum command is especially helpful when we have a large number of cells to add. For example, if we had data in cells A1 down to A200 and wanted to add them, we would use the command =SUM(A1:A200). If we had data in cells A1 across to W1 and wanted to add them, we would use the command =SUM(A1:W1).

The data can be in a rectangular array instead of just in one row or one column. See the following example.

Example 3—Adding Data Values

Enter the data ...   ... and type the sum command ...

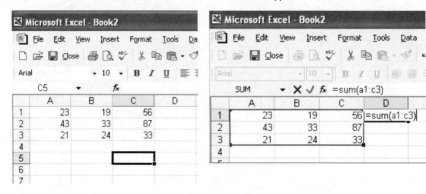

... and then press <ENTER>.

The cells to be added by "SUM" can be chosen by typing, as in the examples, or by typing "=SUM(" and then left clicking on the top-leftmost cell, holding the mouse button down and dragging to the bottom-rightmost cell and then hitting <ENTER>.

Example 4—Other Arithmetic

Using −, / and * allows you to subtract, divide and multiply in Excel. As above, you can do 5 − 3 by typing "=5 − 3" or by typing "=A1 − A2" if 5 is in cell A1 and 3 is in cell A2. There is no command for subtraction or division that are analogous to the "SUM" command. However, for multiplication, there is. "PRODUCT" works the same way as "SUM" if you want to multiply a large number of data values.

If you want to do exponentiation, like 3^2, you would type "=3^2" or "=A1^A2" if the data values are in those cells.

Example 5—Entering Data That Fit a Pattern

Suppose you wanted to enter all of the integers from 1 to 100. It would obviously be time consuming to type all of them. Excel has a nice way to do that.

Enter 1 in cell A1.   In cell A2, type =A1 + 1.

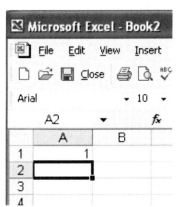 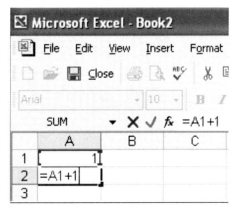

Press <ENTER> and then put the cursor back on cell A2. What we want to do is have cell A3 = A2 + 1, A4 = A3 + 1, etc. Instead of typing all of those we can use the "Fill" command.

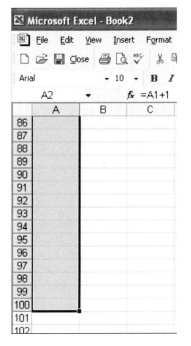

Left click on A2 and, holding the mouse button down, scroll down until you have highlighted all the way down to A100.

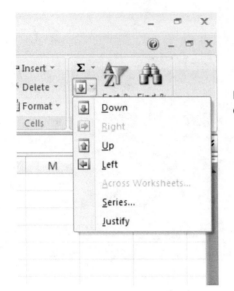

Now, click on the "Fill" button and choose "Down."

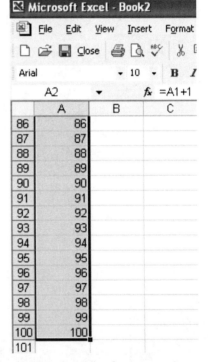

You now have that pattern continued through all of those cells. "Fill" will be VERY useful in some of our exercises.

Note: The "Fill" command automatically changes the cell references as it fills the cells which you are highlighting. There may be times we do not want it to change those references but keep using one particular cell. The symbol $ will allow us to force Excel to continue using the same cell. For example, if you want the commands to all use cell A5, type the cell reference as A5 instead of just A5.

GRAPHING DATA

Sometimes we will want to graph data in Excel. Enter the following data as shown.

	A	B
1	4	
2	6	
3	8	
4	11	
5	15	
6	19	
7	28	
8		
9		

There are a variety of kinds of graphs. We will use a line graph in this case. Highlight the data set.

	A	
1	4	
2	6	
3	8	
4	11	
5	15	
6	19	
7	28	

Choose "Insert" and then click on the appropriate graph icon on the tool bar.

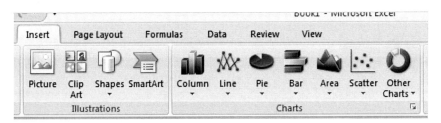

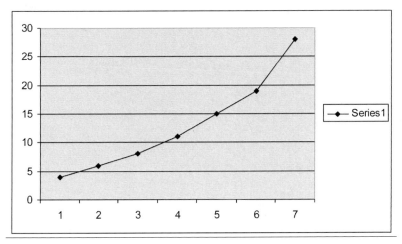

Sometimes the process will be a little more complicated but this will get you started.

Exercise—More Sophisticated Example

Suppose we are going to be purchasing varying numbers of different products. Suppose also that the prices will vary. We may want to set up a spreadsheet that we can use regardless of quantities and prices.

In row 1, put headers for "product," "unit price," "quantity," and "price." In column A, put "product 1" through "product 10" and "Total."

Under "price" set up the calculations necessary for calculating the total price for each product. In "Total" set up the calculations necessary for calculating the total cost.

Exercise—Baseball Statistics and Excel

In 1894, Hugh Duffy played for the Braves. Let us use Excel to calculate some of his statistics.

Set up Excel as shown below.

	A	B	C	D	E	F	G	H	I	J	K	L	M
1	AB	H	2B	3B	HR	BB	AVG	SLG	OBA	OPS	TB	HBP	SF
2	539	237	51	16	18	66						1	0
3													

We now want to calculate the values in the blanks. Let's first do batting average. We know that is H/AB.

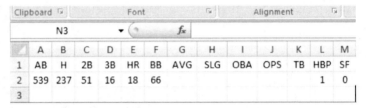

SUM						=b2/a2						
	A	B	C	D	E	F	G	H	I	J	K	L	M
1	AB	H	2B	3B	HR	BB	AVG	SLG	OBA	OPS	TB	HBP	SF
2	539	237	51	16	18		=b2/a2					1	0
3													

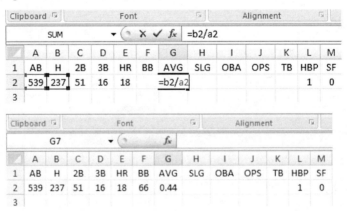

G7						f_x						
	A	B	C	D	E	F	G	H	I	J	K	L	M
1	AB	H	2B	3B	HR	BB	AVG	SLG	OBA	OPS	TB	HBP	SF
2	539	237	51	16	18	66	0.44					1	0
3													

We'd like the average to show three decimal places. Click on that cell, and then click the "Increase Decimal" button on the toolbar. Click it once to go to a third decimal place.

	A	B	C	D	E	F	G	H	I	J	K	L	M
1	AB	H	2B	3B	HR	BB	AVG	SLG	OBA	OPS	TB	HBP	SF
2	539	237	51	16	18	66	0.440					1	0
3													

G2 =B2/A2

Now we will calculate total bases. TB = H + 2B + 2*3B + 3*HR.

SUM =B2+C2+2*D2+3*E2

	A	B	C	D	E	F	G	H	I	J	K	L	M
1	AB	H	2B	3B	HR	BB	AVG	SLG	OBA	OPS	TB	HBP	SF
2	539	237	51	16	18	66	0.440				=B2+C2+2*D2+3*E2		
3													

Since we have TB now, we can now do slugging average.

SUM =K2/A2

	A	B	C	D	E	F	G	H	I	J	K	L	M
1	AB	H	2B	3B	HR	BB	AVG	SLG	OBA	OPS	TB	HBP	SF
2	539	237	51	16	18	66		=K2/A2			374	1	0
3													

On base percentage is next. OBP = (H + BB + HBP)/(AB + BB + HBP + SF).

SUM =(B2+F2+L2)/(A2+F2+L2+M2)

	A	B	C	D	E	F	G	H	I	J	K	L	M
1	AB	H	2B	3B	HR	BB	AVG	SLG	OBA	OPS	TB	HBP	SF
2	539	237	51	16	18	66		=(B2+F2+L2)/(A2+F2+L2+M2)				1	0
3													

Lastly, OPS is easy. That is OBA + SLG.

SUM =I2+H2

	A	B	C	D	E	F	G	H	I	J	K	L	M
1	AB	H	2B	3B	HR	BB	AVG	SLG	OBA	OPS	TB	HBP	SF
2	539	237	51	16	18	66	0.440	0.694		=I2+H2		1	0
3													

	A	B	C	D	E	F	G	H	I	J	K	L	M
1	AB	H	2B	3B	HR	BB	AVG	SLG	OBA	OPS	TB	HBP	SF
2	539	237	51	16	18	66	0.440	0.694	0.502	1.196	374	1	0
3													

(Clipboard — Font — Alignment; cell reference J6, f_x)

If we had multiple players, we could do the commands on one line, as we did here, and then use the "Fill" commands described above to extend the commands to the other lines.

Chapter 12—Exercises

SECTION 12.1—RECORDING STATISTICS

1. Watch an entire baseball game. Keep score of the game. At the end of the game, tally the statistics. Use whatever method you like but try to record the play by play so that someone else can easily follow what happened.

SECTION 12.2—USING EXCEL TO RECORD AND CALCULATE STATISTICS

1. Set up an Excel spreadsheet as follows.

	A	B	C	D
1	Item	unit price	quantity	price
2	A	$4.99		
3	B	$3.95		
4	C	$11.49		
5	D	$19.50		
6	E	$12.99		
7	F	$10.00		
8			subtotal	
9			tax 8%	
10			total	
11				
12				

Set up column D so that, when quantities are entered in column C, column D shows the total price for each item, cell D8 shows the total of the six item prices, D9 shows the sales tax and D10 shows the total price. Have it show two decimal places.

2. Set up an Excel spreadsheet as follows and set up formulas to fill in the blanks.

1930 Phillies

Name	*AB*	*H*	*2B*	*3B*	*HR*	*AVG*	*TB*	*SLG*
Chuck Klein	648	250	59	8	40			
Pinky Whitney	606	207	41	5	8			

Name	AB	H	2B	3B	HR	AVG	TB	SLG
Tommy Thevenow	573	164	21	1	0			
Lefty O'Doul	528	202	37	7	22			
Fresco Thompson	478	135	34	4	4			
Don Hurst	391	128	19	3	17			
Denny Sothern	347	97	26	1	5			
Bernie Friberg	331	113	21	1	4			
Spud Davis	329	103	16	1	14			
Monk Sherlock	299	97	18	2	0			
George Brickell	240	59	12	6	0			
Tony Rensa	172	49	11	2	3			
Harry McCurdy	148	49	6	2	1			
Tripp Sigman	100	27	4	1	4			

3. Set up an Excel spreadsheet as follows and set up formulas to fill in the blanks.

1965 Dodgers

Name	IP	ER	BB	SO	ERA	BB/IP	SO/IP	SO/9IP
Sandy Koufax	336	76	71	382				
Don Drysdale	308	95	66	210				
Claude Osteen	287	89	78	162				
Johnny Podres	134	51	39	63				
Ron Perranoski	105	26	40	53				
Bob Miller	103	34	26	77				
Howie Reed	78	27	27	47				
Jim Brewer	49	10	28	31				
Nick Willhite	42	25	22	28				
John Purdin	23	17	13	16				

4. Set up an Excel spreadsheet as follows and set up formulas to fill in the blanks.

1969 National League East

Team	W	L	PCT	GB
Mets	100	62		
Cubs	92	70		
Pirates	88	74		
Cardinals	87	75		
Phillies	63	99		
Expos	52	110		

Index